BEHIND
THE
SMILE

THE WORKING LIVES
OF CARIBBEAN TOURISM

SECOND EDITION

GEORGE GMELCH

INDIANA UNIVERSITY PRESS

Bloomington and Indianapolis

This book is a publication of
Indiana University Press
601 North Morton Street
Bloomington, IN 47404-3797 USA

iupress.indiana.edu

Telephone orders 800-842-6796
Fax orders 812-855-7931

Manufactured in the United States of America

Library of Congress Cataloging-in-Publication Data

Gmelch, George.
  Behind the smile : the working lives of caribbean tourism / George
Gmelch. — 2nd ed.
      p. cm.
  Includes bibliographical references and index.
  ISBN 978-0-253-00123-8 (pbk. : alk. paper) —
  ISBN 978-0-253-00129-0 (electronic book)
  1. Tourism—Caribbean Area—Anecdotes. 2. Tourism—Caribbean
Area—Employees—Anecdotes. I. Title.
  G155.C35G63 2012
  331.7'619172981—dc23

                                          2011042309

        1 2 3 4 5   17 16 15 14 13 12

To
Ermine Greaves,
Jerry Handler,
Susan Mahon,
Marcus O'Neale,
and
Janice Whittle,
who contributed so much to
my Bajan education over the years

CONTENTS

Preface

When people talk about tourism, they usually talk about their own holiday experiences and the places they have seen. Rarely do they consider the people who serve them and make their vacations possible. *Behind the Smile* is an inside look at the world of Caribbean tourism—specifically Barbados—as seen through the working lives of twenty-one men and women. The workers come from every level of tourism, from maid to hotel manager, gigolo to taxi driver, redcap to diving instructor. Their stories reveal the work of tourism and the encounters between "hosts" and "guests," as workers and tourists are known in both the travel industry and academe.

The tourism dealt with in this book involves travelers from the most developed parts of the world who are vacationing in an economically less developed region—the Eastern Caribbean. In Barbados, the guests are primarily British, American, and Canadian. Through interviews with the tourism workers, we learn how they interact with the visitors and what they think of them—of their affluent lifestyles, their moral character, and the manner in which they pursue leisure. We learn what they admire about them and what they shun. We discover the generalizations or stereotypes they make about nationality and gender. Do women on vacation complain more than men? Americans more than Europeans? Are Canadians cheaper than all others? Are Americans less curious? Brits more prejudiced? We also hear how Barbadians assess the costs and benefits of international tourism for their island and society.

My interest in tourism evolved slowly over a two-decade span of research and teaching in the Caribbean. Initially I went to Barbados in 1982 to study emigrants who had returned home after spending many years living abroad in England and North America. I was interested in comparing the experiences of Barbadian returnees with the return migrants I had studied earlier in Ireland and Newfoundland (Gmelch 1992a). Since then my wife, Sharon Bohn Gmelch, and I have taken groups of anthropology students to Barbados every other year on field-training programs (see Gmelch 1992b). By merely living in Barbados, a small island, we were routinely exposed to tourism. Many residents of the villages where we lived worked in tourism. Most afternoons, we took a break from our village life and went to a large resort near Speightstown to swim and walk on the beach. Although I hated being identified as a tourist myself, I enjoyed observing and talking to visitors and the staff at the resort. When friends from home visited us in Barbados, we became real tourists as we took them around to see the "sights." But it wasn't until we collaborated on a study of culture change in rural Barbados that I developed a scholarly interest in tourism. In *The Parish Behind God's Back: The Changing Culture of Rural Barbados,* Sharon Gmelch and I wrote briefly about tourism as an agent of change. Doing that research piqued my interest in the lives of my village friends who worked in the "industry," and eventually led to the interviews for this book. I hoped that interviews with these individuals, edited into narratives of their working lives, would be an effective way to get an insider's view of the work of tourism and its impact on individuals. As several scholars have noted (Crick 1989; Stronza 2001), a major shortcoming in the literature on tourism has been the lack of local voice. I hope this work will be a step toward filling that void.

The twenty-one narratives in this book are divided into four primary sections that reflect the different settings and workplaces in Caribbean tourism—airport, hotel, beach, and the attractions. A fifth section looks at the government's effort to collect information on tourism and a trade association's efforts to promote it. Each section is introduced with a brief history or description of the setting.

Preface to
the Second Edition

The research for the first edition of *Behind the Smile* was conducted between 1998 and 2000. A decade later, in the summer of 2010, I returned to Barbados to see how tourism had changed, if at all. Despite the global recession (2008–2010), which reduced the numbers of visitors to Barbados, tourism remains essential to the economic well-being of Barbados. Returning to Barbados gave me an opportunity to catch up with many of the people whose narratives are included here. For those I was able to locate I have added short epilogues. I have also added two new narratives, that of Rosie Hartmann, who offers a colorful description of her life and work organizing excursions for cruise ship passengers and locals, and Colin Jordan, who as president of the Barbados Hotel and Tourism Association (BHTA) describes his work trying to educate Barbadians about the importance of tourism to the country. This new edition also includes a description of the tourists who visit Barbados, thus addressing an unfortunate omission in the first edition, and an epilogue describing my field school students' encounters with tourists and tourism.

BEHIND THE SMILE

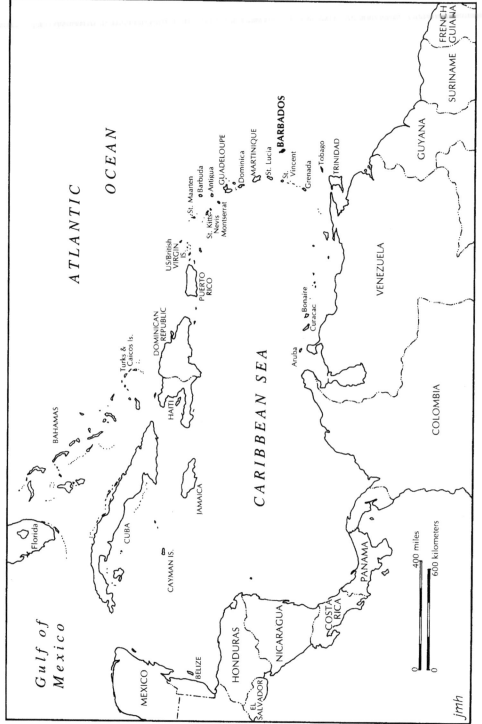

The Caribbean.

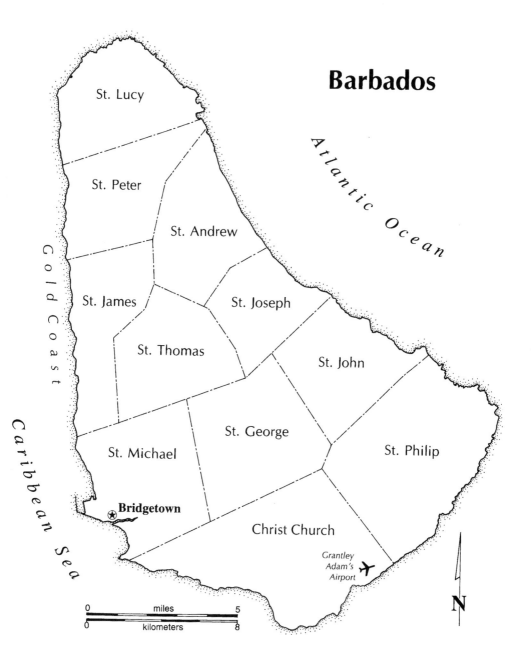

Barbados

St. Lucy

St. Peter

St. Andrew

St. James

St. Joseph

St. Thomas

St. John

St. George

St. Michael

St. Philip

⊛ **Bridgetown**

Christ Church

*Grantley
Adam's
Airport* ✈

Atlantic Ocean

Gold Coast

Caribbean Sea

N

| miles | | 5 |
| 0 | | |

| kilometers | | 8 |
| 0 | | |

Barbados with parish boundaries identified.

1 ISLAND TOURISM

Tourism is travel dedicated to pleasure. Although the *Oxford English Dictionary* dates the term's first appearance in print to 1811, the concept of traveling for leisure dates back several thousand years to the ancient Greeks and later the Romans, whose elites traveled to exotic places around the Mediterranean. The Romans used the Isle of Capri as a holiday destination in what may be the earliest example of island tourism.

Some scholars argue that most early travel was unrelated to leisure; rather, it was aimed at satisfying other needs, such as pursuing opportunities for trade and commerce or seeking spiritual relief in making pilgrimages to sacred sites.[1] Perhaps. But there can be little doubt that for many early travelers, such as Greeks and Romans visiting thermal baths, there was often a large element of leisure associated with the trip. We must not fall into the trap of believing that travelers always have a single motive. Even my academic colleagues manage to do some sight-seeing while on trips to attend professional conferences.

Thomas Cook and the Package Tour

British entrepreneur Thomas Cook is often credited with having started the modern-day organized tour. First a missionary and

---

1. This review of the history and development of tourism draws primarily upon the work of Malcolm Crick (1989), Erve Chambers (2002), Ovar Lofgren (1999), and Polly Pattullo (1996).

later an active temperance worker, Cook chartered a special train to carry passengers the 17 miles from Leicester to Loughborough for a temperance meeting in 1841. The success of this guided excursion and subsequent organized trips to temperance rallies led to the formation of a travel agency bearing his name. Soon Cook was organizing weekend excursions to British seaside resorts, where the mass arrival of "commoners" and their simple ways horrified the refined upper-class visitors, sending them in search of new leisure destinations. By the late 1850s, Cook had gone continental, offering railway tours to southern Europe. Such tours were made possible by rapid innovations in transportation, notably the expansion of railroad and steamship companies, which originally had been built to serve the needs of Europe's new manufacturing industries. Cook and his meticulously groomed staff of tour guides ferried hundreds of thousands of Englishmen, Americans, and Europeans to historical, cultural, and recreational sites.

Cook's tours reduced the amount of effort individual travelers had to spend in planning and undertaking their own holidays, and they were affordable to middle-class families. "It seemed as if Mr. Cook's helpful agents were everywhere and always ready to arrange hotel accommodations, guided tours, and rail tickets or solve conflicts whether in Naples or in Smyrna," notes Ovar Lofgren (1999). His tours also made it possible for many middle-class women to travel, not only with their families but also with just female friends. In short order, Cook had become an institution, laying the foundation for mass travel by offering affordable prices and well-organized tours. His success encouraged a host of emulators on both sides of the Atlantic, and the organized tour became common. Some argue that Thomas Cook's great contribution was not so much the package tour (before his time, successful pilgrimages had also required similar skills and organization) but his creation of new markets for tourism. There was now a demand for travel opportunities where none had previously existed. Soon travel agencies, transportation companies, hotel chains, and entire governments began to mediate tourism in new ways.

As Europe's elites vacationed farther afield, some went to the Caribbean. The choice of destination was mostly determined by the reach of Europe's colonial empires. The British, for example, frequented Barbados and Jamaica; the French vacationed in Martinique, the Dutch in Curaçao, and the Americans in Cuba and the Bahamas. The cost and length of the sea voyage to get to such destinations meant that only the well-off could travel. And they stayed for substantial periods of time, weeks and even months. Although there were a few large hotels, most visitors stayed in guesthouses or in small exclusive colony, or club, resorts made up of individual bungalows, which fostered an intimate friendliness between visitors and local staff.[2] The tourist season, as in Europe, was limited to the winter months. By 1900, tourism was a small but notable feature of the economy of Barbados, and no fewer than eleven steamships carrying visitors made regular calls.

Before the eighteenth century, there was not much interest in the beach as a place of recreational leisure (Lencek and Bosker 1998). After all, sand is hard to walk on, it gets into your clothes and food, and it blows in the wind. Early seaside resorts were developed primarily for their health-giving properties—dips in the sea, known as "sea bathing," were salubrious and were prescribed as general pick-me-ups as well as for serious medical conditions (Lencek and Bosker 1998). Healers and tourists alike swore by the vivifying effects of what they called "ozone"—sea air charged with saltwater vapor formed by wind passing over cresting waves. In fact, the wealthy Britons and North Americans who came to Barbados in the nineteenth century did so principally for the warm air and ozone-laden sea breezes. Medical opinion held that a heavy dose of sea air and sea bathing could help restore one's constitution. As early as 1751, the young George Washington, the future "First Father" of his country, accompanied his ailing older brother Lawrence, who was suffering from tuberculosis, to Barbados, hoping for a cure. (The plantation house—Bush Hill House—where they stayed for two months is today a national landmark and tourist attraction.) Guidebooks for tourists extolled the virtues of Barbados as a health resort, referring to the island as "the sanatorium of the West Indies." In the words of the 1913 *Tourist Guide to Barbados*, the "ozone greatly contributes to recuperation from any ailment." Barbados was also praised for its "copious supply of pure water" and for being free from malaria. Consider this testimonial from an American visitor:

> In the fall of 1911, I found myself badly run down, after years of excessive work. I have contracted chronic bronchitis. My physician rec-

---

2. Some of the rich even bought their own islands, such as the Rockefellers in the Virgin Islands. Mystique and Palm Island, in St. Vincent and the Grenadines, were also sold or leased.

Hastings Baths, Barbados

Victorian-era bathhouses (for men only) at the famous sea baths in Hastings. *Courtesy of Mary Kerr.*

ommended that I leave the northern climate. . . . I consulted with friends, one of whom recommended Barbados. After a most exhilarating passage among the beautiful islands of the British West Indies I finally settled in Barbados. Two months of such bathing as I know of no where else, the genial climate and the freedom from the horrors of the northern winter resulted in a complete change in my physical condition. (Barbados Improvement Association 1913)

Going into the sea involved immersion, not swimming as we know it today. Before the nineteenth century, most bathers were naked because swimsuits had not yet been designed, and once they took their sea baths, they did not linger on the beach or sit in the sun. Heat and sunshine, it was believed, dried up the body's fluids and left it debilitated and prone to physical and moral ailments (Lencek and Bosker 1998). Moreover, since pale skin was valued as a sign of delicacy, seclusion, and idleness (and therefore wealth), nineteenth-century beachgoers ventured to the waters only in early morning or late afternoon. Off the beach, they walked and sat under covered walkways, gazebos, and verandas seeking protection from the dangers of the sun.

All this changed in the early 1920s. Among the upper classes, sunning became desirable, and tanned skin became associated with spontaneity and sensuality. It was the sun rather than the sea that was now presumed to produce health and sexual attractiveness. Beaches, preferably with fine white or golden yellow sand, were the ideal place to take the sun. As this view diffused down through the social classes, holidays at the seaside became popular.[3]

The Airplane and the Era of Mass Tourism

Other than the industrial revolution itself, which introduced new ideas of leisure and new modes of consumption, nothing changed tourism more than the airplane. In the 1960s, long-haul jet service brought the Caribbean within reach of the ordinary holiday-maker. It reduced travel time from Europe to the Caribbean from three weeks by sea to eight hours by air. Postwar affluence and the adoption of guaranteed holidays with pay for most North American and European workers gave people the time off and the money to travel. Travel agencies and tour operators sprang up to package and promote Caribbean vacations. They popularized the idea of winter vacations in "exotic" tropical places and helped bring a Caribbean holiday within the price range of middle-income families. The new visitors, for whom the term "mass tourism" was coined, overtook in number and importance the elite travelers of the earlier period. Throughout the Caribbean, tourist accommodations and resorts sprouted along the seacoasts. (Inland areas are usually mountainous and too wet to attract visitors, other than those looking for nature and wishing to experience the rain forest.)

Jet airplanes also brought other Third World destinations within reach, but few attracted visitors like the Caribbean, with its fine beaches and natural beauty. And many Caribbean islands offer a diversity of landscapes in a small area. The Caribbean is relatively safe from disease and pests, and European and North American visitors can speak their own language (English, French, Dutch, or Spanish) yet still be in an exotic foreign place. The friendliness of Caribbean peoples has also helped draw tourists to the region. The travel brochures project an image of the Caribbean as a warm, sen-

---

3. "This mass impulse to expose the body to the sun," suggest Lencek and Bosker (1998, 201), was to a great degree the result of global trauma inflicted by World War I. Today we see a return to the idea that too much sun is harmful to the skin.

sual, escapist place. They feature colorful photos of pristine coral reefs whose waters are loaded with tropical fish, fruit stands dis playing colorful papayas and mangos, foursomes playing golf on iridescent green courses beneath bright blue skies, sailboats skimming over azure blue waters, and couples walking hand in hand on the beach at sunset. It is an image of an alluring paradise, a simple place with happy, carefree, fun-loving people. In the collective European imagination, notes Polly Pattullo (1996), the Caribbean conjures up the idea of "Heaven on Earth" or "a little bit of paradise." It is no surprise that weddings and honeymoons are now big business in the Caribbean, or that the average holiday-maker has little awareness that the real history of the Caribbean is one of the annihilation of Amerindians, slavery and the plantation system, poverty, and underdevelopment (Crick 1989).

Caribbean governments began to welcome the visitors with open arms in the 1950s.[4] Government leaders were almost unanimous in their enthusiasm for tourism. So were local elites, who identified with the consumerist lifestyle of the international tourist; indeed, some were themselves members of the international jet set (Crick 1989). Many governments viewed tourism as the key to their economic development, a notion shared by developing nations elsewhere. They were encouraged by international organizations, notably the World Bank and the United Nations, who endorsed tourism for the Third World as a "promising new resource" (Crick 1989, 316). But the World Tourism Organization (WTO) was the biggest cheerleader for the industry and for governments interested in developing tourism. Some organizations touted tourism as having almost limitless growth potential in attracting foreign currency. Tourism was also said to be attractive because it relied on natural resources that were already in place—sand, sun, sea, and friendly people—and it was thought to require low capital investments in infrastructure. Some advocates argued that by developing tourism, Third World nations could leapfrog the normal industrial phase of economic growth, advancing directly from a primary-resource-based economy to a service-based economy (Crick 1989).

In a 1973 publication titled "Tourism in the Americas: Road to a Better Life," the Organization of American States asserted that in-

---

4. For an excellent review of the development of Caribbean tourism, see Polly Pattullo's *Last Resort* (1996).

tcrnational tourism would "not only help raise the standard of living of the host country, but encourage integration of people through the interchange of ideas, drinking and eating habits, and styles of clothing" (Hiller 1976, 98). Even Pope Paul VI gave his blessing, declaring world tourism a "passport to peace," stating that it had a "civilizing mission" that would bridge the gaps separating social classes and cultures (ibid.). The private sector also touted the benefits, as it stood to profit most. In a lengthy press release titled "Tourism Is Number One Bread Winner for Many Lands Around the World," Pan American World Airways boasted that tourism created new agricultural markets, that it stimulated domestic infrastructure, and that "tourism money goes directly into the hands of the people—boot blacks and beauticians, maids and merchants. . . . It spreads widely and quickly . . . 80 cents or more of every dollar a tourist spends is left in the countries he visits" (quoted in Hiller 1976, 96).

Such widespread enthusiasm for tourism helped overcome the reservations of some in the academic community who were concerned about the social impacts of tourism. The timing for tourism was right because the traditional plantation economies of the islands, which were tied to exports such as sugar, bananas, and bauxite, were in decline. Crick reminds us that these distorted monocrop island economies were initially created by the very European colonial powers who were now sending tourists. Prices for the Caribbean's commodities were falling as the world rearranged itself into free-market trading blocks, notably the European Union (EU) and, in the 1990s, the North American Free Trade Agreement (NAFTA). Caribbean manufacturing and agricultural industries were no longer competitive. Hence, governments throughout the region, anxious to diversify their economies, viewed tourism as an attractive alternative. Ministries of tourism and development corporations were set up to promote hotel and infrastructure investment. Tax incentives were offered to encourage foreign capital to develop tourism.

The Barbadian government—encouraged by a paternalistic elite who recognized the island's strengths of an ideal climate, natural beauty, political stability, and a friendly people—promoted the new tourism as a major sector of the economy. Spurred on with government incentives, hotel construction boomed, unemployment dropped, and visitors began to arrive. Before the tourism boom, most rural Barbadians worked in agriculture on nearby sugar plantations while also cultivating small private plots of sugarcane and vegetables at home. That pattern changed as tourism expanded, the economy diversified, and new jobs were created. Today, more Barbadians work in tourism than in agriculture, and most young people now disdain agricultural work altogether. The number of sugar plantations has shrunk to under 100 (there were 244 in 1961), the acreage in sugarcane production has dropped by over half, and sugar's contribution to the economy is now less than one-tenth that of tourism ($14.5 million versus $167 million in 2006).[5]

Throughout the Caribbean, tourism has attracted increasing numbers of visitors from North America and Europe. Before World War II, the annual number of tourists who came to the region was hardly more than 100,000; by 1959, the region received 1.3 million visitors, by 1965 close to 4 million, by 1985 10 million, and in 2000 over 17 million. The economies of many Caribbean islands now rely heavily on tourism, which is often referred to as the engine of their growth. Tourism is the primary earner of foreign exchange in the region. By 1992, tourism in Barbados was earning more than all other sectors of the economy.

Beyond the hotel belt, tourism stimulates other sectors of the economy, the so-called multiplier effect. (The term "multiplier" comes from macroeconomics and is used to describe the total effect that an external source of income, such as tourism, has on an economy.) Simply put, the outward ripple of tourist dollars fosters demand for goods and services in other areas. Farmers, fishermen, and merchants benefit because they must grow and supply more fish, meat, poultry, eggs, vegetables, and fruit to feed the large number of visitors. The tourists' desire for curios and souvenirs generates work for local artists and craftspeople. Early on, the largest ripple effect is in the construction of hotels, guesthouses, restaurants, and other facilities needed to cater to visitors. By the mid-1960s, for example, over half of all the construction on Barbados was associated with tourism.

The few Caribbean nations that did not embrace tourism in the 1960s and '70s, such as oil-rich Aruba and Trinidad and Tobago, became converts by the 1990s when oil revenues declined (Pattullo 1996). A shift to tourism also took place in the agricultural economies of the Windward Islands following a crisis in the banana industry in the early 1990s. Likewise, poor performances in sugar and

---

5. Annual Statistical Digest, 2007. Central Bank of Barbados.

bauxite exports pushed Jamaica toward greater tourist activity. And today Cuba is embarking on rapid tourist development in hopes of shoring up its faltering economy following the collapse of the Soviet Union, its former patron. Tourism is generally more important to island than to mainland destinations. Tourism in Germany, for example, represents only 0.17 percent of the gross domestic product (GDP), in the UK 1.5 percent, and in Spain 5.2 percent, whereas tourism in an island such as Bermuda represents nearly 50 percent of the GDP (Lockhart and Drakakis-Smith 1996).

The Downside

While tourism's importance to the economies of the Caribbean is unquestionable, the picture has not been as rosy as the early proponents predicted in the 1960s. Tourism has contributed less to long-term economic development than expected. Too often governments jumped in feet first with no planning, feasibility studies, or any idea of what costs might be involved. Many were influenced by those early optimistic statements on tourism, and the early econometric arguments were not always based on good science (Hiller 1976). Tourism has required larger capital outlays for infrastructure than expected, as governments and investors discovered they needed modern, Western-style amenities to attract tourists (Pattullo 1996). That has meant airports (ideally a large international airport to handle wide-bodied jets), roads, sewage treatment plants, landfills, electricity, and telephones. Tourism has required facilities not just to make the tourists' journey possible but to make it convenient and comfortable as well. To raise the enormous sums of money required to build new infrastructure, Caribbean states have borrowed from foreign governments. Paying off those loans, and the cost of maintaining the expensive new infrastructure, have stretched some Caribbean governments and their taxpayers to the limit. On the brink of bankruptcy, some have required bailouts by the International Monetary Fund (IMF).

Sometimes the expense is worthwhile because some of the new infrastructure, such as better water, telephone, and electricity supplies, also benefits local people. But there is much that locals make little use of, such as the large tracts of land turned into golf courses and large international airports that offer little benefit to poor locals who do not travel.

Yes, building an infrastructure for tourism is expensive, but shouldn't the profits from tourism be enough to meet the cost?

After all, didn't the World Bank and others predict in the 1960s that tourism had unlimited potential to earn foreign exchange? Unfortunately, the advocates of tourism did not realize, or did not care to admit, that much of the profit from tourism leaves the region. This "repatriation of profits," or "leakage," as it is referred to in the tourism literature, means that there is a large discrepancy between gross and net tourism receipts. Hence, the real economic benefits of tourism to a country are not revealed by gross foreign-exchange earnings but by what is left over after deducting the amount that stays or returns overseas. Most of the leakage is due to foreign investment and foreign control of the Caribbean's tourism industry. Two-thirds of the hotel rooms in the region are foreign owned, and the tour companies who arrange the visitor's activities are often foreign owned. The international airlines (American, KLM, British Air, Air France) that bring visitors to the Caribbean are also foreign owned. The small, underequipped, state-owned regional Caribbean airlines have never had the capacity or marketing to compete overseas. The foreign carriers, based in New York, London, and Paris, can influence which destinations get the most traffic by availability of seats, price, and schedules. It was a blow to Trinidad, for example, when British Airways withdrew direct flights to Port of Spain in 1994.

In a pattern referred to as vertical integration, airline, tour company, and hotel chains may be owned by the same overseas firm. Such firms retain many of the profits, thereby reducing the economic gains of the Caribbean countries. The worst is the all-inclusive package holiday, in which travelers make a single payment in advance (to the New York, London, or Paris office) that covers airfare, accommodation, food, and services (and sometimes even tips). With all-inclusives, much of the foreign exchange never reaches the Caribbean. Tourists at all-inclusive resorts have no need to eat out at locally owned restaurants, rent water-sports gear from local entrepreneurs, or arrange island tours with local taxis. Having already paid for their holiday at home, they act as if they left their wallets there, too. The impact on local businesses dependent upon a tourist clientele is devastating. I witnessed most of the small restaurants in Speightstown, Barbados, shut down after a nearby large resort (Heywoods, now called Almond Beach) became all-inclusive. Many locals who are positive about tourism are deeply resentful of the all-inclusives. Since the late 1980s, eleven of Barbados's large hotels have gone all-inclusive, and several more are planning to.

Leakage also happens because Caribbean islands do not have the facilities or the means to produce the kinds of goods required by visitors, especially luxury items for the upscale traveler; hence, much of the food, furnishings, and equipment for tourism must be imported. Pattullo (1996) reports that the Caribbean has a miserable record of attempting to supply its tourism sector from local and regional goods and services. The foreign management of most Barbadian hotels, for example, contributes to leakage by serving their guests a European menu that relies heavily on imported foods. In the dining rooms of Caribbean hotels, where millions of meals are consumed daily, why are tourists not served more mangos, breadfruit, citrus, and bananas grown locally? asks Pattullo. A few countries such as Jamaica and Dominica have succeeded in putting more local products on the tourists' dining tables, but they are the exception.

The leakage of profits is greatest in upscale, or first-class, tourist facilities such as the west coast hotels of Barbados. With rooms going from $500 per night, the guests require many goods expected with high-cost accommodations, which must be imported. While the gross receipts of these luxury hotels are high, the amount of money that stays on the island is low. Conversely, low-end, or back-packer, tourism relies more on local products and has less leakage. In the Caribbean, on average, for every dollar earned in foreign exchange, seventy cents is lost overseas—the antithesis of the Pan Am press release that predicted 80 percent of every dollar earned would stay at home. Sadly, this drain of hard-earned foreign exchange is one of the distinctive characteristics of the Caribbean tourism industry. And tourism profits that remain on the island are not distributed equally among all citizens but go disproportionately into the hands of local elites who have invested in hotels, restaurants, and other tourism attractions and facilities. While all citizens of island destinations must put up with the negative impacts of tourism, only some share in its profits.

Tourism development has also meant inflation in food and land prices, irritating locals. Land for the construction of hotels, marinas, and other tourist facilities commonly sells for more than the current local price. It thereby inflates the price of land in general, putting it out of reach of most local people, especially for property near the sea. The cost of land is also driven up when individual tourists buy vacation homes and cottages. On many islands, locals can no longer afford to live along their own coastline. Unchecked development along the tourist belt can make it difficult to even get a view of sea. The visual loss has been so great in Barbados that a pressure group formed, calling itself Windows to the Sea. Their goal is to preserve the remaining views that are not obscured by hotels. They would also like to see some old buildings razed to give more people physical and visual access to the ocean and its beauty.

Some economists who were ardent supporters of tourism early on later admitted that they were naive. Their multiplier analysis, for one, generated some highly misleading claims about the beneficial effects of tourism on employment and economic growth (Crick 1989). Some also admitted the political naiveté inherent in their one-dimensional asocial conceptual world. Much of the early work on tourism written by economists read like a "series of press releases" (Crick 1989). One economist acknowledged that his colleagues were too preoccupied with classical concerns of economics "and less conscious of the sociological aspects of development. . . . One might feel that we should have been more articulate about these—but we were economists" (quoted in Hiller 1976, 99).

In her critique of tourism development, Deborah McLaren (1998) writes that tourism exerts a greater, more pervasive influence on the countries and cultures of the world than any imperial power ever has. As McLaren has noted, "The sun never sets on the tourist empire" (1998, 26). Today some West Indians are seeing features of the colonial situation resurrected by tourism. Locals are denied access to their own beaches, the best jobs go to non-nationals or those with the lightest skin, and humble service roles and low-wage jobs predominate in the tourism sector. Not surprisingly, the travel industry takes a different view. They still see tourism as salvation. "Without the large hotels, most of the islands would dry up and blow away," exaggerated one American travel-industry spokesman (Pattullo 1996, 10). With equal hyperbole, another commented, "Only tourism and drug traffic keep these islands from going down the tubes" (ibid.).

They also argue that the critics of tourism overlook the lack of economic alternatives open to most Caribbean islands and the desires of many Caribbean leaders to promote and encourage tourism. But even many ardent supporters now concede that tourism has promoted dependency and that efforts must be made to reduce foreign influence and control over tourism in the Caribbean, such as by promoting local ownership of small hotels and developing regional airlines and regional marketing. Some governments, like that of Barbados, are moving in that direction.

Setting the Stage: The Island of Barbados

Now that we have a sense of the history of tourism and its development in the Caribbean, let us turn to the setting of this study—the island of Barbados—and the look of tourism there.[6]

Barbados is the most easterly of the Caribbean islands. It lies outside the great arc of volcanic islands that sweep a thousand miles from the Virgin Islands in the north to Trinidad and Tobago in the south. Unlike its volcanic neighbors, which are steep and mountainous, Barbados has a gentle terrain and one that is favorable to agriculture. Its tractable and fertile landscape allowed early English settlers to quickly bring most of the island under cultivation. As sugarcane plantations spread, African slaves were brought in as a source of cheap labor.

Barbados is the only Caribbean nation to have had a single colonial master. The appellation of "Little England," which has become a hackneyed phrase of the tourist trade, has some legitimacy. It was coined in part from comparisons between the landscapes of the two countries, both green and rolling and everywhere showing the hand of humans. As residents of one of the cricket-playing former colonies, Barbadians take pride in things English as reflected in numerous place-names, a tea-drinking tradition, and the dominance of the Anglican Church. Its orientation toward England, however, is losing ground to American tastes and popular culture. The parliamentary democracy, political stability, and quiet conservatism of Barbados make it attractive to North American and English visitors, overseas tour operators, and foreign investors, as does the island's well-developed infrastructure, which includes good roads, an international airport, and reliable electric supply and telecommunications technologies.

Today, Barbados is better known to North Americans and Europeans for the white sand beaches and sunny tropical climate that have made it a popular tourist destination. The temperature varies little throughout the year, from an average of 77°F in January to 81°F in August and September. The proximity of all parts of the island to the sea ensures comfortable year-round breezes. This, combined with the purity of the groundwater and the absence of pestilence, led one nineteenth-century English traveler to rate Barbados as the healthiest place in all of the British Empire, which then included half the nations on earth (Moxly 1886).

6. Much of the description of Barbados is taken from Gmelch and Gmelch (1997).

Carlisle Bay and Bridgetown. *Courtesy of Acute Vision.*

Over 265,000 people live on the island, which measures just 21 by 14 miles, making Barbados one of the most densely populated countries in the world. The population is unevenly spread, however. Most Bajans (the colloquial term Barbadians use for themselves) live in the capital city of Bridgetown and its suburbs, while most of the rural parishes are thinly settled. Most Bajans are direct descendants of the Africans who were transported to the island to work as slaves on the island's five hundred sugar plantations. About 20 percent of the population are of mixed black and white heritage, while most of the remaining 5 percent are whites, mostly descendants of English colonists and their indentured servants. There are also recent immigrants from South Asia and the Middle East. Whites have always controlled the economy of Barbados and, until the island's independence from Britain in 1966, its politics as well. After independence, nonwhites moved into all the important positions of government. While the economic power of the whites has been diluted in recent times, they still control the majority of the island's large businesses and most of the tourism industry that is not foreign owned. However, education and overseas experience have

done much since World War II to level out the influence of race in
Barbados by elevating the position of nonwhites.

Like most small developing countries, Barbados has one princi-
pal city—Bridgetown—that overwhelms the island's other "urban"
places in size and importance. Stretching outward from Bridgetown
along the west and south coasts is the tourist belt—two long strips
of hotels, restaurants, and shops catering to visitors—the new
mainstay of the island's economy. The hotels of Barbados are not
the high-rises seen in San Juan or Miami; most are low, often sin-
gle-story resorts and cottages with lush grounds planted in
flowering trees and shrubs. Their names evoke images of tropical
paradise that every Caribbean tourist board likes to project—Golden
Palm, Coral Reef Club, Sandy Lane, Coconut Creek, Paradise Beach,
Glitter Bay. Beyond the city and tourist belt, the scene changes; the
rest of the island is fairly rural. The bustle of tourism gives way to
fields of sugarcane that form corridors of tall stalks and grass-like
blades rippling in the wind ten feet above the road. Here everyone
is Bajan. Along the roads are people waiting for buses or walking
home from work and school. Most are well dressed, but some wear
the soiled clothes of road and field workers. Here and there groups
of young men "lime" (hang out) on the roadside, while older men
sit under the shade of a tree or in front of a rum shop, slamming
dominoes down on boards resting on oil drums. The rural settlement pattern is predominantly of small villages separated by fields
of sugarcane, occasionally broken by deep tree-filled gullies. In
these villages live many of the maids, security guards, cooks, taxi
drivers, and the other minions of the tourism industry. Their stories
are the stuff of this book.

Who Are the Tourists?

Thanks to annual surveys of departing visitors conducted by the
Barbados Ministry of Tourism, done at both the airport and the
cruise-ship terminal, we know something about visitors to Barbados.[7] There are two basic types of visitors—first are those who ar-

---

7. All of the demographic data on the tourists come from two Ministry of
Tourism reports: "Barbados Stay-Over Visitor Survey" and "Barbados Cruise
Passenger Survey," both prepared by the Caribbean Tourism Organization and
published by the Barbados Ministry of Tourism in 2008–2009.

rive on cruise ships and are only on the island for a day, and second are those who *land* or what are commonly called *stay-over* visitors. All island tourist destinations that attract cruise ships make this important distinction. Unlike some tourist destinations, such as Alaska, where cruise passengers comprise the vast majority of visitors, Barbados has about equal numbers of cruise and stay-over visitors. In 2009, 635,212 visitors to Barbados came by cruise ships, slightly more than the number of stay-over visitors. The Caribbean is the number-one cruise destination in the world, although it has stiff competition from Europe.

Compared to other Caribbean nations, Barbados has twice as many visitors annually—cruise and stay-over combined—as Bermuda, St. Lucia, and Antigua, but only a third as many as the Bahamas and Jamaica. A coral island, Barbados is endowed with miles of excellent white sand beaches. The other islands in the eastern Caribbean are volcanic and have fewer beaches of the same quality. The low relief of Barbados also allows nearly constant trade winds to produce a delightful climate and cloudless skies during much of the year. There is a high level of basic services—water, power, telephones, and television—that are important to many tourists who want to travel to an "exotic" place without losing the comforts of home. The island's extensive road network also makes its plantation houses, gardens, historic places, and other sites accessible to more adventurous visitors. Also, Barbados is deemed by Caribbean visitors to have higher levels of safety and security than many islands, such as Jamaica.

Where do the tourists come from? Their origins have changed over time. In the early years of the island as a British colony, most tourists came from Britain, the mother country. Then in the post–World War II years the flow shifted, such that by 1958, the first year statistics were compiled on the national origins of tourists, there were more visitors from the United States and Canada than from Britain. Since then, however, the numbers coming from Britain have steadily increased relative to North America, and by 1998 the number of Britons (187,000) once again exceeded the number of North Americans (166,000). Today the majority of stay-over tourists continue to be from Britain; cruise-ship visitors, however, are overwhelmingly from the United States and Canada, probably due to the greater popularity of cruise tourism to North Americans and the closer proximity of Caribbean cruise embarkation ports, notably Miami, to North Americans.

Tourist arrivals in Barbados, like all international tourist desti-nations, are highly dependent on the global economy, political sta-bility, and events at home. The terrorist attacks of 9/11, for example, fueling a worldwide financial slump and concerns about the safety of international travel, caused a 7 percent drop in visitor arrivals to Barbados in the year following the attack and a 2 percent drop the following year. By 2004, however, tourist numbers in Barbados had returned to their pre-9/11 levels. At the time of this writing in the summer of 2010, the U.S.-precipitated worldwide recession has once again curbed tourism, and, in turn, affected related economic activities such as construction and trade and raised unemployment.

The stay-over visitors are the bread and butter of Barbados's tourism industry. According to the Ministry of Tourism's surveys, the primary motivation for coming to Barbados for most stay-over visitors to the island is to "vacation." (About 20% come for business and/or to visit friends and relatives.) About half (54%) of survey respondents were repeat visitors to the island, including 35% who had been to Barbados four or more times previously. When asked what influenced their decision to come to Barbados rather than some other tourist destination, the stay-over tourists overwhelm-ingly (72%) mentioned the beaches and climate, with heritage/cul-ture a distant third. For nine out of every ten North American visitors, Barbados was their sole destination, and they had no plans to visit other islands; in contrast, one out of every four Europeans surveyed were visiting other islands or destinations. The difference is probably due to the greater distance the Europeans must travel to reach the Caribbean; making fewer trips to the region, they are more likely to want to see more than just one island on their trip. Europeans also typically have longer vacations or holidays than North Americans.

Over two-thirds of all stay-over visitors made their own ar-rangements; one-third bought a prepaid package. What sources of information did they use in planning a trip to Barbados? The survey found a heavy reliance on doing their own research on the Inter-net, along with talking to friends and relatives. In sharp contrast to earlier decades, only 20 percent used a travel agent, and just 6 per-cent made use of information from newspapers and magazines. Tourists from elsewhere in the Caribbean were somewhat less likely to rely on the Internet and to rely more on friends/relatives. Typi-cally a lot of preparation went into planning their Barbados vaca-tion. Nearly half had planned a trip to Barbados for three months or more before traveling. Visitors from elsewhere in the Caribbean were more spontaneous and devoted less time to planning their trip; those from the UK and Continental Europe, who were traveling greater distances and at greater expense, spent the most time planning.

The Ministry of Tourism's surveys also tried to capture what visitors do after they arrive in Barbados. The data show that, consistent with the visitors' reasons for coming to Barbados, the most popular activity was visiting beaches, followed by sight-seeing (this was true for both stay-over and cruise-ship visitors). Apart from the beaches, the most popular sight-seeing destinations were Harrison's Cave, a popular fish fry on the beach at Oistins, and Plantation Great Houses and gardens. Next in importance were shopping (41% of all visitors), water sports, cruises, and other boat trips. (Most of these sites and activities are described in the forthcoming narratives.) Comparing the activity data by nationality, North American visitors are far less likely to go fishing or to visit gardens and nature than are Britons and Europeans. But North Americans are more likely to make a boat trip or engage in water sports.

On average, the non-cruise visitors stayed 7.4 days on the island. When asked how satisfied they were with their stay, they gave high marks to the beaches, their accommodations, and the friendli-

Pool and beach at Crystal Cove Hotel on the west coast.

ness of the locals. They gave lower ratings and were sometimes critical of the service and local handicrafts and souvenirs. When asked if they would come back to Barbados, 60 percent said "definitely" and 31 percent said "probably." A majority of the cruise-ship visitors surveyed also expressed interest in returning to Barbados, and next time for a longer stay

The Ministry of Tourism survey data on how much the visitors spend each day in Barbados reveal why governments everywhere tend to value stay-over tourists more than cruise tourists.[8] The stay-over visitors to Barbados spent (2009) an estimated average of $181.00 per day, more than three times what cruise passengers spent per day. The difference is due to the accommodation, food, and entertainment for the cruise passengers all being provided on board ship. Most of the onshore expenditures for cruise passengers were for duty-free purchases, other shopping, and transportation, notably taxis.

As noted earlier, tourism has been indispensable to the island's economy. Tourist expenditure is now the most important growth-inducing factor in the economy, and its receipts are a major contributor to the country's GDP. Tourism has created new employment at the rate of about one job for every hotel bed on the island. Ten percent of Barbadians are directly employed in the industry as maids and security guards, waitresses and barmen, receptionists and gardeners, and so forth. Others work on the margins of the economy as self-employed food venders, beach vendors, jet-ski operators, and even beach boys. Still other people sell locally grown produce to hotels and restaurants that cater primarily to the tourist market. The rest of the population experiences the indirect effects of tourism on the infrastructure, environment, and social climate of Barbados. Everyone on the island is touched in some way by tourism. Tourism has enabled Barbadians to have one of the highest per-capita incomes in the Caribbean.[9] Over 90 percent of Bajan

---

8. The government's Ministry of Tourism collects information on visitors to analyze trends and market developments in tourism, identify "bottlenecks" or problems with their tourism product, and to design better marketing strategies to attract more visitors to the island. The data is also used to compare Barbados's "tourism product" with other countries, particularly its neighboring and competing Caribbean islands.

9. The Central Bank of Barbados gives per-capita income in Barbados as $7,350 in 2007; other sources cite a higher figure, such as the United States Department of Commerce's Commercial Services, who estimated the GDP per-capita income to be $17,300 in 2006.

The cruise ship terminal, Bridgetown. *Courtesy of Barbados Tourism Authority.*

households have a television and a refrigerator, and nearly half own a car. In addition, by creating consumers for art and entertainment, tourism has encouraged the development of local music, dance, performance, visual arts, and crafts. The quantity and quality of live entertainment on Barbados is high considering the island's small population. Tourism is responsible for the creation of a major cultural event that has been embraced by Bajans. Crop Over was originally a celebration held among plantation workers at the end of the sugarcane harvest. This tradition was introduced as a national celebration in 1974 to promote tourism during the slack summer season. Held at first in hotels with dancers dressed in colorful Trinidad-style carnival costumes, the new holiday was later reoriented to the local market. It is now a popular national holiday that entices even Barbadians living abroad back home.

But not all the impacts have been positive. The influx of large numbers of visitors to a small-island destination such as Barbados has a more profound effect in cultural, social, and environmental

Local vendors deep-frying fish, chicken, and pork on Baxter's Road, Bridgetown. Known as "the street that never sleeps," locals and visitors gather here to sample the offerings of vendors, tiny rum shops, and restaurants. *Courtesy of Barbados Tourism Authority.*

The rugged north coast of St. Lucy. *Courtesy of Barbados Tourism Authority.*

terms than is true of mainland destinations or of large islands such as Jamaica. Locals are likely to have more contact with tourists on small islands, and the island's physical resources are more susceptible to the negative effects of tourist development and usage. More than mainland destinations, islands can be damaged for generations by unplanned and uncontrolled tourism; they simply do not have the depth of resources to allow for a recovery period (Mowforth and Munt 1998). Island tourism, generally, is also more vulnerable to the vagaries of the market than mainland destinations and is in the unhappy position of having to rely on the services of airlines, shipping companies, and tour operators that make decisions in the best interest of shareholders and often do not consider the very real concerns of their island hosts.

The environment of Barbados has not always fared well. The large number of visitors has contributed to traffic congestion, exhaust fumes, and noise. The south and west coasts have been overdeveloped with hotels, condominiums, and tourist-oriented restaurants, boutiques, and gift shops. (Only the heavy surf, strong undertow, and steep cliffs have saved the north and east coasts from the same fate.) Along some stretches of the tourist belt, it is difficult for local people to even catch a glimpse of the sea for all the development. Many Barbadians are beginning to feel they are losing access to the seashore, cut off from the most desirable areas of their own island. Many of the island's prime beaches have been taken over by tourists. By law, all beaches up to the high-water mark are public in Barbados, as they are in most of the Caribbean, but in practice, access to the beaches has sometimes been restricted. Some private homes and hotels on the west coast have roped off swimming areas in front of their properties, ostensibly to protect guests from jet-skis. But it also has the effect of keeping away local beachgoers and fishermen, who use these areas to catch bait.

Many locals feel uncomfortable or unwelcome sitting on the sand or taking their sea baths among tourists. A student of mine, Karin Wirthlin, who had offered to teach a young girl from the family she was living with how to swim, described their trip to the beach:

> On the day of the first lesson we left for the beach. . . . She was walking beside me, and was so excited she could not keep her anticipation to herself. She was laughing, talking, and swinging my hand in hers. However, when we arrived at the road that leads to the beach you can turn either right to the beach where the tourists are, or left to the

beach without a nearby hotel. Without thinking I went to the right. My little friend tensed up and became very wary; she squeezed my hand and whispered, "Karin why are we going to the white people's beach?"

In the 1980s, conflict over the beaches became the subject of a popular calypso. The chairman of the Barbados Tourist Board, Jack Deer, introduced wardens to the beaches in an effort to reduce sexual harassment of women by local beach boys, causing some critics to interpret the use of wardens as a strategy to discourage black Bajans from using the beach. A hard-hitting calypso attacked Jack Deer and reflected the fears of Barbadians about the future of their beaches. "Jack," the calypso begins:

> I grow up bathing in sea water
> but nowadays there is bare horror
> if I only venture down by the shore
> police telling me I can't bathe anymore.

Garbage is another impact, as tourists produce several times more waste per capita than do locals, overburdening the island's one landfill. The island's ever-increasing number of golf courses, which primarily serve tourists, consume enormous quantities of water and can reduce the flow to household taps to a trickle, irritating local residents. The golf courses also use inordinately large amounts of harmful fertilizers and pesticides, much of which gets washed into the sea, damaging the coral reefs. Water pollution from hotels, despite the hotels now being required to have on-site sewage treatment plants, contributes to the problem; so do the hard surfaces like roads, parking lots, and roofs that come with development—they reduce the opportunity for rainwater to percolate into the ground; instead much of it runs off directly into the sea, thereby transporting surface pollutants into the sea and losing a valuable source of freshwater to the island's aquifers.

The pollutants are killing the reefs and eroding the beaches. Although wastewater is not yet a public health risk because it is being treated, the large amounts of phosphates and nitrates remaining in the water stress the living coral, and particulate matter in sewage retards the growth of corals by blocking sunlight. (Modern agriculture is also damaging, as the runoff from fertilizers and pesticides harms the corals.) Over time, the corals die and the reef begins to break down. Healthy growing corals are vital to tourism because their calcium carbonate skeletons form the very material from which beaches are regenerated. When they die, the beaches are doomed. In the meantime, as the reefs deteriorate there is no barrier to absorb wave energy and nothing to prevent beach erosion.

Hotel developers have unwittingly hastened the demise of their beaches by building too close to the shoreline. At high tide, the waves strike the hotel's seawall instead of the beach, preventing the sand particles that would normally drop out as the waves run up the beach from doing so. The government did establish set-back requirements for coastal construction (30 meters from the mean high-water mark) in 1972, but these restrictions were sometimes ignored and enforcement has been lax. Also a lot of coastal construction was in place prior to 1972, and today there is so little space between the coast and the road that there is limited opportunity for landward reconstruction of these properties.

Until recently reefs used by scuba divers were being damaged by the anchors of dive boats that drag along the reef, breaking off coral heads. A new program called the Mooring Buoy Project now requires commercial dive boats to connect to buoys instead of dropping anchor, thereby reducing damage to the reef. Personally owned yachts, however, have been harder to control, and they continue to drop anchor wherever they please, according to the government's Coastal Zone Management Unit. Not only is an important underwater tourist attraction diminished in this way, but because corals are nurseries for many fisheries, their deterioration also threatens another resource—reef fish.

Oddly, while tourism degrades the environment on one hand, it can also lead to greater environmental awareness. The tourists' appreciation of scenery, coral reefs, and wildlife has stimulated government agencies and planners to do more to preserve the environment, and not just natural places but also the built environment. To cite just one example, the government has enhanced the appearance of some major roads and roundabouts, particularly the highway from the airport to town (the route most heavily traveled by visitors) with flowers, landscaping, and sculpture. Coming from the metropolitan countries, most tourists are familiar with the consequences of pollution, and through conversations with locals and in frequent letters to newspapers, they remind Barbadians of the beauty of their island and the costs of degrading it. Tourism has also provided support for the preservation of natural resources (e.g., a proposed national park on the east coast, protecting the reefs with boat moorings, and banning some types of reef fishing). And entry fees have been used to conserve and improve some resources, such as plantation houses, the Barbados Wildlife Preserve, and several botanical gardens.

Tourism has social impacts as well, though they are far more difficult to measure than the economic ones, a fact that probably delayed their study. Privacy has been lost in villages and neighborhoods near tourist attractions. Along the routes traveled by visitors, locals may feel the intrusion as tour buses and tourists in their cars gawk at people. The tourists, of course, are interested in seeing the "living culture," such as locals cutting sugarcane, slaughtering a sheep, or playing dominoes outside a rum shop. It is authentic, unlike the contrived things and events that comprise most of their touring activities and tourist attractions. But many locals tire of being photographed and of being asked endless questions.

In every community there are others who welcome interactions with tourists. Some see such contacts as a way to broaden their horizons. Interaction and exchange of information is often entertaining to the unemployed who hang out on the roadside and at the rum shop because the visitors relieve the tedium of inactivity. And some profit from the tourists' curiosity, such as makers and vendors of jewelry, beachwear, pottery, and paintings. In fact, they manufacture their wares in public spaces, hoping that some of the gawkers will become buyers. Tourism creates a market for crafts that often would not exist otherwise, and one can cite examples from all over the world, from Samoa to the Arctic, where local or ethnic art is sustained by tourism (Pearce 1982).

But how locals feel about tourists depends largely on the sheer numbers of people visiting. Small numbers are easily tolerated and may be enjoyed, as I have often witnessed in the remote village where I live when I am in Barbados, in which tourists occasionally arrive at the village rum shop having taken a wrong turn. But too many tourists can overwhelm locals and produce considerable indifference, if not hostility and antagonism. Friction sometimes occurs when locals and visitors share beaches and other recreational areas. Tourists expect to be treated well no matter how they act, and they expect local people to be cheerful and courteous. "I was startled to be spoken to in a gruff manner by a man behind the counter," groused a surprised Canadian tourist in a letter of complaint to a local newspaper, "telling me that I had no business coming in his shop without a shirt."

One consequence of tourism that worries some Barbadians is its effect on the work ethic of the youth. Tourism not only raises expectations and the desire for material goods, it also gives some youths an opportunity to make "easy" money quick. The beach-boy phenomenon discussed elsewhere in this book is one example. Others are drugs and crime, especially burglary and theft. The attitude of a growing number of youths is, "Why should I work all week when I can make the same money in one drug deal or by hustling tourists?" "There is a feeling out there among the younger guys," elaborated Wayne Hunte, a professor at the University of the West Indies,

> that there's a lot of money to be had and that "we want part of it, and we want it now." Serious steady work is not fast enough for them and doesn't pay well enough. So there's a tendency to hustle and perhaps cut corners for it [money]. There's a thin line between hustling and cutting corners and doing illegal things. . . . I think [tourism] has had that kind of impact, although it's hard to separate this from the impact of television which has changed expectations—expectations that are unrealistic given the resource base of this country.

Because tourists have money and come to Barbados to have a good time, they provide a ready market for drugs. Selling to them has become a quick way for unemployed youths to make money. Indeed, the first four drug arrests in Barbados (for marijuana) occurred in 1971 just as mass tourism was getting under way; three of the four individuals arrested for buying drugs were tourists. By the 1980s, cocaine and "rock" (crack) had arrived on the island. Both drug-dealing and other crimes occur primarily in areas with heavy concentrations of tourists. Barbados is now one of many drug transshipment sites in the Caribbean, although it is a minor one compared to the Grenadines and Antigua. Many Barbadians say that without tourism the drug trade would never have developed on their island.

The social impact of tourism on locals, much like economic impacts, is greater when host societies are small, unsophisticated, and isolated. Because of the island's small size, Barbadians are likely to have more contact with tourists than, say, people on the much larger islands of Jamaica and Trinidad. But the impact that contact has on a society also depends on how wide the gap in education and modernity is between tourists and locals—the greater the gap, the more the impact. And in this regard, the impact may be less in Barbados than in many other, poorer Caribbean islands.

2 WORK AND ENCOUNTERS IN TOURISM

The workers' narratives that comprise the bulk of this book relate to important issues in our understanding of tourism. This chapter strives to frame and provide context, beyond the mostly macro-level issues dealt with in chapter 1, for the stories that follow.[1]

Tourism Work and Encounters with Guests

What makes the work of tourism distinctive from most jobs, and particularly interesting, is the frequent interaction its workers have with guests. Workers, who are mostly from modest educational and social backgrounds, intermingle with guests from distant lands and cultures who have widely different lifestyles and levels of income. What also makes the interaction unique, as Malcolm Crick (1989) notes, is that during the interaction one is at leisure while the other is at work. One has economic assets but little knowledge of the local culture, while the other has knowledge (cultural capital) but little money. One is usually white and the other usually black. One is from the First World and the other from the developing or Third World.

---

1. Sources that were particularly important in writing this chapter were review articles by Erik Cohen (1984), Malcolm Crick (1989), and Amanda Stronza (2001).

The encounters between host and guest are mostly transitory, nonrepetitive, and asymmetrical (Cohen 1984). Most visitors are interested in achieving immediate gratification rather than in developing a relationship. They need not consider how their present actions will affect their relationship in the future, because there isn't likely to be one. Hence the relationship is prone to exploitation and mistrust. One exception is the hotel guest, especially repeat clientele, who intends to return.

That most tourists are white and most Barbadians are black influences many interactions between tourists and locals. Racism or expectations of it based on the country's colonial history sometimes complicate interactions. Workers in positions of authority, such as hotel manager Martin Barrow in chapter 4, find that some guests have a difficult time accepting managers and supervisors who are black. Sometimes it becomes comical, as in an incident described by one of my students, in which an unhappy guest went to the front desk to lodge a complaint. The hotel manager, a black man, just happened to be at the desk when the visitor approached, loudly demanding to see the manager. The manager said, "Yes, that's me." The visitor refused to believe that a black man could be the manager of a luxury hotel. When the manager repeated that he was indeed the manager, the visitor left in a huff. Other tourists may simply make statements or ask questions that reveal how salient race is to them. For example, I once saw an American tourist walk directly up to two hotel barmen and ask, "How do you guys feel about waiting on white people? Does it bother you?"

Some scholars (Phillips 1999; Mowforth and Munt 1998) argue that merely having to serve white vacationers, many of whom believe themselves and their cultures to be superior, puts black hosts in an inferior position and that many acquiesce to a view of whites as dominant. The history of the Caribbean has been one in which its people were taught the superiority of things white and the inferiority of things black. It is not surprising then that many workers do not see the difference between merely providing service (doing one's job) and espousing a subservient mentality. As one manager explained, "Too many of my people equate service with servitude." Hence, a focus of the training within the tourism industry has been teaching employees to be friendly and courteous and to look beyond race. As one government leader warned his fellow Barbadians, "I urge you to reflect on the damage which even a ten to fifteen percent decline in tourism expenditure will do to the Barbados

Visitor having her hair braided.
Courtesy of Franklin Otto.

economy and to further reflect on . . . the impact of such [racial] confrontation on tourism activity. National pride, yes. Racism, no."

While urging its employees to be color-blind, the tourism industry in Barbados itself has its own record of racism. Hotel management still remains disproportionately white. Service provided to local black Barbadians in hotels and restaurants is often slow or indifferent. Many resorts discourage locals from using their beaches. Hotels that have converted to all-inclusive plans no longer allow people who are not guests onto hotel premises to eat in their restaurants, drink at their bars, or dance in their nightclubs, effectively banning all locals. On the other side, race is sometimes overtly manipulated by Bajans in dealing with white tourists. Beach vendors occasionally use it as a sales strategy, challenging tourists with the accusation, "You don't want to buy from me because I'm black." Beach boys may say to female tourists, "Hi, I called to you earlier, but when you didn't answer, I thought maybe it was because you don't like us black boys" (Karch and Dann 1981).

Complicating interactions with locals is the fact that tourists are not themselves when they are vacationing. As Jeremy Boissevain

(1996) observed, one of the thrills of being abroad is temporarily permitted illicit behavior, made possible by the anonymity that visitors enjoy in foreign lands. When on holiday their world is inverted from what it is at home—from work to play, normal morality to promiscuity, saving to conspicuous spending, structure to freedom, and responsibility to self-indulgence (Crick 1989). Some types of tourism, however, such as the package tour, may actually involve less freedom and more structure than normal life.

The relationship between guest and worker is also largely commercial, as one is paying for the services of the other. But it must also involve hospitality, which is essential to the success of tourism. It is no surprise that tourists prefer destinations where the hosts are friendly and where they feel welcome and safe. For this reason, it is important to the tourism industry that interactions between guests and workers go smoothly. There is a keen awareness that guests are unlikely to return, whether to a specific hotel or to the country, if they are not treated well. The Barbados Tourism Authority (BTA) encourages locals to make guests feel welcome with awareness programs and tourism slogans such as "Tourism success means Bajan progress." Aired on radio and television, the slogan reminds Barbadians of the importance of being courteous to tourists, which includes smiling and helping tourists when they ask for directions or have questions. Another popular slogan is "Tourism is our business, play your part." "Treat them well and they'll come back," advised one public service announcement on television in the 1990s.

Whatever the specific slogan, the message is always to be nice to tourists. It is not just aimed at hotel employees and taxi drivers but at all Barbadians who come into contact with visitors. One Barbados television advertisement titled "Tourism and You," put on by the Government Information Service, features two men playing dominoes on a beach (Wirthlin 2000). "We need all the tourists we can get," says the first character. "We all got a part to play." "But I never come into contact with tourists," says the second character. "You'll get your chance," says the first. "If they come and talk with you in the street . . . make them feel at home."

I have often witnessed the kind of behavior that such ads aim to eliminate. Near the village where I live when in Barbados, boys hang out on the roadside and enjoy giving wrong directions to tourists looking for the St. Nicholas Abbey plantation house, a popular attraction. In my field notes, I described one incident that I observed at the Barbados airport:

I am at the American Airlines counter when a well-dressed American couple in their late thirties rushes up and asks the agent if the 3:55 flight to New York has already left. It is eight minutes before scheduled departure. The couple is very agitated. They say it is a medical emergency, that the man needs a special blood transfusion and that if he doesn't get to New York tonight he might die. The airline agent, a woman in her late forties, takes their tickets and begins to do the paperwork, but without urgency and without saying anything. She never tells them their chances of getting on the flight. Both man and wife urge her to call the gate to hold the plane. "Please, please call the gate." The agent mumbles something. The couple grow more agitated and annoyed with the agent's casual attitude. The agent asks for $50 for departure taxes. The man throws down twice that amount in U.S. bills and says keep the change. The agent proceeds to make him change. At last, she finishes their ticket and sends them to the gate. At no point did she ever express concern for his predicament or speed up the ticketing.

Training for Tourism

In an effort to do a better job of training its tourism workforce, and to avoid alienating guests like the airline passengers above, Barbados established its own Hospitality Institute. Barbados opened its first "hotel school" in 1964; it initially was without a campus and did its training on site in various hotels. As the government and some industry leaders began to appreciate the importance of training programs to providing a professionalized workforce—deemed essential to enhancing the island's reputation and to ensuring the long-term benefits of a continuous and growing flow of tourists—it made the hotel school part of the Barbados Community College. Then in 1997, in a joint project with the European Union, the government opened a beautiful new campus—the Barbados Hospitality Institute—on the site of a former luxury hotel. An impressive peach-and-white building with a spacious central courtyard, pool, and tennis courts and elegantly appointed rooms leading out to wrought-iron balconies, it evokes memories of the grandeur of colonial architecture. It has 350 students and a 20-room student-run hotel.

The institute offers several degree programs: tourism and travel, hotel catering, and culinary arts. The following list of courses that students may enroll in says much about the institute's mission: Principles of Food Preparation, Food and Beverage Awareness, Social Skills, Sanitation Safety and First Aid, Alcoholic Beverages, and

Caribbean Politics. "In terms of waiting on guests," said one instructor, "we teach our students to be friendly but not to over-fraternize; to be punctual, neat, tidy, and clean. We teach them social skills and we try to motivate them."

While experts say that human resource development and training is the single most important issue facing world tourism, there are still many in the private tourism sector of Barbados who view training as a cost rather than an investment for the future. The result is that training programs are often underfunded and are often canceled during economic slowdowns. Some hotel managers still don't feel that training is as important as marketing.

In the larger society there is some stigma attached to tourism training. Some head teachers of the upscale older secondary schools are not keen to have their students gravitate toward tourism. "It's mostly because they do not understand what tourism is," said the Hospitality Institute's director, Bernice Critchlow-Earle. "Even some of my academic colleagues on the main campus visualize us down here stirring pots and doing menial things. They don't think the degree we offer has the same importance as a degree in history or economics." But when I returned to Barbados in 2010 it was pretty clear that working in tourism was becoming more respectable. With the economy so dependent on tourism, more young people were seeing tourism as the sector with the best job prospects. "In long-term internships in places like Disney World and Nantucket Island," noted Critchlow-Earle, "our students have seen very talented people make money and good careers in tourism, which has had an impression on them."

How to interact with tourists and the importance of tourism to the nation are now taught in school alongside reading, writing, and arithmetic. The Caribbean Tourism Research Center (CTRC) holds workshops for teachers so that they can introduce tourism into the school curriculum. Heading the CTRC's list of recommendations is teaching students to be aware of their demeanor and of the need to change their deportment in order to match the expectations of visitors. That students have to be told indicates something of the unnatural strain that tourism can place on locals.

Close Encounters: Sex and Romance Tourism

The most intimate and talked-about guest-host encounters are those between female tourists and beach boys. (See the narratives of Rosco Roach and Ricky Hinds in chapter 5.) These relationships are so well known that many Barbadians believe that any foreign woman who arrives on the island without a male companion has come with more than tourism's "three Ss"—sun, sand, and sea—in mind. Some women do come to Barbados hoping to have a relationship with a black man. Locals say it began in the early 1960s when many French Canadians began to visit the Caribbean on inexpensive charter flights. French Canadian women are still thought to be the visitors most eager for sex. A study of beach boys and their clients in the Dominican Republic by Herold, Garcia, and DeMoya (2001) also reported that French Canadian women were eager clients. Fantasy notions of the sexual Other play a part in these beach boy–tourist interactions. Some white female tourists regard black Bajan men as "fantastic lovers," as more "exotic," "natural," and sexually endowed than white men—which is the idea behind popular expressions such as "once you go black, you never go back."

While some women undoubtedly do have no-strings sex in mind, other women fall into romantic relationships with local men that they believe are genuine and unique. The latter do not view their activity as hustling or prostitution; rather, they emphasize the romance aspect of the encounter.

Beach boys initially approach female tourists by offering something to sell, such as jet-ski rides, shell jewelry, or aloe for sunburns. Most are young and muscular and roam the beaches in revealing swimsuits. Some wear dreadlocks, enhancing their exotic and natural appeal. Women tourists who at home might be considered plain, overweight, or too old for such a young man may be especially vulnerable to the beach boy's "sweet talk." "You married? You have a special friend?" he asks. "A beautiful girl like you should have a boyfriend," he responds, no matter how she has replied. "You need a Bajan boyfriend," he insists. "How you goin' to experience Barbados, if you never sleep with a Bajan man?" Beach boy–tourist encounters reverse conventional gender and class roles, because a Barbadian working-class male would never be invited by a middle-class educated Barbadian woman for a drink in a hotel or a meal in a nice restaurant, much less to a nearly all-white resort.

Anthropologists Deborah Pruitt and Suzanne LaFont (1995) refer to the behavior surrounding these liaisons as "romance tourism" and argue that it is quite different from the "sex tourism" found in underdeveloped countries such as Thailand or the Philippines, in which male tourists travel explicitly to avail themselves of the paid services of local prostitutes, most of whom have been forced into prostitution by poverty. In contrast, relationships between beach boys and female tourists usually involve a discourse of romance and the possibility of a long-term relationship. The beach boy has some leverage in the relationship. He is on familiar ground, while the tourist is in a foreign land. He is knowledgeable about such relationships, while she may be unfamiliar with them. But ultimately it is the female tourist who has control, since she pays the bills, can break it off, and will leave the island to return home. She may be emotionally vulnerable, but it is the beach boy who is financially dependent and who must show deference and appreciation in order to maintain the relationship.

For beach boys, relationships with tourists provide money, sex, intimacy with a foreigner, short-term comforts (e.g., dinner, drinks, a nice room), and enhanced status among their peers—as self-styled nicknames such as "Dr. Love" suggest. Barbadian masculinity is defined largely by sexual prowess that includes the ability to satisfy women, and what better evidence than being able to attract foreign women. Besides good sex, the women get a glimpse inside Barbadian culture. He tells her about his life growing up in Barbados and shows her a good time by taking her on a tour of the island (in her rental car), showing sights that ordinary tourists do not see, such as the sea turtles that beach boy Ricky Hinds mentions in chapter 5. Sometimes they will stay in contact after the woman returns home, often with the beach boy hoping for financial support. The following excerpt from an e-mail sent to me in January 2011 describes the experience of one American woman in her early 40s with a beach boy:

> Within one week of being in Barbados I fell hard for a guy. I liked him so much and we had so much fun together. I think it was partially the simple and slower pace environment and the beauty of Barbados that I loved too. After I returned home he contacted me with many stories of his need and requests for money. I didn't send money mostly because I do not have excess funds to part with. Though I saw lovely qualities in him, I also believe that he plays games with female tourists . . . I don't like to judge people, so I try to just remember the fun times we had and let it go. He claims he is not trying to play me, but that when the storm came through in Oct. a tree fell on his house and then his grandma who he lives with recently died of diabetes. I don't know if these things are true, but it doesn't matter. I hope we can be friends when I see him again when I go in June, but I do not expect anything else.

Recall the early proponents of tourism in chapter 1 who talked about tourism as a modernizing influence. Pope Paul VI, for example, asserted that world tourism had a "civilizing mission" that would bridge the gaps separating social classes and cultures (Hiller 1976, 98). What impacts do encounters with guests really have on the hosts? Do these encounters influence change? Most scholars say yes, and some even suggest that we should think of international tourism as a modern agent of acculturation (Crick 1989). When tourists and locals come together—an intermingling of peoples of diverse backgrounds—both have the opportunity not only to glimpse how others live but also to reflect on their own lives through the lives of others. As the narratives show, tourism exposes locals to a lifestyle that is appealing because it is based on the consumption of luxuries and on leisure activities. Some tourists flash their cameras, sports equipment, and money around, wear expensive clothing and jewelry, stay at expensive hotels, and eat at the best restaurants. For most Barbadians, just going to a full-service restaurant is an extravagance, done only to celebrate major family events such as a child passing the Common Entrance Examination, graduating from college, or getting married. "The locals see what the tourists have and how they're living, and they want it," explained one hotel worker. "They don't see the fifty weeks of work behind it. They think it's easy."

Of course the tourist lifestyle is a distortion of the normal lives of most visitors, but unless locals have been abroad themselves, they may not know the difference. Tourism, like television, has the potential to transfer outside values and patterns of behavior to Barbadians through its "demonstration effects." That is, tourists become a reference group for the host society; they are living manifestations of the wealth Barbadians so frequently see in movies and on TV. But what exactly do guests communicate in interactions with their hosts? What aspects of the visitors' behavior do hosts observe and mimic? Might there be negative influences such as the injection of lavish consumption habits into a developing society that can ill afford it? In the workers' narratives, we get a sense of the kind and content of the interaction and some clues to the types of individual change it produces.

Jobs, Gender, and Social Mobility

The tourist industry, in general, offers a broad base of unskilled and semiskilled jobs but a narrow upper echelon. (Of the twenty-one workers represented in this book's narratives, only four are from top management.) In the Caribbean, management positions are often held by non-nationals. Many locals believe the hotel industry has a glass ceiling, making it difficult for Barbadians to become hotel managers or executive chefs. "Although tourism is necessary to our very economic survival," notes Critchlow-Earle, director of the Barbados Hospitality Institute, "jobs in tourism still don't count for much; they do not have high status. Barbados is a highly class-conscious, stratified society, and parents would rather see their sons training to be lawyers and accountants than working in hotels." As one hotel manager commented, "No Barbadian ever aspired to being a waiter" (Lerch and Levy 1990, 360).

In a review of the tourism literature, Erik Cohen (1984) notes that one of the most ubiquitous effects of tourism worldwide has been the creation of jobs for women. In the Caribbean, many women have found employment in hotels, as guides, and in ancillary economic activities such as the production of crafts and souvenirs for the tourist market. Some of them did not have a wage-paying job before being employed in tourism. The overwhelming majority of the applicants to the Barbados Hospitality Institute are also women. Though many women are employed in tourism, they have even more difficulty than men breaking into the ranks of management (Lerch and Levy 1990). As Critchlow-Earle put it, "There are a lot of women coming up in Barbados, getting better opportunities at the top levels, but not in tourism. You won't see women head chefs. You won't see women managing the hotel. . . . You go to the Hotel Association meetings and it's mostly men."

The opening of employment in tourism to women often raises living standards, but it can also produce tensions in traditional families. A study of former plantation women who obtained jobs at a beach resort in Hawaii found that their employment stirred conflicts in their rural lifestyle and family social order (Cottington, cited in Gee, Makens, and Choy 1997). Jealousy was noted among some husbands whose wives had to dress up to serve hotel guests. A subsequent study of the same population three years later, however, reported increased family income, greater independence, an increased sense of self-worth, expanded contacts with fellow employees, and an expanded worldview. Moreover, the wives' husbands had assumed more household and child-rearing chores and had developed more respect for their wives as competent individuals able to hold good jobs. In short, the initial effects of new employment in tourism were negative, while the long-term effects in this case were beneficial.

Stereotyping

As local people sustain contact with tourists over time they begin to make finer distinctions, developing categories or stereotypes that are often based on nationality. In a study of tourism in a Spanish maritime community, Oriol Pi-Sunyer (1977) found that the earliest tourists to arrive in a new destination were treated as individuals in a personalized relationship. But with the advent of mass tourism, locals became incapable of relating to each visitor individually and began to create an "ethnic typology." Pearce (1982) notes that it is often the negative attributes of tourists that are noted by locals, which then crystallize into a stereotype that is uniformly applied. Evans-Pritchard (1989) has noted that scholars have largely ignored how locals perceive guests. In the narratives, however, we often hear Barbadians expressing their stereotypes of tourists, based principally on nationality, such as the British being "reserved," Canadians "thrifty" or "cheap," and Germans "disciplined." Stereotypes also exist for gender and age and for cruiseship visitors (they are believed to be less independent, less adventuresome, and less knowledgeable about the island). Locals readily acknowledge that stereotypes are just that and that often there are exceptions, that not all guests fit the mold. Nonetheless, stereotypes can influence how locals, workers and nonworkers alike, interact with tourists.

Is Tourism Neocolonialism?

Many observers of Caribbean tourism have raised concerns that tourism is a form of neocolonialism or leisure imperialism (Hiller 1976; Crick 1989; Chambers 2002). Tourism, they say, involves relationships of power in which the metropolitan countries have the upper hand over the developing tourism-dependent nations. Tourism reawakens memories of race and labor relations of the colonial past and so perpetuates resentments and antagonisms. As early as the 1970s, some intellectuals had criticized foreign influence in the Caribbean region as "demeaning and a recolonization by other means" (Pattullo 1996). "Tourism is whorism" was a phrase coined in the 1970s.

There are two issues here. One, discussed earlier, is the social issue of Afro-Caribbean people—waiters, maids, taxi drivers, and so forth—serving predominantly white guests, which some say is reminiscent of the old plantation system in which black slaves attended to their white masters and overseers. The second, an economic issue, concerns mastery at the national level in which the metropolitan countries of the North exercise control over the less-developed and dependent nations of the South. They do so in part through their domination of international tourism, achieved through the vertical integration described in chapter 1. Neocolonialism takes power from the local and regional levels and concentrates it in the hands of foreign-owned companies. Foreign interests also induce Caribbean tourist destinations to supply whatever their tourists want—fast food, air-conditioning, swimming pools, and imported food and beverages—under the threat of directing their clients elsewhere if these commodities and services are not provided. At the operational level, the higher-paying positions in the hotels and attractions are given to foreigners, ostensibly because they possess the necessary experience and expertise. The lower-paying, more menial jobs go to the local population.

Some scholars argue that tourism development, in its structural form, often follows the preexisting socioeconomic structure (Crick 1989). For the Caribbean, according to this line of thought, tourism recapitulates its colonial past (and, as in the colonial past, it is defended with the rhetoric of development). Amanda Stronza (2001), however, cautions that in the absence of analysis we sometimes wrongly assume that tourism was entirely imposed on developing societies. As we saw in chapter 1, international tourism in the Caribbean was actively sought by regional government officials and elites after they were convinced of its merits (although some analysts feel they were conned) by international agencies. Tourism development was not a grassroots movement or something citizens voted for in a democratic process. That Caribbean governments invited international tourism does not excuse its lopsided power relationships and its tendency to promote dependency in the region. Though these issues are complex and not readily discernible on the ground to the average Barbadian, or even to many who work in tourism, I nonetheless asked most of my interviewees their opinions about the notion of tourism as "the new slavery." As the narratives show, most did not see a connection.

The Research Methods

Before turning to the workers' stories, some explanation of how the research was conducted is in order. After some months of mulling over the idea for this study, I made a list of the key occupations in the industry and divided them by workplace—airport, hotel, beach, and so forth. Once I had the list, I began asking friends and village neighbors who worked in tourism to recommend individuals who might be good subjects. I was primarily looking for individuals who would talk openly about their lives and work. I then contacted the individuals and requested an interview at their workplace.

Some found it difficult to understand why I would want to record their lives. Not being politicians, performers, sportsmen, or rich or famous, they had difficulty grasping why their lives would be of interest to readers in North America. I explained that the subjects of oral history are often ordinary people and that I was mostly interested in getting an insider's perspective on the work of tourism. I also said that the research aimed to enter into the scholarly record the everyday lives of tourism workers, who had heretofore been overlooked. That was usually enough to get their consent.

The interviews were conducted in an inductive fashion in that my questions were not guided by any particular hypotheses. I came to the project with a general interest in tourism that emerged over fifteen years of visiting Barbados to teach and do research. I also had a longtime interest in the anthropology of work and a specific interest in doing oral history. I had just finished an oral history project on workers in professional baseball (Gmelch and Weiner 1998) and was interested in doing something similar.

The interviews were done at the subjects' workplaces, for their convenience and because I wanted to see their work environments. They were conducted with a general interview guide, a sort of shopping list of major topics and questions. The guide functioned more as a topical road map than an explicit set of questions and was constructed from the ground up; that is, the topics were ones that had come up in the many informal conversations I had with tourism workers before the oral history work began. I wanted the narratives to reflect as much as possible the workers' own perspectives and concerns rather than mine. In general, the topics covered the subjects' upbringing and education, how they became involved in tourism, their work history, the job itself, their encounters with guests, and the impacts the work and interactions with guests had on them. Oral history research is, above all else, an extended process of asking questions and then permitting the narrators to take them wherever they want. Some interviewees also offered their own analyses of the tourism industry.

The interviews usually lasted sixty to ninety minutes. The interviews were then transcribed, and follow-up interviews were done to flesh out and fill in missing or unclear details. Because tourism workers are accustomed to speaking standard English to visitors, and did so with me in the interviews, translating or editing Bajan dialect was seldom an issue. My approach in editing the interviews was to ensure that the narratives were faithful to the subject's story while making them topically coherent and interesting for readers. Invariably, the transcripts were condensed by well over half to enhance clarity, avoid repetition, and eliminate material unrelated to the themes of the book. As a rule, I tried to preserve the style of each person's speech. I have sometimes retained in the narratives the questions asked when dealing with a topic that the subject would not have raised independently. I asked the subjects to check the edited narratives for accuracy and to delete anything they regarded as embarrassing. Only a few minor changes were requested.

My role, apart from getting people to tell me their stories and editing them into a coherent form, has been to provide a framework—to describe for the reader the historical and social contexts of tourism and later to offer my own observations. The decision to use oral history interviews rather than a survey or an ethnographic approach that combines several data-collecting strategies was largely one of personal preference. I enjoy doing in-depth interviews and then editing them into narratives. This preference also grows out of early frustrations with survey research. The first research I did in Barbados in 1983 was a survey of return migrants (Gmelch 1987). The results were disappointing in that the survey data, in which all behavior was reduced to statistical patterns, seemed so far removed from the reality of the lives of the migrants that I knew. The generalizations I made glossed over some enormous variation I knew to exist in their experiences. Two years later, I restudied Barbadian return migrants, this time collecting oral histories (Gmelch 1992a). The new approach captured the lives of my subjects and the diversity of their migration experiences, and I enjoyed the research more. Through the in-depth interviews I got to know the subjects well, and two have become long-term friends.

Oral histories are subjective documents that lack some of the detachment and objectivity of historiography, ethnography, or social survey—though even with these methods the a priori notions and biases of the researcher leave their imprints. The aim of oral history is not *explanation,* as is generally the case with the approaches mentioned above, but rather *understanding*. In providing an insider's account, oral history reveals the subjective world of attitudes and feelings. This is a perspective not often found in the etic methods frequently used to study tourism, where the emphasis is on the general rather than the individual. In place of varied individual experiences, survey-based studies of tourism, for example, produce abstract descriptions and statistical frequencies of what is normative. The chapter 1 profile of tourists who visit Barbados, based on government survey data, is a good example of this. Of course such generalizations are essential to our understanding of tourism and to developing theory. Oral history data are quite unsuitable for determining frequencies, averages, and relationships between variables. But from narratives we learn the particular, and we can understand what the abstract categorizations and generalizations about tourism look like on the ground, from the local or actor's point of view. In the pages that follow, for example, we get a sense of the degree to which workers are free actors shaping their own destinies rather than pawns merely responding to constraints imposed upon them by their employers, the guests, and the larger society. Oral histories give voice to local people—to the "little tradition." I believe oral history offers an invaluable alternative to the tendency in many of the social sciences to reduce people to categories and abstractions.

3 THE AIRPORT

On islands, the airport is the gateway for most travelers. Other than cruise-ship passengers and the small number who arrive on private boats, everyone arrives by air. The airport in Barbados, Grantley Adams International, is named after the island's elder statesman, Grantley Adams (1898–1971), who was instrumental in modernizing the antiquated system of government in Barbados in the 1940s and '50s and in moving the country from domination by a white planter class to a democracy. The airport, which is on the south coast, was opened in 1939, modernized and expanded in 1979, and modernized again in 2007. For many years a steel band would greet arriving passengers as they made their way from the tarmac into the large immigration hall. Although it is one of the largest and most efficient facilities in the Caribbean, immigration formalities can take time. A lot of time. The delays getting through immigration, which are of considerable concern to people in the tourism industry, are unfortunate for a country that spends millions of dollars in advertising to entice people to visit Barbados.

Emerging from the arrival hall during the winter peak season are pale-skinned travelers weary from their long journeys from Europe and North America. A few have slipped into shorts on the plane, but most are still in long pants and sleeves, having come from the cold. Once they clear immigration, they find their bags on the luggage carousel, stop at the *bureau de change* to get local currency, pass through customs, and go to the curb outside to engage a taxi or bus to take them to their hotel.

On the opposite side of the airport is the departure area. There, refreshed from a one- or two-week holiday on the beach, their skin bronzed by the sunshine, the visitors begin the journey home. Many are wearing shorts and bright-colored shirts, or T-shirts emblazoned with tropical scenes and products, such as Mount Gay Rum. Some of the women and children have braided and beaded hair, a souvenir of native style, although it sends an unintended message—"I am a tourist." Last-minute shopping is done at the duty-free shop before they board their flights home.

This section contains interviews with a redcap, or porter, and a teller in the *bureau de change*. The names of the interviewees have been changed, except for those who requested that their real names be used (these interviewees are listed in the acknowledgments).

REDCAP | Wendy Husbands

After clearing immigration at the Grantley Adams International Airport, passen-
gers enter the arrival hall to claim their luggage from the carousel. Redcaps dressed
in red hats, red shirts, and black pants stand by to carry their luggage through
customs and outside the terminal to the curb. Wendy Husbands, 33, single mother
of two children, has been a redcap for the past ten years. She grew up in a tough
neighborhood of Bridgetown.

I don't just approach any passenger. I look at the person. I look at
the way they're dressed. It can give you an idea of how they might
tip. And in this job all we have is tips; there's no salary. So if you can
select the right people, you can do a lot better. Most times I look for
men wearing jeans, leather shoes, and a jacket. Not suits. Anybody
can wear a suit. And for women you want a somewhat different
standard, too. I don't go for the glossy ones with all the makeup. I
like working for elderly women; they're pretty good tippers. And I
like family jobs because if it's a wealthy family you can be sure
they're going to have many pieces of luggage. It's the norm here
among the redcaps that when you see Gucci bags, you go for them.
But even they don't always pay well.

Young people are poor tippers, so they're usually your last
choice. And some young people, as strong as they are, don't even
lift their own luggage off the conveyor. They'll be standing there
talking to someone and see their bag there and shout, "That's mine,
that's mine." They want you to lift it off and put it on the trolley.
You do all the work. And it's a lot slower getting through customs
with them because their baggage is more likely to be checked.
When it comes to students, a lot of porters are like "Tsk, tsk," because you know they'll only give you the minimum, a dollar (BDS)
per bag [$2 BDS = $1 U.S.]. But you can never be sure. In Decem-
ber I had this Rasta guy, a student, who came in on the 4:15 from
Jamaica and needed some help. I don't usually help Rastas, because
you never know what's going to happen at customs, with drugs and
all. It can be very slow. But this guy was a student and he began

talking to me about his studies and things like that. I could see he was on the right track, so I decided to help him. Well, when we got outside, didn't he give me 20 dollars for just three pieces of luggage. I wouldn't take it. I said, "You only have three pieces of luggage and it's just one dollar a bag, and you're a student, you need the money."

The biggest tip I ever got was 100 U.S. dollars from a man on the Concorde with fourteen pieces of baggage. But then you have others where you carry all their stuff and you get outside and they say, "No money." [She says this with great emphasis.] Some give you foreign coins that are of no use here. What am I going to do with Swedish coins? No bank here is going to accept them. I had one American guy who gave me coins worth five and ten cents. I said, "Sir, it's one dollar per bag." He said, "What do you want me to do? The bank is closed. What do you want me to do? Is this paradise? Is this the beautiful Barbados you all talk about?" I just said, "Okay sir, you go along and enjoy your holiday." He was a very miserable-looking fellow.

Winter is the best season, especially around Christmas. You can bring in over 200 dollars (BDS) a day. But last night [late March] I worked for less than 50 dollars. And I've got to pay 16 dollars every day out of my own pocket to the guy that rents the trolleys to us.

Overall, I think Canadians are the worst tippers. The British can be hostile. Maybe it's because they've traveled such a long way and they're really tired when they get here. And when you have passengers from England, sometimes you've got to safeguard your trolley. Over there they have self-service trolleys and they're used to just putting their stuff on any trolley they see. Sometimes I've got to say, "Excuse me, can I have my cart back, please?"[1]

I like Americans. They'll chat with you. You can tell them that you're in the middle of helping someone else but that you will come back to them in a minute, and they'll wait instead of finding another redcap. Most of the Germans pull their own luggage, except for the elderly ones. It's the same with the Swedes and the French. With Caribbean people you get all types. Some are very generous, but then you have others that are not okay. Like the person who is originally from St. Vincent but is living in New York and is in transit, coming home. He doesn't know, and he won't listen to

---

1. A government proposal to introduce self-service trolleys was dropped because of the job losses it would cause the redcaps.

you when you tell him, that he has to remove his baggage from the conveyor and take it to the check-in counter.

Some Bajans are very good tippers, but some are terrible. And when they're coming for Christmas, Crop Over,[2] or a holiday, they usually bring a ton of stuff from New York, so their bags are extremely heavy. They fill them to the maximum seventy pounds. And then customs will want to check them for things that are subject to duty, like electrical stuff. So that slows you down. And then sometimes they have to go pay duty and when you finally get outside with their bags they say, "Oh, sorry, I don't have much money left. They charged me sixty dollars duty." Or by then, they're so annoyed with the long wait and having to pay duty that they snap at you. Big, heavy bags, a long wait, and a small tip.

With the heavy baggage you've got to watch your back. A lot of redcaps have hurt themselves. You want to raise heavy bags onto the trolley with both hands, supporting them with your knees. I used to have backaches before I began weight lifting at a gym.

When you're dealing with visitors you've got to slow down and speak regular English so they'll understand you. Sometimes when I speak quickly they'll ask, "Do you not speak English?" Like when I say, "Come-ah," which is "Come here." I believe people should try to speak as well as they can. I'm no scholar but I speak my best. And I don't just do it here. I try to speak standard English to my children at home.

You're dealing with people who can be very grumpy, especially if they've been traveling a long time and are tired. And then maybe they had to stand in line for an hour trying to clear immigration and then wait some more for their baggage. You can imagine that sometimes they're very frustrated, and things upset them. Recently, I had a couple from the 9:30 American [flight]. They had ten pieces of luggage. The lady put some pieces on my trolley, which tied me up because I could have done another job while she was waiting for the rest of her luggage. Then some of her bags passed by on the conveyor and she missed getting them off. Then one of her bags never showed up and she blamed me. That was wrong; it had nothing to

---

2. Crop Over originated in the early days of plantation society, a summertime celebration of the completion of a successful harvest. It was revived in the 1970s and now plays a major role in promoting new cultural awareness in Barbados. It is also credited for having revived the calypso tradition.

do with me. The bag hadn't made the flight. She was very grumpy, and when we got outside, she said, "I won't pay. I'm not paying you a cent." I said, "You either pay or I take your luggage back inside." She finally did pay up but just the minimum.

When I'm doing arrivals, I start working at 3 P.M. I'll get seven flights during my shift—American [Airlines] from New York, American from San Juan, Air Canada from Toronto, British Air from London, American from Miami. Then you get some that aren't international, like the 4:15 from Kingston, Antigua, and St. Maarten. And you finish up with the American flight from New York at 9:30, if it's on time. If you're really hustling you can get eight jobs from each flight.

When I'm doing departures, I get here around 6 in the morning. You're just carrying the person's baggage from the curb to the check-in counter. Usually mornings are very, very slow. But the people are friendlier as they're not yet worn out from the plane ride and they're just finishing up a relaxing vacation. They say nice things like, "I'm sorry to leave, I enjoyed your island."

I like talking with people. I like helping visitors when they first get to the island. Sometimes they ask you about things to do on the island. I always tell them to be careful because they're not at home. I tell them when they're out sight-seeing to not leave their diamonds and cameras in the car. To take everything with them. And when they're on the beach and go inside the water, don't leave their handbags lying out. Some want to know about the nightspots, but because I don't party I don't know much about them. I tell them about Harrison's Cave, Andromeda Gardens, and Heritage Park, but I don't know the nightspots.

One thing I've seen about black people is that those who returned home from living in England build houses here. Those who return from living in New York go in for the clothes and style and brand names. They're into flashy things. As a black person I've visited London on three occasions and carried around a survey in my mind so I'm totally right in saying this. In England, people just put on clothes and go to church. They don't look to see if they have on this brand or that. The ones from New York are into expensive clothes, they've always got on the flashy. When they're here visiting in Barbados they go to church in $300 dresses. But at the end of it, what do they have? Nothing. They're wasteful. I fit in better with the English type because I'm not interested in flash and I'm not a party person.

The redcaps are a good service. A lot of them, though, are very backward. They can't carry on a decent conversation with the tourists. A lot of them don't know things about Barbados, so when visitors ask they can't tell them. It's a pity they didn't do any reading or try to move on to better themselves. I got a lot of encouragement from my boyfriend, who is a teacher. I probably would be in the same boat as the others if it weren't for him.

Growing up, I wanted to do nursing but my mother wasn't too helpful. She was never there for me. I got pregnant at 18 and had to move out of the house, out on my own. Things weren't too bright. I moved into the St. Michael area, which is pretty rough, and the conditions weren't healthy for a child. So my mother came back and took my son to raise him. I worked for four years in a school canteen before I got this job. Being a redcap is on the bottom as far as jobs go. But I've never been embarrassed about doing this work because I'm a very strong person. It's an honest dollar and you work hard. You meet a lot of different people and you learn about things that are happening worldwide. And, I think, having to deal with difficult people who are very tired and grumpy has made me a better person.

No, I'm not sorry I went this route. But I would never want to see my kids doing this job. My boy is 15 now, my girl's 11, they're both very smart and will make something of themselves. In the thirty-three years that I've lived my life I've not done bad. I have bought my own home. Of the ninety redcaps, I don't think twenty of them own their own homes. A lot of them have kids and they're still renting. So like I said, I'm happy for myself. I've done well. Last year I won some money in the lotto, and I invested it in a car which I hire out. Some English girls have it now for the next six months. My plan for this year is to save enough money to get another car on the road to hire out.

Epilogue

One year after this interview, Wendy quit her job and enrolled in a child care certificate course at Wedgebridge College in Essex, England. After living abroad for several years, she returned to Barbados and now works in a children's home in Bridgetown.

TELLER AND MONEY EXCHANGER
Joyann Springer

As they leave the immigration counter at Grantley Adams International Airport, some passengers stop at the bank window to exchange their money for local currency. Joyann Springer, 35, is one of the tellers there. She has been working at the airport for eight years and serves about 300 people a day, mostly tourists.

Most passengers are cashing traveler's checks, but we also take a long list of currencies, like Deutsche marks, Austrian shillings, Australian dollars, and so forth. We don't take Trinidad, Guyanese, or Jamaican currency. Those are restricted currencies, meaning people aren't supposed to take them out of those countries. Some tourists don't know that, and they get annoyed when they can't change their Trinidadian dollars. They are stuck, and those monies have no value unless the tourist goes back there to spend them. Those countries should do a better job of informing visitors that their money has no value outside of their borders.

I sometimes work in departures [the bank window serving departing passengers], but I'd really rather be in arrivals. In arrivals you can be of more assistance. The people have had a long plane ride, and maybe they've had to make one or two connections to get here. Then when they get off the plane, the air is so hot and they have to stand in the immigration line for a long time. They are pretty beat. They want to get some cash, get to their hotel, and relax. But a lot of them ask you questions, too. If they are arriving for the first time they may be nervous, not knowing what to expect. They need someone to reassure them and give them good information. Some of them ask you a lot of questions, about the taxi fares, what the food is like, if you can recommend a nice restaurant. They'll say, "I'm staying at such and such a hotel, are the rates there good? Is it an okay place?" It's mostly Americans and Canadians asking questions. The English, nine times out of ten, are staying at an all-inclusive hotel, where everything is provided for them, so they don't need to know as much. I find that women like to ask about the cost of things, and the men more often ask about places to go and things to do. The middle-aged and older people ask a lot more than young people, even though young people know a lot less. Either way, by the time they get to my window, they need a friendly face.

I think I always wanted to work in tourism, always wanted to be able to help people. It probably goes back to when I studied French in school. We used to have an exchange program where we would go to Guadeloupe or Martinique—the French-speaking islands. They would entertain us when we went there, and we'd entertain them when they came here. One year they made me leader of the group. The leader plans activities for the visiting students and acts as a tour guide on the bus. I found myself always giving advice or directions. I really got to like making their visit pleasant. I really didn't mind putting myself out as long as they were happy. After that first year, I was always the group leader. On those trips I discovered that I liked mingling with people. I liked learning about their culture and language.

Although my job is changing tourists' money, I also see my job as promoting tourism. The airport is the main entrance area for the island, other than the harbor. I believe you should always be as helpful as you possibly can. I like to say, "It's nice to be important, but more important to be nice."

You should be as helpful as you can because how you treat visitors reflects on all of Barbados. Just one person can determine what a visitor is going to think and say about Barbados. Whether he says "Barbadians are like this, or Barbadians are like that" may depend on how you treat that person. Let's say the person has been traveling all day and is grumpy and aggressive when he gets to the window. Well, if I'm cold and aggressive back, he is going to think, "I'm sorry I'm here, because these Barbadians are not as nice as I was told." So when passengers come to the window I try to be very friendly; I ask them about their trip and if they are new to the island; I try to give them some tips that might really make their holiday. That's just me; I'm not saying every bank teller is the same. Some just do their job and don't care about the visitors. They don't remember that the people they're serving have just had a long trip and are tired. They think it's not their problem.

Earlier this year I had a group of ten black Americans who had never been to Barbados before. They knew nothing about the island. When they changed their money I gave them lots of ideas about things they could do. When their holiday was over and they were leaving they came by to thank me and tell me what a splendid holiday they'd had and that everything I'd recommended had been great, even the fish fry at Oistins. One of them said to me, "I think you are in the wrong profession. You are far more informative than any of those ladies at the Visitors' Bureau." Well, that made my day, because some of my co-workers say that when I am at the bank, helping visitors shouldn't be my job. But I don't see it that way. If it's not busy, why shouldn't I take the time to help them?

The other day, there was a gentleman and his wife who had come here to stay but were told that their hotel was full. The girl in the Visitors' Bureau was recommending another hotel way down in Bathsheba. Now what is a couple wanting a holiday on the beach going to do in Bathsheba, where you can't go into the sea over your knees because of the undertow? What was she thinking? Two of us found them a guest house in St. Lawrence Gap, right on the beach. They were so grateful they wanted to give us money, but we wouldn't take any. When they got back home they sent us two cards and their addresses and told us any time we wanted to visit them in the British Virgin Islands we were welcome. Those are the things that make you feel your job is worthwhile.

In all my jobs since leaving school, I have dealt with the public. First I worked as a cashier in a supermarket, and then in a shop which sells to tourists, and now the bank. So I got used to working with people. I met a lot of tourists working in the shop, Walter's World in St. Lawrence Gap, but I prefer the bank. In the shop, people have no reason to talk to you unless they need help. But when people come to the bank window they have to talk to you. At the bank, there is always talk.

But not everything about the bank is rosy. Like the money is dirty and you get a lot of muck and grime on your hands. The money can carry germs. I have already gotten chicken pox from handling money, from a German. A few days after I changed his money I realized I had the same kind of piles on my skin that he had. Everybody that worked in my section got it, too. The bank gives us gloves to handle money, but they are hard to wear all day. We use disinfectant to wash our hands, and I am careful not to put my hands near my face.

And we have to deal with little complaints, such as traveler's checks. If people got them in the mail they are supposed to sign them before they bring them to the bank to cash. If not, they are supposed to produce a proof-of-purchase slip. Well, a lot of people forget and don't bring it with them. When you tell them they have to provide it, they think you are giving them a hard time. Some men say, "You're just wasting my time" or "You're trying to make my trip difficult, aren't you?" Sometimes they'll complain that the shops will give them two Barbados dollars for every U.S. dollar, and why is the bank only giving them $1.98? They'll make a fuss over those two cents. I try to tell them that there is not anything I can do about it, that the Central Bank governs the rates. And sometimes the arriving passengers are unhappy when you can't break their U.S. $100 or $50 into smaller U.S. dollar denominations.

Some people can be very difficult, like they don't want to show you their identification when cashing a traveler's check. I say, "Sir, this is a traveler's check and we need to verify that the person cashing this check is you." And they'll say, "So do you think I stole it?" I just stand and bear it because I don't ever want them to think I'm rude or being difficult. Eventually, after all their fussing, they'll give in. You can't let one grouchy visitor affect your feelings toward other customers. The next customer is not responsible for what just happened. If you treat each with a happy smile, sometimes it will pull you out of the bad mood the last person put you in, and if you are happy, the visitors might say nice things like "Oh, you look so pretty today," and that can really boost you.

Do you ever encounter racial prejudice?

Hardly ever. But I did have an elderly Australian fellow say to me one day that he didn't know why he'd come to Barbados because he doesn't really like black people. I said, "Sir, didn't you know that Barbados is a black-people country, that a black man is going to serve you your meals, a black lady is going to make your bed, and that wherever you go you are going to see black people? I don't think you made a wise choice for your holiday if you don't like black people." I didn't snap at him, I responded in a very decent way even though what he said really hurt me.

Another time I had this older Englishman who was going on a side trip to Mustique and wanted to exchange Barbados dollars for pounds. I told him we couldn't because he was coming back to Barbados, that we could only exchange his money for EC [Eastern Caribbean currency]. He said, "I know, I know, you don't like white people! Right? You don't like us because we are better off than you." Some silly remark like that. He said that I needed to remember that black people were once slaves to white people. He started going on the slavery line. It was not very pleasant, and my co-worker was very annoyed with him. I told her not to get vexed, because getting angry would make him go away feeling good knowing that he had upset her. I smiled, I didn't fret with him, but just smiled. At the end of it I said, "Anyway sir, despite how you feel about black people, you still enjoy your trip and I'll see you [to convert your EC to pounds] when you get back." That's the best way to handle that type. When you get that type of race thing, it's usually from older men.

Overall, I have fewer problems working in departures. People are coming off their holiday, most of them have a smile on their face, some have gotten married—a lot of hotels are now advertising for a beach wedding in Barbados. They are relaxed and easygoing. Even so, I would rather work in arrivals where I can be of help to people beyond just changing their money.

Like, I had this one incident with a doctor from Michigan who exchanged some money. There was a long line, and after he was gone I saw his wallet sitting there. When I looked at it I realized it was the doctor's and all of his documents and his cards and cash were there. I was able to call him because when you purchase currency you have to say on the voucher where you are staying in Barbados. So I called his hotel. But when I reached him he was adamant that he had not left his wallet. So I left my name and number and told him that if he didn't find it, he would know where it was.

Well, the next day didn't he come back to the bank to get it, and he was so impressed that everything was still intact. When he took the cash out of his wallet, well over a thousand dollars, my head started to grow because I knew that if he had lost that it would be the end of his twenty-one-day holiday in Barbados. He wanted to give me some money, but I wouldn't take it. When he got home to the United States he sent me a thank-you card and put the cash inside. That's what I like—people coming to Barbados and being able to say, "Despite whatever happens, the people in Barbados are nice, they are friendly, and they are honest." It starts with me, but then it ends with Barbados as a whole, if you get my meaning. I know it's not always that way, but that's the way it should be.

Does it make any difference to you which nationalities you are waiting on?

It doesn't make any difference, but I find Americans and the English are a little bit nicer than the Canadians. We don't carry Canadian coins, so when they are converting the money back into Canadian dollars we round the money off to the nearest dollar. A few of them think you are swindling them.

Has interacting with tourists changed how you think about Barbados?

Of course it has. It has caused me to appreciate Barbados a lot more than I used to. One tourist who has been to many Caribbean islands said that no place has a cave as good as our Harrison's Cave. She was also fascinated by our *Atlantis* submarine. When she and her husband hired a mini-moke and drove around the country they saw women in their yards washing on a juking board [an old-fashioned heavy washboard]. It was the first time in her life she had ever seen a juking board. Those are all things we take for granted in Barbados.

I've learned a lot about currencies, like Swedish kronors and Dutch guilders. One night, a passenger gave one of the redcaps a tip in guilders. The redcap was complaining that the money had no value and he was going to throw it away. I knew better, and it turned out to be quite a bit of money for a tip. Through the currencies I have also learned about some countries, like the Arab ones, that I never knew existed.

Has dealing with tourists changed you in any way?

When I was working at the shop, I got a few ideas from visitors that I have used at home. Like, a Canadian woman told me that I could cover my slices [table mats] with clear plastic and keep them fresh, and that you could do the same with your tablecloth, so that if you spill a drink it won't dirty your tablecloth. I now do that all the time. Someone else told me how to make a bottle lamp by filling a bottle up with sand and shells. I have three of them at home now and some of my friends have come in, seen them, and done the same thing. I've learned to use bolder colors than most Barbadians do. A lot of visitors, especially North Americans, like really bright colors. Sometimes I say, "Well I'll try that and see what happens." It takes a little exploring sometimes, but it often turns out to be fun. I think, too, that interacting with tourists has made me realize how Americanized Barbados is becoming, that a lot of our true Barbadian culture has died out. Everyone today wants to be on a par with other countries, and that's killing our roots. Killing the things that are really and truly Barbadian. That's why today, when I have the chance, I tell people to go see "1627" [a dance performance about the island's early history], or to the museum, or to the Morgan Lewis Mill and the other places where they will see the true Barbadian culture.

Sometimes I just feel like telling Bajans to stop trying to match up to something else and to value what we have. We need to appreciate what is unique about Barbados. If we become just like everyplace else, like St. Vincent or St. Lucia, then visitors are going to say, "Why go to Barbados? It's so expensive, why not go to St. Vincent?" Now, when I go to another country in the Caribbean I want to learn about their culture and their history. I want to know all about it, and I want to eat their food. Like in St. Lucia they don't take the skin off dolphin when they cook it, where here in Barbados we do. When I go to these places now, I am not just interested in purchasing a T-shirt.

Epilogue

Six months after the interview, the bank transferred Joyann to their branch office at Sam Lord's Castle. Several people had resigned from Sam Lord's, and the bank wanted a teller they wouldn't have to train. Unfortunately, the Sam Lord's branch does mostly commercial banking. Joyann, who was such a valuable asset to the tourism industry, is now mostly serving locals, who come in to cash paychecks and government pensions and pay their utility bills. She misses dealing with tourists and exchanging foreign money. She hopes someday to have her own tour business: "I don't want to be behind a desk, I want to be out dealing with visitors, making sure that they have a splendid holiday in Barbados. And I want them to come back and bring back ten more people with them."

4 THE HOTEL

Most visitors to the Caribbean stay in hotels, though guest houses, resort cottages, and apartments are also available. Barbados has 150 hotels; most of the island's medium-sized and large hotels are owned by international chains headquartered in Britain and the United States.[1] Because hotels are the preferred form of accommodation, their development is key to the growth of local tourism. Rather than being nucleated, as on some islands, the hotels of Barbados are spread along the south and the west coasts, where the island's best beaches are located. In the hyperbole of one tourist brochure, the hotels "embrace the Caribbean coastline like a strand of glittering gems."[2] Often interspersed with other urban development, the hotels of Barbados allow for more mixing between locals and visitors than is true on many Caribbean islands.

The most luxurious hotels are on the west coast in the parish of St. James, an area variably referred to as the "Gold Coast" or "Platinum Coast" because of its abundance of wealth. Many are cottage, colony-type resort hotels and are among the finest in the Caribbean. These upscale properties have luxuriant tropical gardens brimming with colorful hibiscus and bougainvillea and fragrant frangipani. A few of the resorts are located on former sugar estates,

---

1. Most of the island's hotels and related services (restaurants, tour operators, travel agents, and department stores) are members of the Barbados Hotel and Tourism Association, the organization that most actively promotes tourism. The Association regularly places large supplements in the island's two newspapers to promote the tourism industry. The supplements also remind readers of tourism's importance to the economic health of Barbados.

2. *Barbados Indulge*. Pamphlet. Barbados Tourism Authority.

which some observers view as a visible symbol of the link between the old plantation colonialism and the new tourism-dependent neocolonialism (Pattullo 1996, 136).

Hotel development came to the west coast well after it did on the south coast. Prior to World War II, few people built there due to a fear of tidal waves and dislike for humid summer heat (the west coast does not benefit from the strong trade winds that hit the island from the south and east). The west coast's negative image changed for good, however, when the luxury Sandy Lane Hotel was built in the 1960s. The five-star hotel ranked among top resort hotels in the world and soon became the preferred winter resort of wealthy Britons and Americans in the eastern Caribbean, supplanting the Mill Reef Club in Antigua. The popularity of the west coast grew as affluent Americans built homes alongside the wealthy English winter settlers who preceded them on the island. In *Last Resorts,* Polly Pattullo (1996, 137) aptly describes some of the differences between west and south coast tourism:

> West coast tourists like luxury in bucketfuls. They stay in places such as Sandy Lane, tucked away from normal life behind heavily guarded perimeter gates, with private drives of royal palms sweeping down to marbled reception halls, swimming pools and fountains and always beyond there is the Caribbean Sea. . . .

> They do it differently on the south coast at places like the Firholme Hotel whose clientele is about as likely to tuck in to a Sandy Lane buffet as a Barbadian cane cutter is. The south coasters pour off the charter flights on the cheaper package tours. They tend to stay in modest self-catering hotels and condos (not all on the beach), nip across to the supermarket for tins of spaghetti hoops . . . drink rum punch at a pirate party aboard the *Jolly Roger,* dine on ribs and pasta, burgers and garlic bread. . . . At night, they disco and karaoke at the Reggae Lounge.

The only hotel ever built on the rocky and rugged north coast was the North Point Resort. Because it was too far from town and the airport and lacked sheltered beaches, it closed in 1977 after only a decade of operation. Only a few hotels exist on the east coast, mainly because dangerous currents and a strong undertow make its otherwise beautiful beaches unsafe and therefore unattractive to overnight guests.

Barbados tourism officials would like to attract more of the up-market visitors that stay at the west coast resorts. Not only do these

Colony Club Hotel. *Courtesy of Elegant Hotels Group.*

A room at Sandy Lane. *Courtesy of Barbados Tourism Authority.*

tourists spend more money on their vacations, but they also create fewer problems. They are less likely than the down-market tourists, who stay on the south coast, to look for drugs, be rude and boorish, or disrespect local customs by wearing inappropriate beach attire in shops and on the street.

The upmarket guest is also more likely to return, even in a global recession, whereas a Caribbean vacation for a working-class family is often a once-in-a-lifetime experience. Having a high repeat clientele is a much-sought-after status marker in the hotel industry. In this chapter, Errol Sobers and Martin Barrow boast about the high level of repeats their hotels enjoy. What makes visitors return to the same hotel often has less to do with the amenities than with the guest's relations with the staff. Nothing is more satisfying for a guest than walking into a hotel and seeing a familiar face and being greeted by name, notes John Urry (1990) in *The Tourist Gaze*. Industry analysts say these "critical moments" greatly influence the guests' feelings about the place, and they ultimately determine the success of a hotel. Hence, having congenial staff is essential for management wanting to present a favorable image to guests.

As a rule, the more guests pay for a service, the more they expect and demand. In elite hotels, such as Sandy Lane, the expectations of customer service are particularly high. Consequently, management in these hotels exercises more control over the appearance, speech, and personality of their employees. In the dining rooms, for example, the staff are not just expected to serve meals but also to provide a tangible ambiance. This requires what is sometimes loosely referred to as "emotional work," involving the need to smile in a pleasant, friendly, involved way to the guest. One of the ironies of tourism is the reversal in dress, in which smartly attired working-class hotel staff often wait upon and interact with wealthy guests in shorts and sandals.

For some hotel employees, their hotel is a home away from home. In a study of labor relations in two large Barbadian and Maltese resorts, Godfrey Baldacchino (1997) found that large hotels function like small villages in their lack of privacy among employees and rampant gossip. Even though many Barbadian hotels are owned by multinational firms, there are so many local Bajans working there, some of whom are related, that it can feel as Bajan as the local parish church.

Hotel work has not attracted the best and brightest students of Barbados. The children of the middle class are much more interested in becoming economists and lawyers than food and beverage managers. Many workers believe the hotel industry has a glass ceiling, with the top management jobs going to white non-nationals. The lack of enthusiasm for jobs in tourism is also a legacy of colonialism. As noted earlier, there is still a tendency to confuse service (as in serving white guests) with servitude. The following interviews are with men and women who represent all the major hotel jobs, including housekeeper, bartender, chef, taxi driver, security, guest service, and hotel manager.

TAXI DRIVER | Trevor Mapp

All Barbadian hotels of any consequence have their own taxi stand and a fleet of drivers who wait for requests from hotel guests for transportation. Each fleet has its own captain, and its drivers work together as a team. Trevor Mapp, 53, drives for the Glitter Bay Hotel taxi stand. The Glitter Bay stand, hidden by palm trees and tropical flowers at the back of the hotel, has a parking area and a white shed with scattered chairs and tables on which the drivers play cards and dominos. It has the ambience of a clubhouse. Trevor was raised on his family's 156-acre sugarcane plantation in the parish of St. Thomas. At age 16 he became the bookkeeper and did the "accounts and wages" until the declining fortunes of sugar led him to drive a taxi.

I didn't set out to be a taxi driver. My cousin's best friend had a stroke, and he had a wife and family to feed. Me being 19 years old and not having diddly-squat to do, they asked if I would drive his cab and be what we call a jockey—a person who works for somebody else on commission. I worked the whole season the next year, and then I was able to get a loan to buy my own car. I've been driving ever since, thirty-four years.

The job varies. Someone can book you up for the morning and keep you all day. Or you may have a series of drops to Holetown [1 mile away] where you take them down, say for shopping, and bring them back, with maybe a few other trips out to Harrison's Cave or up to Speightstown. There are certain jobs you'd rather have, like Harrison's Cave because it's a return job. You take them up there and you wait until they're finished and you bring them back. That's a lot better than a one-way fare. On a really good day you might start out with a fare to the airport at 6 A.M. and never stop running until midnight. Your cellular phone always ringing. You may even have to refuse some rides.

But we haven't had good days like that lately. Glitter Bay has a lot of repeat clientele and that's not good for us. After a guest has been to Barbados a few times they know what the sight-seeing is about. They've been to Animal Flower Cave, they've been to Andromeda Gardens, they've been to Harrison's Cave, and they don't need to go again. They're coming for the beach, and they don't need no taxi to take them there. It's the same at the all-inclusive hotels—most of their guests eat on the property since they've paid for it, so they don't need a taxi to take them to a restaurant. Plus the hotel provides its own shuttles to shop and its own tours of the island. So when we read in the paper about the bustling tourist season, we laugh. Sure, we have a lot of jobs on the weekend getting people to and from the airport. But during the week it's not as busy as it used to be.

It's nice to get someone who wants a tour of the island, because you're good for that day. Some people have the notion that they can see the island in two or three hours. But if you're good at it, you can keep them out all day. First I check to see if they have a list of things they want to see. If not, I show them the island and I explain the history, the change from colonial British leadership to independence, and all of that. After having traveled to the great New York City, Washington, D.C., Miami, the great America—I wouldn't live there for anything. I'm honored to show off my island. I'm honored to tell its history. I like making people realize that Barbados is not just a tourist trap, like Miami with skyrises on the beaches. That Barbados is a community of black people living their own independent lives.

A lot of visitors can't believe our history is 350 years old. They can't believe that this island once produced more riches than all of the North American colonies. A lot of Americans have only heard of Bacardi and Malibu, they've never heard about our distinguished rum, Mount Gay. I think a lot of people, when they hear about our heritage, change their opinion of Barbados. They realize that we're not just down here like a bunch of monkeys in grass skirts, but we're actually an industrialized and developing nation trying to come around and make honest livings. I really like the role of educating tourists about my island.

You'd be surprised at how ignorant some people can be about Barbados. I was driving a man around and he asked, "You guys have television? You guys have running water? You guys got electricity?" One guy was even surprised to discover that we have cats here on the island. I don't understand how people can think we're so backward. I just smile and take it in, keep my mouth shut, because these things can lead to arguments. I remember one day taking people on a tour and they were saying how dilapidated and dirty everything was. It bothered me. I told them I'd spent a long time in Canada and that the streets there weren't any cleaner. In

Toronto I saw a guy lying on the street, asking for a quarter. I said I'd seen apartments in Canada so small you can't move around. A big country like that with tiny little apartments. So stop making silly remarks about Barbados.

The best part is when I encourage someone to come back to the island and they call me up. The other day I saw a woman at the airport and she hugged and kissed me up. When the husband gets in my car he says, "You're lucky I didn't shoot you with all that hugging and kissing." But the husband was there patting me on the shoulder, telling me how nice it is to see me again. That's the best part about driving a cab—clients who come back from all parts of the world and are happy to see you, who tell you they enjoyed themselves so much the first time that they've come back.

Driving a taxi is a long day, fourteen hours some days, especially during the tourist season [mid-November–March]. Some days you're finishing up at midnight and it's almost time to start again. But there's usually downtime when we're at the taxi stand and sit around, play cards, curse each other, watch the VCR, and argue shit. Also, you wash your car and clean out the insides. And if you need rest, you get in your car and take a sleep. Them long days are why most of us ain't married. [Trevor points to each of the drivers sitting around the taxi stand and says, "He ain't married, he ain't married, he ain't married, and I ain't married."] Women these days demand time from their men. This is the kind of job where you don't have time to give. Sure, you can take your job easy, go slow, take your sweet time, but you're not gonna make no money. If you want to make money you've got to put in the time. If a client calls me up and wants me, I'll go flying there. I'll fly there and I'll fly here. It's the only way to maintain business.

Things do slow down out of season. Sometimes there will only be twenty people staying in the hotel. Every night we look at the hotel's list of departures, arrivals, number of repeat guests, and then decide if we need to cut back. Well, maybe tomorrow's a good day to stay home, or maybe I'll put my car in the shop and get it repaired. We work it out among ourselves.

Our aim is to provide the best service we can. Every time that phone rings somebody should be here to answer it, to do the job. We try always to be punctual. If you want me at 9:00, I'll be there at 8:45. You always try to get there ten minutes early in case something happens on the way. Anyway, most of the time the client is early. Most clients are ready five minutes before. If you're punctual and if you're courteous to the guest, they will come back for more service.

When a guest isn't punctual, he can really trip you up. Suppose I take someone down to Holetown to dinner and they say, "Pick me back up at 9:00." You get back there at 9:00 and they're not ready yet, and you've got another couple waiting for a 9:30 pickup. Pretty soon you can't make that 9:30 pickup and you've got to call the stand and say, "Charles, you've got to cover this one for me." It means I'm losing business, you're chillin' doing nothing waiting for your fare to finish dinner. And you can't go up to them and say what's going on here. And you can't leave them because they're staying at your hotel and you can't raise his fare because he kept you late. Then after keeping you all that extra time maybe they don't even give you a tip.

One thing I've learned about tips is not to expect them. Some days you get a guy who gives a small tip and says, "Here you go, that's for a good driver." And then he expects you to break your back carrying all his luggage. Sometimes you have a guest in the car and you have a good conversation and you think that they're going to give you a tip. Then they just say thank you and walk away. So you really can't tell who's going to tip, unless it's a repeat client that you know.

Do you ever have problems with tourists?

You get the odd one. Like I had an English guy a while back. I picked up his party at Crystal Cove to go to the airport. On the way everyone's flashing their lights at me and I think there are police up ahead checking for speeding, so I look at my speedometer and I'm doing okay. Still more people flashing their lights, then another cab driver honks at me. I look in my mirror and see my passenger has his head completely out the window, just having a jolly good time. I said, "Man, what do you think you are doing? You're gonna have your head taken off." And he starts ragging on me, like what's my problem, mind my own business. I said, "See if you can get your whole body out the window." When we got to the airport he says to me, "How dare you speak to me like that. Who do you think you're talking to!" He wouldn't pay me, and finally one of the other passengers did. You find people like that, who want to make their own rules, who don't want to listen to you.

But most tourists are genuine. You look at them and know that you don't have to worry about them being in your car and that they're going to pay the fare. Mind you, there are a few that will cheat you if they can. When you're leaving the hotel, going to the airport, you state what the price is. You tell them, "It's 45 dollars." But maybe they don't hear, or don't understand, or whatever. You get to the airport and he hands you a 20-dollar bill. Some will say I only paid 20 dollars to come down and I'm not paying you more than 20 dollars to get back up [to the airport]. When they don't want to pay, they will tell you all kinds of stories. I try to keep my mouth shut, I try to avoid any kind of confrontation. But if I'm not in a good mood, I'll say, "I'm gonna call the police on you. I don't want you to miss your flight but that's what's gonna happen." But with the average guest, I'll show him the price sheet from the hotel, to remind him. Some budge after seeing that.

Experience has taught me who the troublemakers are. Like smokers. Most of us don't smoke and don't want people smoking in our cars. It's offensive. The other day I had a lady from England. When she got in the car I specifically told her no smoking. I get her halfway to the hotel and I smelled a cigarette. I turned around and said, "Madam, we discussed this already." And she says, "Well, you must understand, I can't go without a cigarette." I tell her that we can stop the car so that she can get out and smoke and then we'll carry on. She says, "No, you carry on and I'll get rid of the cigarette." So she flicks the cigarette outside but the wind must have blown it back in and it burns a hole in the seat. When she got out of the car at the hotel she gave me $150. I said, "Let me see if you left anything in the car," and when I looked in I saw where the cigarette had bounced here, there, and there, marking the seat.

Then you get the beachers that get sand all over your car. I had this woman going from the beach back to her cruise ship. She put her hat up on the dashboard and there was sand all over it. And then she puts her feet on the dashboard, like I want to see what's under her skirt. I tell her to put her feet down, but she says she doesn't speak English. Her man says, "I'll pay you double if you let her keep her feet up there." Finally I stopped the vehicle and she puts her feet down. But when we get to the seaport the man tells me, "It's people like you that stop people like us from coming to Barbados." I said, "No problem, it's tourists like you that we don't want coming to Barbados."

You get a few that come off the beach that are wet. They sit on your seats and get them wet. I tell them to put their towels down and sit on them, but they don't want to do that. You've always got to watch out that they don't complain to the hotel management. Because in the view of the hotel, the guest is always right. That is gospel. You've got to be careful because one bad report and it could be your job. Say you've been driving for a whole season, right, everybody's content and happy, and then you have to yell at a man for getting sand all over your car. There's a confrontation and he tells the hotel. His story is always better than yours. Manager will call you to talk, then it goes to the general manager. It keeps burning. Man! We don't have a union, the taxi stand is their place, not ours, and they can kick us out any time they want. Walk the plank, Jack!

I'll tell you what vexes me about some visitors. They'll spend the whole day on the beach sitting in the sun. Then the rain starts to fall when they're going out for dinner, and they'll ask you for a weather report. "How's it gonna be tomorrow? Sure hope it's not going to rain." It doesn't matter to them that we need rain for the vegetables, for the fields, that we need water to survive. They figure they're here for a week and it shouldn't rain, and God should curse Barbados if it does. That's the hardest thing for me to understand.

At the stand, we tell one another about the guests. Like, this guy doesn't like to be driven slow or this guy is always in a hurry, you can't drive him too fast, or this guy is always late. If he books a car don't bother to come on time, because you're just gonna wait. It helps you to know what to expect.

Do you think you've learned anything in conversing
with North Americans and Europeans all these years?

I'm an island man, educated here. I can read and write, I have e-mail. I've traveled—I've been to Canada, to the States, and I've just come back from Japan. I get to see other cultures, too. You learn a lot more from traveling than you do from listening to tourists talk about it. People can rub a lot of things into your head, but it ain't the same until you've seen it for yourself.

Epilogue

Trevor is now CEO of his own small taxi-transport company.

BARTENDER | Sylvan Alleyne

Sylvan Alleyne has been tending bar for over forty years. Much of that time he has served wealthy guests at the deluxe Cobbler's Cove Hotel on the west coast of Barbados. Hugging the curve of a crystalline cove and set amid tropical gardens, Cobbler's Cove is one of the island's finest small beach resorts. It is English in its tradition of serving afternoon tea and thoroughly Caribbean in its open-air dining next to the sea.

Sylvan, or Raccoon, as he is known to friends, laughs easily, revealing a full set of teeth encased in gold. He takes pride in being able to converse with tourists from a wide background. He is equally proud of his knowledge of alcoholic drinks—he can make over a hundred mixed drinks and has invented two of his own. At 62, he is quick to point out that most people don't believe he is that old. During our interview, however, he sent a barman off to fetch his blood-pressure pills. Sylvan has three years to go before mandatory retirement, then he'd like to open a small beach bar: "I still want to be in a bar, mixing drinks and telling stories."

I left school at 14. My mother was a fish seller, and we were fairly poor. She couldn't afford to send me to a trade or a secondary school. Today, education is free from primary all the way through university. All my children finished secondary school, and my boy got all As and Bs. When I was a boy in the '40s young people would do construction or work in the fields. I didn't want to be digging up the land or cutting cane in the hot sun all day long, so I started out in the hotel industry. I was a messenger at a little restaurant called John's Place. From there I got a job working in the kitchen at the Hotel Royal in Christ Church washing pots and dishes. But I couldn't take the kitchen; cooks are miserable people. Everything's fine in the morning, everybody's happy, then a pot boils over, something gets burned, something else happens, and everyone starts cussing. It's not for me. I like people, I like talking to people. I didn't want to be looking at pots and pans and cooks storming around all day long, so I moved out of the kitchen and became a waiter. But I didn't like that either. All a waiter does is carry plates back and forth all night long. I wanted to be able to make something.

Sometimes I helped out at the bar, mostly cleaning up, sweeping, and stuff. I was fascinated with the idea of being a bartender some day. In those days, bartenders wore white pants, white shirts, and white jackets with black shoes and black bow ties. I really liked the uniform. My aunt had a boyfriend who was a bartender and he used to bring home a book about making drinks. I got very interested in all the different cocktails.

One day the owner of John's Place, a gentleman named John Hammond, said the bartender was going on vacation and that he'd heard I knew how to fix drinks. He offered me the bartending job. I could mix some drinks, but I didn't yet know liquors, like the difference between rye, scotch, and bourbon. I had a lot to learn. And Mr. Hammond taught me everything. Ninety percent of the things I know about bartending, the real technical stuff, I learned from him. He is dead now, God bless him, but he sure did teach me a lot. He was a very cultured man who knew about wines, food, antiques, all the fine things in life. He had owned two antique stores, one in Washington, D.C., and one in London. When he retired, he moved down here and opened up John's Place, a bar/restaurant. It got very, very popular. Besides tending bar, I worked as his butler and waiter when he had houseguests. I was 15 or 16 at the time and here he was teaching me all about cutlery, liquor, and glasses; how to set a table; fingerbowls; and all that. He taught me about eating things, like oysters. I never thought I'd eat that slimy raw thing, but he showed me they are delicious. Yes, he taught me the fine things in life. A lot of poor black boys get their bellies full, but they don't have the opportunity to learn about the niceties of things like I did. He entertained some big-name people that I served, like Harry Belafonte and Joan Fontaine. These days you don't see the kind of service that we put on.

I learned a lot about dealing with people from watching Mr. Hammond. He had a terrific sense of humor, a gift with people. He insulted people, his friends and guests, and it would be okay. There was a lady from America who used to come. She was in her 60s or 70s, but she was very well kept, very upright. She'd say, "Hello John, darling," and he'd say, "Oh, you old bag, come here, how are you?" She'd say, "John, I don't mind you calling me an old bitch, but don't call me an old bag." He could say things like that and get away with it. Mr. Hammond died from cirrhosis of the liver. Everyone who came in was buying him drinks, and he was drinking from morning until closing. Too bad, because he could carry on a conversation about anything.

The bar at a south coast hotel. *Courtesy of Barbados Tourism Authority.*

When you come to my bar, I'll serve you whatever you want, but I'd prefer you to order a mixed drink. Mixing drinks is like making food, it gives me satisfaction. When I mix a drink and the customer tells me how good it is, it makes me feel good. I don't get that when I pour a bottle of beer. And when a real problem crops up between three or four different liquors or Latin drinks—tequila, samurais, margaritas, and stuff like that—it's a challenge. I like that because I have to keep going over and sampling things to see what works. I probably know how to make 90 percent of all mixed drinks. And if I don't know one, I've got a book, *The Bartender's Bible,* by Oscar Hamill.

What's popular in drinks changes. Harvey Wallbangers and Yellow Birds were hot thirty years ago. So were martinis, Rob Roys, Mint Juleps, and Singapore Slings. Today, at least here in Barbados, people like rum drinks. Lots and lots of rum today. But we serve a lot of other mixed drinks, too. And some we developed down here, like the Cobbler's Cooler, Bajan Green Monkey, Camelot, Duppy Parasol, Crop Over Calypso, and the Speightstown Market.

The weather affects what people order. If it's a lovely day, people will be out sunbathing on the beach and they'll be drinking lots of piña coladas, coconut punches, and fruit drinks. But when it's raining, they won't go out, they'll lime around the bar, bored, and drink rum punches.

In an average day I'll mix about twenty different drinks out of the one to two hundred drinks that I'll serve during my shift. But being a good bartender is not just mixing drinks, you gotta be friendly and you gotta speak properly so that people understand you. When you're dealing with tourists you've gotta speak English in the way they can understand. You can't speak dialect. You need to be well groomed. People don't feel safe if you look rusty, like you haven't shaved in a few days.

I always say that a good bartender has to be a therapist, counselor, pimp, loverman, ambassador, and even a bush doctor. You've gotta have knowledge of what's going on so you can converse with people. You've gotta be able to talk to people and make them feel okay. When somebody comes in that is bored or has a problem, you try to help. He might have had a fight with his wife, or maybe he is just looking for some Bajan comfort. I try to break the ice, "How are you sir? How long you been in Barbados? Are you enjoying it? What do you think about Barbados?"

Now maybe there's something about Barbados that's annoying him, and he might see me as someone he can talk to. Maybe he's been ripped off by somebody. I tell him there are black sheep in every town and that most Bajans aren't like that. Pretty soon he tells me they have the same problem at home in America or England. Maybe he's annoyed over something like the slow service and I can make him feel better by explaining how things are in Barbados. He has a few more drinks and we become buddy-buddies. And maybe by the time he leaves, he's feeling okay again. Sometimes they even apologize to me when they leave. You've got to remember when people come into the bar, they don't come to hear your problems. They come to tell you theirs. When I have a problem at home, I leave it at the hotel gate. I don't take it into the hotel. Visitors come to enjoy themselves. They want to be merry and if they're not, they want you to listen to their problems. So when I talk to them I'm always happy, laughing, ha, ha, ha. I never let them know that I've got problems, too. I really don't mind listening to theirs, because I love knowing that I can help in some way.

A lot of times people want to know what they should see while they're on the island. I'll suggest the Animal Flower Cave, the Flower Forest, and Harrison's Cave. I tell them, "Don't go down no dark alley and think you won't get mugged just because you're in beautiful Barbados. You'll get mugged here just like you would in a dark alley in New York." And I tell them that if they're going out to bars in town, there are two prices. Locals will pay 2 dollars for a beer and tourists will pay 3 or 4 dollars, so try to go with a local person if you don't want to pay extra. If they have a car and they're going to drive around the island, I'll tell them places and remind them that they can ask directions of most people but, like in every flock, there will be some black sheep. Some might want to snatch their purse or bag, so I tell them to always stay alert.

Sometimes a barman has gotta pimp, too. Single men will want to know where the action is, where they can get some girls. You can't just look at them and say, "I don't know." You got to know where to tell them to go. I may send them to a place in town where they have wicked young things that do naked dancing. The girls slide down a banister naked and you put two dollar bills in their [laughter]. You'd be surprised at the things that go on down there. If they want to help themselves afterwards, that can be arranged, no problem. But I don't get too many requests for that sort of thing because I'd say half of the people staying here are over 60. The older people are here for the rest and relaxation, they don't want too much dancing and wild things like that.

Sometimes you gotta be bush doctor, too. We call it primitive medicine. Some will step on a black sea urchin on the reef and get spines in their foot. It hurts bad, and I can help them by pulling the spines out and by rubbing a lime on the wound. And you get others who have a sick stomach and I'll mix up bitters and soda water with a little lemon juice to make them feel better. If they have a hangover you give them a spicy Bloody Mary with tomato juice, a little vodka, Worcestershire sauce, with a little salt and Tabasco. That'll make them feel better.

🌴   🌴   🌴

Though I've never been to the States, never been to England, never been to Canada, by talking to the people from those countries I've learned a lot. I can speak a couple words in French, a couple words in German, a couple words in Spanish. And like I said before, Mr. Hammond taught me the niceties of life, like food, wine, and music. I listen to all kinds of music now.

Some wealthy tourists can be very nice, very nice. Then you meet some who think they own you, body and soul. It can be miserable having to serve that type. But I hardly ever think about color.

Sometimes a person will say to me, "Oh, wouldn't you like to be on this side [of the bar] and me on that side?" I say, "Of course not, this is my job." Some people think we're uptight about having to serve white people all the time, but really, it's my job and I don't think about it. It's like the doctor who's got to cut off someone's leg. He's gotta do it, so he does it and he doesn't think much about it—if you know what I mean. All that race stuff is much bigger in the States than it is down here.

GUEST SERVICES | Marilyn Cooper

Marilyn Cooper, 40, is an energetic and outgoing single woman. She is a white Barbadian but was mostly raised in Canada. Her parents, like many middle-class Barbadians of their generation, went abroad for university. They returned to Barbados after their degrees, but later re-emigrated to Canada for jobs. Marilyn's passions are people and sports. She runs, plays tennis, water-skis, dives, and sails. After she completed a degree in languages, with an interest in translation, Marilyn had hoped to go to Geneva to study at the International School of Interpretation. But she later realized it didn't fit her personality. "I could no more be a translator than a nuclear physicist. To shut me in an office working by myself would kill me. I have to be with people." Today she looks after guests at the luxurious Royal Pavilion and Glitter Bay hotels.

I'm a bit of a nomad in that I seem to change jobs and residences every few years. It probably goes back to my childhood. We moved to Canada in 1969 when I was 9. In high school I was an exchange student in Brazil. I survived Carnival in Rio de Janeiro but had to return home when I got very sick with hepatitis. I did my third year of university in Grenoble, France. After graduation I moved to Calgary to work for the Olympic Winter Games for four years, then it was on to Los Angeles, then Hawaii, then Banff [Alberta] where I worked on celebrity sporting events, then Vancouver to work for the Hong Kong Bank of Canada, then back to Calgary to work for a travel company, then to Toronto to work for another travel group, and finally home to Barbados. It was 1993.

I really had no intention of coming back to Barbados. I was here on holiday when I met some businesspeople at Sam Lord's. They were saying how difficult it is to find good people in sales and marketing, and we just started talking. When they found out I was Bajan and therefore could live in Barbados, they offered me a job. I wasn't really that interested and went home to Toronto. But they kept hounding me and finally they made it so attractive that I thought, "Well, why not give it a try; if I don't like it I can always go back to Canada."

Once I got back here, there was no way I was going back to Canada. The quality of life here is far better. Of course, at first it wasn't easy. The heat made me very lethargic and tired for the first three months. Also, coming back was like living in a small town again, where everybody knows everybody else's business. In fact, people make a habit of knowing your business, and what they don't know they make up. As we Bajans say, "Why disturb the story with facts when you can make it up?"

For a single woman it can be a very difficult society to live in, especially coming from North America where you're so used to being independent and free-spirited. In Canada it's okay to go out to a movie or a bar by yourself. But down here, people watch your movements, especially if you are a single woman. And you have to be very careful about what you say, and I'm not very good at that. I'm an open, free-spirited person, and I am prone to shooting my mouth off and saying what I feel. Here you must mind your p's and q's.

It also took me a while to get reaccustomed to the work ethic here. In the Caribbean, because it's a warm climate, people don't operate as swiftly, decisions aren't made as quickly. I'm used to zipping in five million different directions at once, I move faster than people here, and that's been an adjustment. It's also an adjustment learning to live with lizards and mosquitoes and other tropical critters in your home. And the prices of things are out of sight. You can buy almost anything you want in Barbados, it just costs a fortune. I had to buy a paintbrush the other day at a hardware store and it cost 40 dollars. That's highway robbery, and I resent being ripped off like that.

On the flip side, it's a small-town community where people look out for one another. If you need something, you just pick up the phone and call a few friends: "Do you know someone who's got arugula in their garden, or do you know a good seamstress, or do you know someone who can fix my car at a reasonable price?" People are connected and they help you out. Another good side of small-island living is that everything is pretty accessible. I also like that it's a more relaxed society. The rules aren't as rigid as in Canada. You can go for a drive and sit under the stars with a bottle of wine or a beer and not get harassed by the police because you're drinking liquor outside your residence, like you would in Canada.

Once you get used to the heat, it's wonderful living in perpetual sunshine, not waking up and hearing the pitter-patter of rain for six months of the year, not having to scrape ice off your car, winterize your house, buy winter clothes. Sometimes I do miss the change of seasons, but then I think that on any day I can go to the beach, go swimming, go sailing.

Barbados is a cocktail society, and in many ways that suits me. Here you're meeting people all the time, often really interesting people. My offshore [foreign] friends might not agree; they often say it's hard to get to know Bajans, that Bajans are cliquey. But offshore people are also cliquey. Bajans tend to keep to themselves because the offshore community is so transient—here today, gone tomorrow. Many are just here for two years and then off to the next port. I'm more fortunate in that I have family on the island, but also I've lived abroad. I can see both sides, and I have a mixture of friends from both communities.

Being white, are you often mistaken for a tourist?

All the time. Absolutely. Most of the staff at the hotel still don't realize that I'm Bajan, but that's largely because of my North American accent. Whenever I meet people for the first time they just assume I'm not Bajan because of my accent. If I'm on the beach getting harassed by a vendor, I just put on my Bajan accent. "I's Bajan, I live here, and I don't need dat." I find them incredibly annoying. When I'm on the beach reading a book, minding my own business, I don't want somebody coming up to me, trying to sell me things, sitting down in the sand next to me and carrying on a conversation. It's very irritating. They just assume they have the God-given right to strike up a conversation with anyone they please! And then when you're walking to your car you've got to listen to, "Aw, sweetheart, you is lookin' good, can I help you with dat." Man, that irritates me.

Glitter Bay and Royal Pavilion are smallish hotels, what I call boutique hotels, where the guest's experience is paramount. It's the repeat clientele that they try to develop. You want people to keep coming back. To do that, it's important that they feel like this is their home away from home. You want them to know the staff, love the staff. When our repeat guests arrive, the staff give them a big hug, "Oh, Mr. and Mrs. Barrow, it's so nice to have you back." It's almost like coming into your own house and throwing down your suitcase; bam, you're home.

My job is director of guest services, which on any given day can involve everything from general management to hauling boxes. For instance, I just organized a library in our lounge, for guests to drop off and pick up books. This week cricket is starting, so I had a large television put out and organized lunches for the cricket fans each day. I kind of run my own show. I work with everybody, but I don't have to manage anyone. I prefer that. I like managing projects, situations, and environments, but I don't like managing people, and I particularly don't like managing women. Women can be bitchy, catty, and I'd just rather not have to deal with them. I've discovered that managing people is a talent, and one that I am not good at.

One of my roles is information. Anita Thorpe organizes our entertainment, and I get the information out to the guests and all the department heads so they know what's happening. I also take travel agents and tour operators around the property on site visits so that they can get to know us and sell us better. I oversee press trips—journalists, writers, and photographers who we show the hotels in the hope that they'll promote our property in their publications. We just had a super article in *Gourmet* magazine, and there's one coming out in *British Homes and Gardens,* and another in *Condé Nast Traveler.*

I also have some involvement with reservations. Charmaine, our reservations manager, handles the everyday stuff like assigning rooms. I deal with the extras, like when we have honeymoon or anniversary couples, I make sure we send a nice bottle of champagne and a card to their rooms wishing them a happy anniversary. I do it for their travel agent as well as for the person that books the holiday. The agents fax me requests like, "Can you put a bottle of wine in their room?" or "Can you make sure they have a really nice room?" The other day I organized dinner in Palm Terrace for a lady who brought down her husband for his 60th birthday. So I got balloons, cake, brought in a singer, and the whole bit. It makes me happy when I can make dreams come true. When they thank you and tell you how beautiful the hotel is and how wonderful the staff has been and say that they're planning on coming back, that makes me really satisfied with the job.

What I don't like is dealing with complaints. However, I suppose they do help you to understand where the hotel can improve or where you've made a mistake. When I get a complaint I try to trace it back and find out what really happened. There are always two stories, the guest's version and the staff's version. It's important to find out what happened from both sides before you respond. Fortunately, we don't have too many complaints. Thank God!

Every Monday, Wednesday, and Friday morning we have meetings in which the heads of different departments get together. We go over the guest comment forms, we discuss any problems in the hotel, what needs to be done for the physical plant, the reactions of the travel agents and tour operators that have been shown through the property, what's happening in entertainment, and so on.

A large part of my job is just going out and meeting the guests. We have a huge amount of repeat guests and with them it's very important to take time to chat. They are very familiar with the island, so with them it's more catching up on where they've been and on how their year has been. They always want to know what's new in Barbados—new restaurants, what's good, what's bad, that sort of stuff. With first-time guests, I talk mostly about the island, what there is to see and do. I like to promote the east coast, as that is the most beautiful part of Barbados and is so different from the west coast. What you talk about depends upon how many times they've been here.

I do the cocktail parties for guests every Monday night at Glitter Bay and every Wednesday night at Royal Pavilion. My job is to shake people's hands and move around and talk. "Hi, I'm Marilyn Cooper, Guest Services Manager. It's nice to meet you, have you been here before? How did you hear about our hotel? How is your room? Is there anything I can do?" You know, general conversation. And then you say, "Excuse me for a sec, I have to meet some other guests." So you move to the next group, "Hi, how are you doing?" With the repeat guests that I know very well, I introduce them to new arrivals, "This is Mr. and Mrs. Caldwell, I'd like you to meet the Weakleys, they've just arrived," then I leave them to talk. This way people have a chance to meet one another and learn something more about the hotel and the island.

So I wear many hats. Some days are so busy my head is spinning; other days it's quiet. But I like being busy. I like when I've got sixteen different things going on at once. I thrive on it. I like dabbling in lots of different things.

Winter, between Christmas and April, of course, is our busiest time. There's a lot of seasonality in the hotel business in the Caribbean that you don't get in the North. During peak season you can feel the buzz in the hotels—lots of people around, the restaurants are full, the beaches are full, you can feel a hum, you can feel the property moving, and that carries through until about Easter. Then you feel it calm down. That's when we do a lot of our maintenance and repairs. Summertime is much quieter still. You can almost send a bowling ball down the pathway. The staff works better when it's busy, in wintertime. When it's slow and quiet you have to really push them. They need that pressure, they need to be busy to work hard, and when it's not they just sort of lose momentum. I think they also prefer it when it is busy, when there is the buzz and the excitement of a full hotel.

What are your impressions of the guests? How are they different from the less affluent tourists who stay on the south coast?

About 70 percent of our guests are British or European, whereas you get more North Americans staying on the south coast. Because these are very upscale hotels, most of our clientele are fairly wealthy, sophisticated people. They come here to unwind, to relax, and to be catered to by the staff. Some of them are very demanding, some unreasonably so; others are absolutely wonderful—just gentle, lovely, and kind. Really lovely people. If I were staying at a hotel of this caliber, spending the amount of money they do, I would be demanding, too. When you pay big money you expect a certain level of service.

But some have unrealistic expectations. They come with a European or New York attitude, expecting a level of service which is not characteristic of the Caribbean. Here you can't expect room service to arrive within five minutes of placing an order. You can't expect to send out a fax with the snap of a finger. Things just don't happen as swiftly here as they do in their own countries. If you need that kind of service, then you should stay in New York or London.

The same is true of laundry. We don't do it in house, we send it out, and it can take two days to get it back. Well, for some people that's not good enough, even though it's explained in the Directory of Services and on the telephone. When the waterworks turns off the water and all of a sudden there's no water in the guest's room, all hell breaks loose. It's little things that get under the skin of some guests. But the sophisticated traveler, the one who's traveled around the world, expects the Caribbean to be more laid back, expects there to be problems, and he deals with it a lot better. It's the

Pool cleaner at
Turtle Beach Resort.
*Courtesy of Elegant
Hotels Group.*

new traveler who doesn't realize that things don't move quickly
and don't always work as well in the Caribbean who has trouble.

Are there differences between North American and British guests?

Europeans, on a global scale, speaking very generally, are less
likely to complain than North Americans. Our rooms at Glitter Bay
have air-conditioning in the bedrooms and just a ceiling fan in the
living room. Well, Americans love air-conditioning, they like cold
rooms, air-conditioning throughout. The Europeans will open their
doors and just use a ceiling fan, maybe just use the AC to sleep. I've
noticed, too, that Europeans gravitate more to the beach while
Americans gravitate more to the pool. Maybe it's because Americans are not as used to swimming in the sea. Some of them seem
scared about what's underneath, that there's fish and sea urchins
under there. Maybe the movie *Jaws* didn't do them any great fa-
vors. Maybe it's because a lot of Americans have swimming pools at

home and they're a lot more accustomed to pools. I think it's also the case that Europeans live much closer to the sea than most Americans. Brits, the French, and the Italians flock to the sea on their holidays. Sometimes I get the impression that a lot of Americans simply don't like saltwater on their skin or sand between their toes.

Their eating patterns are also different in that Europeans, particularly the British, will do an afternoon tea—a light snack between lunch and dinner. Europeans eat later than North Americans; they go for the later reservations. And as you know, Europeans come for longer stays, often a couple of weeks, while North Americans will do three- to five-day getaways.

Because Americans are here for a shorter amount of time, they're less likely to go off the property and travel around the island. When you're here for three weeks, like Europeans, you get tired of the beach and you want to go out and explore. Also, I think many Americans are leery about driving on the left side of the road. Brits are used to it, so they can just hop in the car and away they go. But overall, our guests are probably less adventurous than many. The type of guest that comes here is spending a lot of money and wants to be pampered, wants to be looked after, and doesn't want to be zipping and zapping all over the place. They want to take advantage of the property; we have two huge properties with lots of walking space and gardens. It's very comfortable for them to stay right here.

It's interesting to work every day in this kind of luxury, working with people that are very wealthy, very well educated, very sophisticated. But working here does not mean you're part of their society. Mostly you're on the outside looking in. Some of the staff are envious of the wealth that we are surrounded by, but it's untouchable wealth, it's a false reality, one they don't have access to. However, some of the guests have become friends of mine and I've been invited to come stay with them in England or wherever. So some people do cross that line.

I would certainly love to be able to be as wealthy as some of them are, to be able to travel the way they do, and to be able to stay in a hotel like this and pay for it. On the flip side, they're envious of the fact that we live in the sunshine, work in beautiful conditions, see this beautiful ocean every day, and live a simple lifestyle. A lot of the guests are like, "Oh my God, you're so lucky, you live in this every day." I say, "Yeah, but you're lucky to live in Europe, you can zip off to Paris or Rome just like that."

*What do you think Barbados must do to remain
an attractive destination for tourists?*

For one thing, not price ourselves out of the market. We need to give value for money. We need to be very careful because we are already very expensive, and people don't like to be ripped off. People that come to Barbados have other choices—they can go to Hawaii or Mexico or elsewhere in the Caribbean. They come to Barbados because it's safe and they are treated well and we have wonderful beaches. But they'll go elsewhere if they can get better value for their money. I'd love to see the government get rid of the beach vendors, get rid of the harassment on the beach, clean up the crime, clean up the roads. Traffic has become a big problem; there are too many cars on the road. We may have to be like Bermuda and restrict cars to one per family, and we need to do something about speeding. Start yanking licenses and pulling the speeders off the road.

Our survey of the guests' comment cards tells us that the majority of our guests are very, very happy. Most say that they would come back. Sure, there's a few that say we didn't meet their expectations. Sometimes they're disappointed their room didn't look out on the sea or the bar didn't stay open late enough at night. Or they might be disappointed that they didn't get the specific room that they requested. Sometimes the complaint is about service, sometimes it's about the food. But every hotel faces that. You have one person who says the food is fantastic and another who says it was awful. Someone says the service was terrible, and another person is saying that it's exemplary.

The weather can have an influence on you, too. Some get grumpy when the waves are huge and they can't swim in the sea. They get disappointed when the sea stirs up the broken coral and brings it on the beach. Well, those are natural phenomena that we can't do anything about.

When you work in luxury all the time it's easy to forget how nice it is. Sometimes I have to pinch myself and think of my friends who are scraping the snow off their cars right now. I think, this really is paradise, a beautiful place to be and to work. On the other hand, it's sometimes lonely in that I'm single and I don't have a man in my life. And although I'm meeting people all the time, most everybody is just passing through, just here for a vacation, here to kick up their heels. The people you meet here are on a high, they're having fun and are probably very different back home. Besides, the clientele we have are all either newlywed or nearly dead. Mostly the latter. They're all coupled off. There are a few single men that come here—mostly for business—but I'm very wary of meeting men that are just passing through. As a white female, it's very difficult to meet a potential partner on this island. My Canadian friends say that I'm reducing my eligibility by living here. Maybe, but at least I've got a very active, energetic lifestyle here.

Although I love what I do, and this is a wonderful profession to be in, I can't see myself being here in five years. For one, I really need to make more money. The hospitality industry does not pay well. There are lots of advantages and perks, like eating in the finest restaurants, but you don't get rich. My friends in the finance or off-shore sector make three times what I do. I'd like to make their salaries, but then they say, "But you got such a great job, you work in a great place, you eat in the best restaurants, you're always meeting neat people." I say, "Yeah, but."

Also, I think I'm always looking for something new and exciting. I like my little house on the south coast, and the thought of moving is just exhausting and terrifying, but still, if I had to guess, I'd say I won't be here in five years. Maybe I get bored easily.

Epilogue

The year after this interview, Marilyn changed jobs and moved house. Several years later she left Barbados altogether and now works in sales and marketing for an affordable housing project in the Turks and Caicos Islands.

ROOM ATTENDANT | Sheralyn O'Neale

Sheralyn O'Neale, 38, is one of seventy maids, or "room attendants," at the Sandy Lane Hotel. Sandy Lane is the best-known and most luxurious resort in Barbados. Twice it was selected by Business Traveller as the leading international resort in the world. It was built by an Anglo-American, Ronald Tree, who "wanted a place where his friends could vacation in luxuriant tropical surroundings, while maintaining the habits and standards of English upper-class life." Opened in 1961, Sandy Lane's fame grew as it attracted the likes of Princess Margaret, Jackie Kennedy Onassis, Tom Jones, and Mick Jagger. During the winter season, the room rates vary from a low of $880 for a "garden" room to $2,390 per night for a penthouse. There are three staff members for every room.

Sheralyn, a single mother, lives with her parents and her two teenage boys in the remote district of Round Rock on the north coast of the island. Raised in the country, she still helps her parents in their large garden and in tending sheep. She gets up at dawn to feed her children and tidy the house before taking a bus down to the west coast. At the hotel she changes into a green uniform with a white apron, white socks, and white sneakers.

In the morning, before we start cleaning, the supervisor briefs us on our duties for the day, arrivals and departures, and guests' special requests. For instance, if the guests are getting body massages, they need extra towels. Some want an extra chair on their patio and if it's a business guest with a computer, he may want an extra phone in the room. Things like that. After the supervisor's done talking I get my caddy and cleaning stuff and go on the corridor to start my duties. Sometimes you find "Do Not Disturb" signs on the rooms, so you have to wait until they're ready. I may swap some rooms with another attendant so I can get going.

When we enter a room, we don't just push the door open. We enter cautiously. I knock three times and say who I am. Then I enter slowly. If someone's there I say, "Sorry, I'll come back later." When we clean the rooms we always keep the door open so that the guests know there is someone in there cleaning and there's no misunderstanding or anything.

You do the bathroom first. You spray the tub, toilet bowl, and sink top with a cleaner called R-2. Then you use a sponge to clean the tub and countertops; the shower curtain can be the hardest to clean. With the toilet you may need to get your hand really deep into the bowl to get it clean. You replace the little shampoo, gel, lotion, soap, cotton balls, Q-tips, sewing kit, and shower cap from the basket on the sink counter, if any of them have been used. A few guests take them every day, so you have to replace them all. You change the towels—three bath and four hand towels and two side mats for when you get out of the bath tub or shower. Then you do the bedroom—empty the wastebasket, mop the tile floor, mop the patio, straighten up, and change the linens. We change the bed sheets everyday. Sometimes a guest will say, "Oh, don't bother, the sheets are still clean." Sometimes the guest doesn't want any service at all. "Don't bother. I'm okay for today."

Most people are pretty tidy but sometimes you get into the room and, oh Lord, it's so messy. Sometimes they've left their clothes scattered all over the place, and if they have kids, there may be lots of toys about. Sometimes you ask yourself why can't people be a little more tidy? I guess the guests are on holiday and some of them don't want to be thinking about where to put something.

When you pick up their things you try to put them in a place where they can find them easily. But if they have something wet in the bathroom, like a swimsuit, we're supposed to put them on a rack on the patio. Some guests come in looking for their swimsuits and can't find them and have to call housekeeping. Then you have to go to the room and show them where it is. I don't like it when people leave their underwear lying around. Normally we neatly fold the clothes and put them on shelves in the closet. If it's underwear, we'll put them in a laundry bag and leave it there.

Sometimes they leave so much stuff on the bed that you get jittery. Like when they leave money. If there's a lot of money sitting out you call the supervisor and he'll come to the room and put it in an envelope. Last week one room attendant found 500 dollars a guest had left sitting on the dresser.

It takes about thirty-five minutes to do a room, unless it's really messy, in which case it can take up to an hour. When the guests depart, we call it a "DI"—a dirty room. With a DI room you start from scratch and give it a thorough cleaning to get it back to standard for the new arrival. If the guest was smoking, it leaves a very strong odor and you really have to clean the room well and use lots of R-2 and fresheners or the next guest will have that smell.

At 7 P.M. we start the turndown service. You take the bedspread off and put out fresh towels, freshen the sink, replace anything in the basket that's been used, and tidy back the room.

Most of our guests are from England. You can tell from how they speak. And you can tell from the clothing they bring, too. Sometimes they have books with them, and if they're not English you can tell from the writing, like if they're Italian or German. You don't have a lot of contact with them because most of the time you enter the room when they're gone. Sometimes I won't see a guest for the whole week.

There's a service charge so most of them don't leave tips. Maybe one in every ten will leave you something, but it's not expected. I once got 100 U.S. dollars. They presented it to me in person. I was in the room when the guest came in off the beach and said to me, "This is for you, Sheralyn." Usually, they just leave a note saying "For room attendant" with the money on top of the note so that you know it's for you. If you're not on duty that day, they'll put it in an envelope and leave it with housekeeping or at the front desk, so that you're sure to get it.

The guests have nice-quality things. I see them on the table, sitting out, and I might love it, but I'd never think of taking it. Sometimes I see a dress and say, "I would really like this fashion." I take it in my brain and see if it would be easy to make. But it's not like we go into the closets searching because we shouldn't do that. Sometimes I look at the makeup. I've bought cologne that I saw a guest had—Gio. It's very nice.

I've been working here for seven years now but I put in my application three years before I got the job. I had almost forgotten about it when one day I got a phone call saying I was to come in for an interview. I went and they started me in training. Four weeks of training. People lectured us on being professional—on how to deal with guests, how to talk to guests, how to answer the telephone. They even teach you how to greet the guest in the morning, "Good morning, sir, would you like your room serviced?" And, if a guest needs a hair dryer, I should know how the hair dryer operates, to show the guest. They told us about guests who are difficult, that even when you're doing your best, some guests will not be satisfied. That guests can make you jittery, but you must always keep your cool, you must maintain the standard of the profession.

They teach you all the standards for making beds, folding towels, folding sheets, and things like that. Like in making a bed, you use two flat sheets, tuck the first sheet all around, then the second sheet, and finally you smooth the bedspread out and leave a breakfast card on top. A breakfast card is where the guest writes out what he wants for breakfast in the morning. We're taught to have confidence in ourselves when we're doing something, whether it's making a bed or talking to a guest. They want you to always put your best foot forward.

When the guests depart, they sometimes leave things behind, like half a bottle of hair mousse, magazines, sometimes a shirt. If it's something you'd like to read, you can take it home. If it's a magazine about housekeeping, like *Cookery* or *Designs,* I'll take it, and I might take home a newspaper or an unopened drink. But if they've forgotten something by mistake, I take it to housekeeping so it can be returned. A while ago I pulled open a drawer and there were six shirts in a package inside. Housekeeping will get in contact with the guest. We keep everything for three months, and if the guest doesn't ask for it, you can take it.

Whenever we leave the hotel, the security people check our bags. If you take anything off the property that was given to you or that you found in the room, you have to get a note from housekeeping to show to security when you go through the gate.

We don't get many complaints. Sometimes a guest will say that their room wasn't cleaned properly or that it has a smell or that they want brighter towels or that the room attendant wasn't polite to them. It's usually women that complain. Sometimes you get a guest who tells you not to touch their things. That can make it hard to tidy the room. We tell the supervisor that they don't want their things touched so that he'll know why the room wasn't straightened properly. I had one guest who didn't want anything touched. She had moved the luggage rack against the window, which crushed the drapes. I moved it back against the closet where it belonged. She didn't like me moving the rack and made a complaint. She called me back to the room and told me the luggage rack was to stay right there against the window. Some women can really be picky-picky. The English especially.

But all in all I really like my job. I think I love to clean. I love to turn something messy into something clean and neat. When I finish a room, having dusted and swept and mopped and left a fresh odor, I feel very comfortable about it. I hope the guest is pleased. I like pleasing guests. The only bad thing is that making beds puts a lot of stress on my back, and the work can be very tiresome, especially on Concorde days [when Concorde flights depart and arrive from London], when we have a lot of departures and arrivals.

When I get home at the end of the day, I sit down for a little. Then I get up and tidy the house. Sometimes I clip the hedge, do the wash, I do a little gardening. Sometimes I play cricket in the yard with my boys Ezra and Randolph. Sometimes it don't matter how tired I am, I'm not ready to sit back and relax. I don't know why but I find myself doing a lot of work. I just work, work, work, work. But I feel good about it. And by 8:30 I'm pretty sleepy, so I go to bed.

Working at Sandy Lane has been good for me. Before I went to Sandy Lane I found it hard to speak out about things or share my views. Working at the hotel has made me braver, made me feel freer to talk to people that I don't know. I think it enlightened me.

Epilogue

Sheralyn was laid off when Sandy Lane was closed for renovations. She is now a room attendant in another west coast hotel.

SECURITY | Errol Sobers

Tall and rugged, Errol Sobers, 40, is the head of security at the upscale Royal Pavilion and Glitter Bay resort hotels. The Royal Pavilion describes itself in its brochure as having "a whisper of old world grace and a setting of astonishing new world beauty . . . a cloister of calm and serenity overlooking a half mile sweep of golden sand and turquoise sea." Its sister hotel, Glitter Bay, is centered on the former great house of British shipping magnate Edward Cunard of Cunard Lines. The great house, where Cunard entertained celebrities and members of the British aristocracy, now serves as the reception area. The property includes 30 acres of magnificent gardens and grounds. With a staff of five supervisors and seventeen officers, Errol works closely with every department in the adjoining hotels to look after the needs of the guests. Two nights a week he is the manager on duty. Growing up, Errol wanted to be a doctor, but after leaving secondary school he followed in his father's footsteps as a police officer and then went on to hotel security.

I've been working in security since 1978 when I joined the Barbados Police Force. I was just 20 years old. After six months' training and two months on the street, I heard that the Bermuda Police Force was recruiting. I applied, and I became one of the youngest officers to go. I spent fourteen years on the Bermuda force, and I worked in just about every department. I started off on foot patrol. My nickname was Zip because back then I was young and quick on my feet. Many of the guys who had drugs would try to run, but I would catch them in the first couple of yards. Then I went to the traffic department and after that to the cycle squad. We investigated stolen cycles and mopeds. For four years I was in the CID—Criminal Investigation Department—and then the drug squad. A lot of our work was with airlines traveling out of Central and South America in connection with drug smuggling.

I learned a lot about the drug trade and I became an expert witness in court. I gave evidence as to the use of the different drugs— like the value of different cocaine depending on its purity and the supply on the street. And I spent a couple of years talking to community and school groups about drugs. I even did a course on drug investigations at Scotland Yard in London. After four years on the drug squad, I was burned out and needed a break. Drugs are tough, you're dealing with the same people and you're seeing the effects of drugs on them, and after a while it starts getting to you.

In 1992, I came back to Barbados to work in hotel security. It's funny, but my life and my father's life have been very similar. He went from Barbados to Grenada as a police officer; I went from Barbados to Bermuda as a police officer. He worked for some time and came back to Barbados; I worked for some time and came back to Barbados. He became a security officer at a lumber company, and I became a security officer in the hotel industry. To be honest, I wouldn't mind if my son became a police officer. Being in the police helps you see life in a different light, and you learn that things aren't always what they seem. Also, police officers learn to do just about everything. You have to be a counselor because you get into domestic conflicts, you're a medic because often you're the first person at the scene of an accident, and so on. After having been a police officer you think you can do almost anything, and I think that's why I was able to leave the police force and go into the airline security and now tourism.

When I came back to Barbados, my job was head of security at the Hilton Hotel. In many ways, there isn't any difference between being in charge of security at a hotel and being a police officer. A large hotel is like a small village. You have just about everything here that you would have in a village—people, shops, restaurants, a bar, a bank. For the guests, this is their home away from home. They come here and stay for a week or two, during which time everything they need is here. That's why the same kinds of problems that occur in any village or town can also occur in a hotel—break-ins, robbery, and, God forbid, rape. So each hotel has its own security to look after the safety of the guests. You want to make sure the guests feel safe moving around. Around the clock—day and night we have at least four security personnel on duty.

The beach is one of the big challenges. A lot of hotel guests think the beach is private. Well, all beaches in Barbados are public. We don't have any jurisdiction over the beach; that's up to the rangers who work for the NCC [National Conservation Commission]. If our guests are being harassed or if there's a problem with drugs on the beach, we bring it to their attention. We don't have any power ourselves. Even with harassment. By that I mean guys approaching a guest on the beach trying to sell merchandise, jet-ski rides, drugs, or sex. We don't get a lot of complaints about harass-

Beach boy passing a group of visitors playing volleyball on Heywoods Beach. *Courtesy of Emily Sparks.*

ment here because our clientele is older, and a lot of them are repeat guests who know their way around. Even so, there are some beach bums who come up to the women and tell them how happy they can make them. I had one incident where a lady was lying on the beach and a beach bum went right up to her and asked her if she wanted to see his erection. He told her about his size and what he could do for her. The rangers know who these guys are.

But the big drawback to prosecuting people for harassment is that in our legal system you need to have a witness in court. If you don't have a witness, nothing is going to happen. You can arrest the guy and take him to the station, but that's it. The complaint is made by a guest who will have gone home, left the island, and can't be in court to give evidence. Beach bums understand this and know they can slip through. Another problem in hotel security on a small island is that the staff are often hesitant to report illegal activities or otherwise get involved for fear of reprisals. They'll tell you, "No one's gonna come and burn my house down because of that." We've had instances where we've caught the thief, and then when it comes time to testify, all of a sudden the staff person can't remember a thing.

I try to keep the beach bums moving down the beach. As a matter of fact, I harass them. I'm tough and they know it. They don't like me, but that's okay. It means I'm doing my job. A couple of days ago I was driving home and one of the guys who does jet-skis up here called me a dog. I've had others threaten me. Those things don't rattle me.

A lot of the beach rangers just sit back and observe when they should be moving around. They'd be more effective if they would actually patrol the beaches rather than standing in one area. There seems to be an understanding between them and some of the [illegal] vendors on the beach. Right in front of me I witnessed a ranger ignoring an unlicensed vendor going from chair to chair soliciting business from guests. That's not supposed to happen. Many times I've had to go to that ranger and say, "Can't you see what is happening?" Only then will he spring into action.

Some beach bums are selling drugs. Some of the jet-ski guys and some of the guys selling jewelry are also pushing drugs. You see them making trips down the beach, and if you watch closely you'll see a guest walking a few yards behind. They'll go off out of sight, then a short while later they'll come back. That type of thing. There is a perception that people travel to the Caribbean for the sun, the sea, and the sex. But for some it's also for drugs. As an ex-member of the drug squad, I can tell you that if there wasn't a market—if visitors didn't come down here looking for drugs—it wouldn't prosper. You wouldn't have so many guys on the beach selling. At the last hotel I worked at, I had a couple in a room who met one of the beach bums and brought him back to their room. A security officer was passing the room and smelled marijuana. He called me and we went down there and found them in the room with this guy smoking. Hotel management usually doesn't like to involve the police because they don't want any negative publicity, so what we do is meet with the guest and tell him that it's against the law and if he continues we will have to alert the authorities. That doesn't mean the person is going to stop, though. He'll just be more discreet in what he's doing.

Since we don't have much of a young clientele at Royal Pavilion and Glitter Bay, we don't often have a problem with drugs. A lot of younger people's idea of fun is using drugs, meeting people, and going to bed with them. I've tried to educate our room attendants about that and what to look for in terms of drugs when cleaning the rooms.

When I left Barbados in 1978, there wasn't a major drug problem. There was marijuana, but not much else. When I returned in 1992, there had been a major increase in drug-dealing. I can't say that tourism is responsible for this increase, but it seems obvious that if there wasn't a market for drugs, there wouldn't be many guys out there selling them.

Is topless bathing of any concern to hotel security?

At Almond Beach Hotel we had a lot of Europeans, especially Italians and Germans, and it's second nature for them. But toplessness has never been encouraged in Barbados, and there's not much of it. On our property, you'll get one or two who might be topless. If there are a lot of kids running around, I'll ask them to turn over or cover up. But a woman cannot be arrested for exposing herself unless you see the pink. Her vagina.

Sometimes you get a single man checking into the hotels. He calls for room service and when the maid comes up and knocks on the door he says, "Come on in." She opens the door and he's standing there stark naked. That happens quite a bit. There's always going to be some sexual relations between staff and guests, and there are always stories of certain maids who perform sexual duties for male guests. Some of it happens on property, some of it happens off the property. When you think about it, it's quite easy. The room attendants are told to leave the door open while they're cleaning. If the door is open, you eliminate any accusations. Also, if the maid is in there by herself and the door is open there is less of a chance that she'll go through the luggage, since someone could walk by and see her.

A lot of people who come to the Caribbean are not used to mixing sun and alcohol. They don't understand how much stronger the effect of alcohol is in this climate, when you've been out in the hot sun. If you're not used to it, you can really lose it. You can do things that are out of character. We had a gentleman here two Mondays ago who drank thirteen rum punches and toppled over in a garden bed. It's mostly the ones who haven't been to the Caribbean before who overdo it, but most quickly learn their lesson.

Maintaining security at night is pretty challenging. Number one because nighttime is made for sleeping. If you're going to be up all night, you have to prepare for it by resting all day, and a lot of guards don't do that. Almost every night you've got somebody on security falling asleep. I come back to the hotel at all different hours to check up; they never know when I'm going to be here, and that helps keep them on their toes. When I was working at the Hilton, I came across a guard asleep in the bar. Fast asleep. So I took his shoes, his cap, and his radio and went and got his supervisor to come back and look at this guy. We came back twenty minutes later and he was still fast asleep. I worked in airline security in Miami for a while, and we had a system where the security guys had to punch in twenty different positions at intervals. But people always have a way of getting around the system. One guy came in with an alarm clock. He would set it, put his head down, doze off, and when the alarm went off he would get up and punch in. Then go back and put his head down. Wherever you are, security at night is going to be challenging. Like I said, nighttime is made for sleeping, so people will sleep. The other thing about nighttime security is that it's dangerous because people can see you but you can't see them. Two days ago we had an incident where an intruder was checking room doors, looking for one that was open. Two of our security officers confronted him, and he started fighting. One of our guys got two fingers sliced, and it took five sutures to close him up.

Another aspect of hotel security is preventing staff from pilfering. You always find some staff who feel that because they work here they have the right to help themselves to things. Like one night I was walking around the grounds when I heard a thump. When I looked around the corner, one of our staff was lying on the ground with a frozen turkey next to him. Another employee was twenty feet up on the roof of the kitchen. He had dropped the turkey to the guy on the bottom, but the guy didn't catch it and it hit him in the chest. When I first came to Royal Pavilion, we had a cook who was caught one night with sugar and things as she was leaving the property. I had to call the police. Well, the next day there was a handwritten note under my door that said I needed to be killed and poisoned and stuff like that. You see, it can be hard policing your own staff. But I've been around long enough to know that people usually make threats like that just to scare you. Someone who really wants to kill you isn't going to tell you beforehand. When I was on the police force I was told many times that my name was on a hit list. It just comes with the job.

A lot of the hotel staff live not too far from the hotel, and a lot of the staff are related. We have a mother and daughter working in the same department, and the daughter's boyfriend is a waiter here. The mother's father is one of the taxi drivers who operates from the property. The mother's sister works here, too. There are a lot of other relationships like that. I don't think it's a good thing, because when you come to a situation like pilfering you run into a real knot trying to find out what happened. It's like "This person is my mother or my sister, and there's no way I'm going to tell on them."

When you have staff that pilfers from the hotel you also run the risk of them pilfering from guests. We often get reports of things missing from guests' rooms, but I can tell you that 90 percent of the time when the room is checked, the item is found. I can tell you true stories of people who put money in the safe in their room and then say it's missing. "I put my wallet right in there last night and now it's gone." Well, there's only one key to each safe. In fact, if they lose it, we have to drill the lock. On one occasion, when I checked the pocket of the man's trousers hanging in the closet I found the wallet. It's just the same as you putting your glasses on your forehead and then looking all around for them. When people are in a hotel and can't find something, some just assume it's been stolen.

But we also have, and this is a growing trend, people making false reports about things being missing from their rooms. Usually they do it the day before their departure. They'll call the desk and say, "I'm missing my jewelry." And then they'll say, "Since we're leaving, can we have the report for our insurance?" Usually it will be high-priced items that are missing, like jewelry. It used to be that the police would give them a report right away. No problem. The guest would give a statement, and the police would give them a copy to take home. Then people began to realize that this was a scam. Now insurance companies are getting tougher. Now a guest must report it to the hotel within twenty-four hours and obtain a full police report. I find that people are more willing to tell a lie to a hotel security officer than to the police. The police obviously have more power, and if they find out you're lying they can arrest you. Recently I had a lady call up and say her watch was missing. She said she put it right here on the dresser last night and this morning it was gone. She wanted a report to take back for her insurance. I told her she'd also need a report from the police and I would call the police for her. Then she said, "Let me think about it." Funny enough, the following day, when I followed up on the report, she said, "Oh, oh, I found the watch, it was on the beach. I must have dropped it." Now that's unlikely. The beach has heavy traffic, lots of people going up and down. And during the time she had left the beach it had been raked. The woman was British, but we find it's mostly Americans, and mostly younger people, that make these claims. If people in their 50s or 60s report something missing it's usually genuine.

One thing that challenges our security is outsiders coming onto the hotel property posing as guests. It is sad that in this day and age there is a certain mentality that only black people commit crimes. The result is that people of other persuasions, colors, are not looked at as closely as someone who is black. You experienced it today. When you came to the hotel, you drove right through security. They didn't ask you who you were or what your business was. They waved you right through. If you were black you would have been stopped for sure. You take a white guy dressed like a hobo, and he can walk right through this place and nobody will say anything to him, but take a black guy dressed in a suit and somebody's going to wonder, "Who is he? Why is he here?"

The other day we had two guests that were staying together. One black man, one white man. They were walking along the beach and the white guy was in front when he walked onto the hotel property and passed a security guard, who said nothing to him. When the black guy, a couple of yards behind, walked the same way, the security guard stopped him. Obviously he was offended by this. It's unfortunate that people still think that black people don't have a right to be in certain areas. And this is a black society!

To give you another instance, when I was at the Hilton there was a Trinidadian chap who would slip into a room when the maid was cleaning. He'd slip into the bathroom, which is near the entry, then, when the maid knocked on the bathroom door, the Trinidadian chap would say, "I'll be right out." When he came out, he'd go into the living area, sit near the coffee table, pick up a magazine like he is the occupant, and wait until she finished cleaning. When the maid left, the chap then went through the guests' possessions and took what he wanted. Guaranteed, if he was black, he wouldn't have gotten far. A black guy in the bathroom would have triggered something in the mind of the maid: "Hey, something's not right here." Unfortunately, we have black guests who get that treatment.

I've enjoyed working in this industry for some of the same reasons I liked being a police officer. No two days are the same. You meet different people with different challenges every day. It gives me satisfaction when I can turn someone's negative experience around and make it positive. Solve their problem. Like recently, there was an incident where two guys went into a guest's room and stole his expensive designer bag, a Louis Vuitton. We caught the guys. The guest wrote, thanking me for the way it was handled. That's what really gives me satisfaction.

But whether it's police work or hotel security, I always say the outcome has to do with how you treat people. How you approach the problem. If you approach a situation in a hostile manner, it's guaranteed that you're going to end up with hostility. You have to treat everyone the same way. We tend to stereotype people; we think that because a guy is out there on the beach selling aloe that he's a bum. It doesn't necessarily mean that he's a bum. Maybe he really needs the money and isn't able to do anything else. Just because he is shabbily dressed doesn't mean you can go speak to him like he's a dog. No, you treat him like everyone else, and when you do, it disarms him, it knocks him off his feet. He's expecting you to treat him like a bum and then you treat him with respect.

When I was a police officer I was able to arrest people for drugs in some of the worst areas, arrest them on my own without a fight. Then there were other times when I'd go in with three other police and we would end up with a big fight on our hands. All because of the approach. It's your initial approach that often determines how it comes out in the end. So when guests report that they've lost something, have been harassed, or whatever, I am always very polite. I listen to what they have to say. I've had cases like this woman who went berserk and ripped all her clothes off. People went up to her but she wouldn't put her clothes on or cover up. She was singing hymns and stuff. When I got there I stood alongside her and started singing along with her. And eventually I got her to cover up and we were able to take her to the hospital. It's all how you approach the thing.

When you hire in the hotel industry you want people who know how to deal with people. We get guys who apply for jobs and say they worked for a security company. But that doesn't mean they have any real training. A lot of private security companies just get bodies because they have a contract to fill. They hire you, put a uniform on you, give you a radio, tell you to stand here and watch this place for the next eight hours. But there is no training. So when I interview people, I ask them what they actually did in their last job.

"Well, I worked at this factory."

"What did you do there?"

"I watched these tanks."

Well, I know this is not the kind of person I'm looking for. And sometimes we get people who tell you that they don't like white people. Now, hey, how are they going to work in a hotel not liking white people?

I've enjoyed being a part of tourism. But while tourism has brought a lot of development to Barbados, it hasn't all been good. Some of our landscape, especially along the beach, has been over-developed—it's now nothing but hotel after hotel after hotel. Tourism here is different than what I knew in Bermuda. In Bermuda it's really viewed as a business, as a foreign-exchange earner, and people are more sensitized to tourists. Here we're still developing as a premier tourist destination. It wasn't that long ago that a lot of Bajans were working in agriculture. Barbadians are very friendly, but they're not as sensitized to visitors as in Bermuda. I remember coming back here on vacation and I had some friends with me. We were driving around the island and there were people working in the field. We stopped, and my friends wanted to take a picture. The workers all turned their backs on us. They didn't want to be photographed.[3] Even some police officers here refuse to have their photographs taken. That's so unlike Bermuda. One of the highlights of my career as a police officer was working in the birdcage—a little shed in the middle of the street where you direct traffic. Everyone takes pictures of you. People come over and pose with you. I enjoyed that. And some people sent the pictures back to me. We have a long way to go in Barbados, and I think we can learn a lot from Bermuda.

Epilogue

One year after this interview, Errol was promoted to general manager of Glitter Bay Hotel. In the future he hopes to have his own business—a training academy for security guards in which he would do some of the teaching himself.

---

3. When one of my students included pictures of her Bajan friends on Facebook in 2010, she was asked to take them down. They didn't feel comfortable having their images on Facebook for strangers to see.

CHEF | Malcolm Bovell

Malcolm Bovell, 25, is a chef at the fine-dining Orchids restaurant in the Colony Club resort. The Colony Club is a superior-first-class-rated resort set on 7 acres of tropical gardens overlooking a secluded cove. Many members of Malcolm's family have worked in the hotel industry. Malcolm's mother is a waitress and cashier, and his father went to a hotel school and worked in a resort before becoming a police-man. He has two aunts who are high school home economics teachers. Despite the isolated setting in which Malcolm grew up, near the northern tip of Barbados, he was exposed to tourists from an early age. His family's home is on the road leading to River Bay, a popular scenic attraction for both tourists and Barbadians. He doesn't mind the tour buses and rental cars; rather, they make him proud because "they've come such a long way to see my parish and the coastline." Malcolm fondly remembers his first encounters with tourists—an American church group that came to his village to rebuild the pastor's house. "I was amongst them every day. I still have pictures that were taken of me with the Americans."

When I was young I never really had an interest in cooking. I used to play around the kitchen sometimes, but it was nothing. When I was in high school I got a taste of the hotel industry through a little job attachment. The school used to give out summer jobs, and they sent me down the road to Cobbler's Cove Hotel. I worked in different departments—the front desk, the storeroom, accounts—but never in the kitchen. The whole hotel atmosphere was interesting to me, especially the tourists and the way the staff got along with each other. People who work in hotels are very close because they spend most of their lives working together. They seem to have a good time with one another. Plus, tourism is the number-one revenue earner in Barbados, so it's always good to be in that industry. Plus, my mother was working in the industry.

So when I finished school, I applied to the Hospitality Institute at the community college and was accepted. I did a course on food and beverage operations and I really took to the cooking part of it. I liked learning about international foods and dishes. I'd never even heard of some of the vegetables and sauces before, things like asparagus and artichokes, which aren't grown in Barbados. And the kitchen was a fun place and very social.

After graduation I sent out applications to Colony Club, Almond Beach, Royal Pavilion, and Glitter Bay. I was offered jobs at all of them but I chose Colony Club because they contacted me first and because they had a brand-new kitchen. When I first started it was hard. I had to work with this crazy French chef. Very crazy. One day you would do something and he would say, "Perfect, Malcolm. This is perfect." The next day you would do it exactly the same way and he would say, "Malcolm, this is crap." And he would take it up and throw it. I mean he would really throw it. He was very moody. At first I wanted to quit. But my parents would say, "Malcolm, it's not always an easy road. There will always be some rocks sticking out." So I stuck it out. It paid off because I got a promotion, and since then I've been "Employee of the Month" a few times.

Right now my title is Junior Sous Chef. There's a ladder that you work up. When you start out you're a trainee chef, then you're a common chef, then junior sous chef, sous chef, head chef, and finally executive chef. We have five chefs in our kitchen, plus a porter and a steward who washes dishes and mops floors. Then there are the waiters.

Most days I catch the noon bus in order to get down here around 1:30. I like to get here early to get things under way. After I punch my card, I open the kitchen and get the stock from the storeroom, then clean the surfaces to make it nice and hygienic. Then the preparation starts. I specialize in vegetable dishes and sauces. We use lots of sweet peppers, zucchini, eggplant, carrots, and onions. The key to doing good vegetables is to make sure they are fresh, and then don't overcook them. With spices we use lots of cayenne, tarragon, and saffron, which besides giving a nice flavor gives the food a nice yellowish color. Saffron is the most expensive spice in the world. We pay 300 dollars for a tin of it. We try to use a lot of fresh herbs as well, as fresh as you can get them. When we're doing beef and lobster, the head chef will do the meat and I'll do the lobster and another chef will prepare the vegetables. If the pastry chef is out, sometimes I'll help with the dessert, but I'm not really trained in desserts.

We prepare from 2:00 to about 6:30, when we're ready for service. Service starts at 7:00 and goes to 9:30. After the dinner service is over we clean down our work areas and order stuff for the following day. We each have a sheet with jobs assigned for the next day.

About 80 percent of the food we prepare is imported. It's because our chefs come from all different parts of the world—Europe, the United States, England. Sometimes they'll make their dishes with a Barbadian flavor but mostly they stick to what they did abroad. We get most of the vegetables from the United States, the lamb from New Zealand, and we used to get our meat from the UK, but since the mad cow thing we've been getting it from the States. We get lobster and red snapper from the Bahamas, shrimp and pineapple from Trinidad, bananas and other stuff from St. Lucia and other parts of the Caribbean.

You get a lot of comments from guests who say they want more Bajan foods, that they want to experience our local foods. But the hotel owners, who are mostly British, say that the guests don't want to eat local cuisine seven days a week. So they bring in chefs from overseas, mostly British and French. That prevents our local chefs from reaching the top, and I don't see that changing any time in the future.[4] I was told that years ago hotels had a lot of Caribbean food, but not so with the new foreign hotel owners. These owners have totally forgotten about the really good chefs here who do Caribbean cuisine. We could be using our own black-belly sheep instead of New Zealand lamb. We could be serving cou-cou, flying fish, and black pudding and sous. We could use our own locally grown oranges, peas, sweet potatoes, yams, and okras. Why not give the guests local cuisine three days and international three days, especially when so many guests are saying they'd like more Barbadian flavor in the menu? But that's not how the hotel owners want it, so what can you do?

Is working in the kitchen stressful?

[Hearty laugh.] Very stressful! The heat for one, there's lots of heat. If you're gonna be a chef you've got to take the heat, and the burns. A couple of weeks ago I got burned almost every day. Like making salmon, you put a little oil in the pan and then the salmon and you get splashed. If I wore long sleeves I wouldn't get as many burns, but with the heat you gotta wear short sleeves. My worst cut

---

4. Opportunities for local chefs have improved considerably in the decade since this interview was conducted. In 2010, a fair number of local chefs had become "executive chefs," and there was generally less reliance on foreign-born and foreign-trained chefs.

ever is this one [he holds up his left hand]. I was chopping onions very quickly and I sliced off a side of my hand. Then you have to deal with waiters and waitresses coming in and saying, "This person wants this thing and that right now." Well, we're doing fine dining, and that takes time. Then sometimes the waiter or waitress will do dumb things, snatch up the food and spill the sauces. We set our plates to perfection, so it's frustrating to see a waitress come in and mess it all up. Thursday night we got an order for a ten-person table. We filled the order—that's ten meals—and then we discovered that the order was from yesterday and the waiter had forgotten to take it out of the pile. That's ten sets of food wasted. The people weren't even here, they were on a plane flying back home.

Still, I love being in the kitchen. We're like brothers. Five brothers and one girl, and we're very, very close, like family in there. We talk a lot, and it's always lively. We joke around—we get lots of laughs. We do long hours and we work very hard but we do it together, we know what each person is thinking.

The one girl in the kitchen is the pastry chef, but she's been on sick leave for almost a year. She slipped on the wet floor and tore ligaments in her knee. It shouldn't have happened. The dishwasher had been leaking on the floor for some time. Maintenance always takes their sweet time when something in the kitchen wants fixing, but when it's something to do with the guests they'll be right on top of it. She and I have a close relationship, actually she's my girlfriend. We met at the Hospitality Institute; but we were just friends then. Most people say it's not good to be working with your girlfriend. Maybe, but she is a very good pastry chef, and she is a workaholic just like me. The kitchen doesn't run as well without her being here.

They brought in another girl to replace her and she wasn't here long when she fell down the stairs. So she's out too. So now it's just us guys in the kitchen. Working in a kitchen is more of a male job anyway, because of the heat and the stress and the burns. The kitchen is different when it's all guys. We can be loose, you know, we can talk guy-talk all day long. We swear a lot. I don't think you can be a Christian and work in a kitchen. But there are good female chefs and I wouldn't have a problem working under a woman.

How often does a guest send a dish back to the kitchen?

Not often, you get one or two in a week. Some guests are very hard to please. Maybe they take it out on you if their day isn't going well. Sometimes we can overcook the food. If the dish comes back and it's perfectly all right, we use our kitchen language to curse and shout. We say this is totally impossible. We talk to each other about the dish and get all angry and stuff. But there's nothing you can really do because, as they say, "The customer is always right." Now, if we overcooked the food or something, we apologize and offer them something else on the menu for free. Once in a while a guest will want to see the chef. The other day I overcooked this man's beef and he said he wanted to see the chef. The head man who was on that night is about 40-something, he's Bajan, and he's shy. He doesn't like to interact with the guests at all. So he says, "Malcolm, you go, you go." So I went out and we had a good chat. The man said that he was disappointed because this was his last day in Barbados and the beef was overdone. He was from England and we started talking about England and stuff and we had a good chat. He wasn't angry, just a bit disappointed. Sometimes the guests ask us to come out so they can pay us compliments, and sometimes they want to know recipes. I've had them say, "What's a youngster like you cooking so lovely." And the other day a lady said, "Oh, I want to take you back with me." Stuff like that.

What happens to the leftovers?

Some staff take it home to feed to their dogs and pigs. But most of it goes in the garbage because of the paperwork—every night you have to get a release form if you're taking food off the premises, then you have to show it to security when you leave the property. Then security looks in your bag to make sure it's just scraps. So a lot of people don't bother taking the stuff home.

Is the other restaurant in the hotel similar to yours?

No, the Laguna restaurant downstairs in the hotel is much bigger than Orchids. It seats 300 where we cater for only 60. They have a much older staff, and right now there's a lot of tension over the new chef. He's young, 26, from England and he wants everything done his way. The older people in the kitchen who have been there for years are set in their ways. They don't like the new guy telling them what they should do. They don't like change. Even when the chef, who is white, makes things easier for them they don't realize it. They say, "Oh, this guy's picking on us, he's racist," and stuff like that. I don't want to deal with that crap, because most of it is because they don't want change. Like different menus, new dishes. They'll say, "Oh, this is too hard." The younger staff, who are more educated, don't have a problem with that. Some of the people downstairs started working in the dishwashing area and got promoted. They weren't educated, they don't have any knowledge of the French terms used for cooking and stuff like that. They do their eight hours and go home. And some of them are just naturally lazy. They take lots of sick time when they really aren't sick or like if they just have a cold. And if it's raining some of them will stay home for that. In our kitchen we wouldn't think of doing stuff like that. The guys here are dedicated.

Has being a chef in a hotel changed your
ideas about tourism in any way?

Yes, I think people who work in hotels are very underpaid. For an industry that brings in so much revenue, they should pay their workers more. I mean, you can read the newspaper and see that this hotel made millions of dollars in profit, but the workers are not seeing it in their paychecks, and most of us are hardworking people.

Epilogue

Malcolm has moved to England, where he is now a chef in a London restaurant.

MANAGER | Martin Barrow

Martin Barrow, 35, manages the British-owned Crystal Cove and Coconut Creek hotels on the west coast of Barbados. He is one of the few black general managers of a hotel on this island. He is modest about his achievement. Martin explains: "It was the luck of the draw, being at the right place at the right time, and having someone give you an opportunity to prove yourself." Before getting into the hotel business, he played international tennis as a member of Barbados's Davis Cup team for three years.

Crystal Cove and Coconut Creek are both small hotels—fifty-three rooms in one and eighty-eight in the other. Our guests stay about an average of ten days. Most British and Europeans stay about two weeks, North Americans for less, five days to a week max. Most arrive and depart on weekends, so Saturdays and Sundays are our busiest days in terms of both arrivals and departures of guests. Coconut Creek has been around for fifteen years and has a high repeat clientele, maybe 75 percent. It's nice because you get to know everyone. Crystal is a lot newer so we're still trying to build base, but I think Crystal will eventually have a high amount of repeat clientele, too. The guests seem very happy with our product. In fact, they rave about it. I'm not saying that what we have is perfect, and the facilities are certainly not on par with Sandy Lane, but in terms of ambience, service, and interaction with staff we can match any hotel in Barbados.

In school I didn't think of working in a hotel. My dad wanted me to be an engineer. With that in mind, I finished one year of math, chemistry, and physics at the community college. But then I got caught up in the idea of working in the hotel industry; the interest in hotels probably goes back to my childhood. Because my dad was in government [attorney general and a cabinet minister], we had a lot of opportunities to travel all over the world, and we stayed in good hotels. I liked the glamour and glitz of the whole industry, and it looked like an easy life. Obviously the food and beverage was appealing to a young lad, and I liked meeting and interacting with the different people. When you're staying in a fine

Crystal Cove Hotel. *Courtesy Barbados Tourism Authority.*

hotel it's a very relaxing environment, and I think that translated into my thinking it would also be a nice place to work. I said, "Hey, this is cool. This looks like an easy life." I only saw the positive side of it.

So I dropped out of the community college and did a one-year apprenticeship with Sandy Lane Hotel, working in the restaurant, kitchen, and other departments. I liked it. Then I did a four-year degree in hospitality and tourism management at Ryerson University in Toronto. Each summer I'd come home and do a work attachment at a different hotel. After Ryerson, I did a management training program in the UK and another in the United States. Then Sandy Lane hired me back as food and beverage manager. Then I moved up to be assistant manager at Cobbler's Cove Hotel, and a couple of years after that I was offered the general manager's position here at Coconut Creek.

What is a typical day like for a hotel manager?

Well, I go for a run or lift weights in the morning, because I think it's important to start your day out right. That hour and a half I'm exercising I'm by myself and I'm gathering my thoughts for the day, and it relieves stress. When I come in in the morning I stop at Coconut Creek first and check all the departments—guest services, housekeeping, kitchen, restaurant, and bar—to make sure they're fully staffed, that everyone is here, and that things are running smoothly. In the restaurant I'm also looking at the buffet, to see what's on the lunch menu and to see that the preparations for it are coming along. If they're short of any particular item from the store-room then we'll need to go purchase it. Then I go next door to Crystal Cove, where our main office is. I do a quick tour of Crystal and set out work for the various maintenance people and beach people. Because the properties are small, I play a hands-on role. I don't mind clearing up tables when it's needed or going in the kitchen and turning down a burner. Doing what needs to be done. I like doing that, I like getting my hands dirty. Large hotels involve more delegation—there you have department heads, like executive chef, executive housekeeper, and so on, that assume more of the responsibilities. At a large hotel you spend more time in the office than out on the floor. I like being on the floor, and I like having contact with both my staff and with the guests. Because my style of managing is hands-on, these hotels suit me well.

Are hotels in Britain and Canada run
differently than those in the Caribbean?

The style of hotel I worked in up there were mostly city-center hotels, and their approach is quite different from the resort hotels down here. Their working environment is very business oriented, with a strict management structure. They're more professional when dealing with situations. Crisper and sharper. In the Caribbean, we're laid back and more into interacting with our clients, "Yes sir, good morning ma'am, what can I do for you sir," that kind of thing. Obviously the needs of our clients are different. Up there it's more businesslike. In a city-center hotel, guests don't want to sit down and have a three-hour lunch. They want to get in and get out, have their business meetings and go do their shopping. Down here, in resort hotels, people come to relax, and interacting with the staff is a big part of the holiday. There's a real psychological difference in what the guests are looking for. Here they want to switch off, and most are willing to just go with the flow.

As I said before, one thing I like about my job is the interaction with people, both staff and guests. With staff I get satisfaction from seeing people develop, knowing that this person is going on to achieve something and that some of it can be attributed to my style, my help. Often what I'm doing is just forcing them to think for themselves. When they come to me to make a decision, I try to send them back out and hope they will make the decision. The young corporate-management trainees are not afraid to make decisions, but I find that the older people, those who've been here a long time, bring all their problems to you. Maybe it's because they've grown up with managers that didn't allow them to make decisions. But my style is that you need to learn and develop, so go back out there and make the decision on your own.

With guests, the satisfaction comes from doing everything you can to make sure they have a good holiday. As a professional, you know that people come here on holiday and that they want to leave having had a good time and value for their money. For me, there's satisfaction in hearing them rave about our product. Also, because of our small size and repeat clientele, there's good interaction with the guests. A lot of them I consider as friends, and we talk like friends.

What kinds of conversations do you typically have with guests?

Well, apart from the usual one-on-one, I do two cocktail parties a week. One at Coconut Creek and one at Crystal. Generally, I just ask how they're enjoying their stay and what they think of the hotel. However, as I said, many of those who stay at Coconut are now my friends, so we talk about family and we share experiences. They tell me about their kids and where they went on their holiday. When conversations are with friends, it's not work for me anymore. At Sandy Lane [Barbados's most elite hotel], where I worked before, I can count on one hand the number of friendships I developed with guests. It was quite different than here. Maybe it's because at Sandy Lane you get much richer, more affluent guests who see you more as help. At Sandy Lane, it's an "us" and "them" scenario. At both places the guests are mainly British, but here at Coconut they're a cut below the Sandy Lane guests and that makes the interactions more equal. And I find that here they're often genuinely interested in you and your life. I didn't find that at Sandy Lane.

Has all the interaction with foreign guests changed you in any way?

Well, it obviously makes you more open-minded. Also, I think you don't see color anymore. I just see an individual. But that also comes from having traveled so much and having lived in North America and England. But I think, too, getting to know so many guests makes you more tolerant and respectful of other peoples and their cultures, their differences. I certainly have a more open view of life because of it.

How often do you come across somebody who's prejudiced? How does it show?

Not very often. But when you do, it shows in how they talk to you. You'll hear things like, "Well, I'm paying your salary." Often it's a feeling you get more than anything else. But the fact that they've come to Barbados means that they must know the local population is whatever percentage black. So if they're prejudiced, you would think they wouldn't have come here to begin with.

Does your staff see color?

I would say generally no; that's because of the environment they work in. Curiously, there may be some reverse discrimination in some hotels in that when the staff see black couples or a mixed couple they tend to stay away and not interact with them. I don't know why. I don't know if they think that a black person shouldn't be there or what. We had one case where a black couple thought they were given a worse room in the hotel. It wasn't true. When I see a name on the list, it doesn't say John Jones, black, or John Jones, white. You don't know. This couple may have played it up to get a better room.

What do guests complain about?

We don't get many complaints, but when we do it is usually about service or food—that the service is too slow or the waitress was rude or took the order wrong or that the food was overcooked. A lot of these complaints, especially with food, are very subjective. What you like and what I like can be quite different. Still, you have to be sympathetic to the guest. Usually I will try to get more information. I don't want the guest just to say the meal wasn't good. I want specifics. Was the sauce too rich? Was the beef overcooked? Was it not spicy enough? I'll try the plate for myself, to see what the guest's palate is like. I try to get the chef involved, get him to talk to the guests. It helps if they see the chef taking a personal interest in them.

The difficulty is that some guests don't say a word while they're here, rather they'll go back home and write an eight-page letter. At that stage there's nothing you can really do. I can't go back and try the meal or see if the waitress was rude because it's so long after the fact.

When we hear complaints about the service being slow, I usually get my department heads involved. We do comment cards so we can see if there are any trends. If we see a pattern, then it's time for the supervisors to spend more time on the floor to deal with the issue. Sometimes it involves more on-the-job training. We try to hammer home the message that this is our business and that, at the end of the day, if a person doesn't come back, we all suffer. We try to get across the point that we're all in this together.

You must also remember that the style of operation is different at a resort hotel in the Caribbean than at a city-center hotel in London. Most guests are here to relax, not here to eat in five minutes and run off. But guests sometimes have prior notions of how fast a meal should take to prepare and bring to them. And that notion may be based on their stays in big-city hotels; it may not conform to the standard here in the Caribbean. But to be honest, there aren't many complaints.

How do you deal with guests who claim something has been stolen from their hotel room?

Well, I always get the police involved. The guests will want to make an insurance claim when they get back home, and to do that they need a police statement. You get a sense of whether it's genuine or not. If it's a genuine case where there's been a forced entry, we fill out a report and our insurance covers it. But usually there's no evidence of a break-in. In a lot of cases, they may not even have brought the item to Barbados. "Oh, I lost my gold watch and gold chain." Obviously we can't prove it one way or the other, so they just go back and make the claim. Now, I'm not saying that every room attendant in the hotel is honest. In fact, we keep track of all incidents, in what room and who was on duty, to see if there's a trend. If thefts occur in the room that Edna does, then you know there may be a problem. But it doesn't happen often.

> *Both of your hotels are all-inclusive. There is lots of talk about all-inclusive hotels taking business away from local restaurants and other services.*

If you look at what the European and American marketplace is saying, there's a need for all-inclusive. People want to know how much their holiday is going to cost up front. They want to know that when they leave home it's going to be 800 dollars and they won't have to worry about whether or not they can drink an extra rum punch or how much lunch is going to cost them. There's also all the activities that all-inclusives offer with no price attached to them. You can get snorkeling gear, go water-skiing, wind-surfing, sail a Sunfish, play tennis, all at no extra cost. So there is a need for all-inclusives, though I'd hate to see the island go totally that way. There are a lot of restaurants and services that depend on guests and taxi drivers who depend on moving people around to make a living.

> *What do you like least about your job?*

The hours. It's a twenty-four-hour, seven-days-a-week operation. I'm often here from 9 to 10, about fifty-five hours a week. And before when I was a food and beverage manager and someone else would fill out the work schedule, you'd often get penciled in on bank holidays and New Year's Eve. You'd be in there working when everybody else was out partying. That was hard for me. Of course, as a general manager I have a little more flexibility in when I'm here and when I'm not.

When I get home at the end of the day I need some personal space. In this business you interact with people constantly, nonstop everyday—phone calls, staff, and guests. So when I get home I need time to myself to unwind. My girlfriend now understands that, but at first it was hard for her because she'd want to go out or do things together. But for me it's very important to be alone for a while, to read the paper, listen to music, have my own space where there's no one else around. It takes me about an hour and a half, sometimes longer. If she strays into my space, I get irritable.

After I have my bit of solitude, then we'll talk or maybe we'll watch something on satellite television. There's always a North American broadcast, and we watch a lot of U.S. sports, *Dateline,* or *20/20,* that sort of thing. I really only take one day off a week, which is Sunday. Church is a big part of my life, and I try to go every Sunday.

There are many white Barbadians in hotel
management but not many blacks. Why?

There's definitely a shortage of locals in many areas, even in food and beverage. In some cases there is a genuine shortage, but in others I think they're being excluded in favor of non-nationals. There are finance positions, too, where the owners like to hire expatriates. Some of the foreign companies coming into Barbados place certain restrictions on hiring—"If I'm coming to invest I get to choose my own people"—so it's a catch-22 for us. I don't think enough is being done to hire locals. In an industry that's now forty or fifty years old, there should be more local chefs being promoted to executive chefs. Some things are being done, like the government now requires hotels to advertise jobs locally. And if they don't find anyone they have to place an ad in the paper saying no applicants were found. Only then do they go to the chief immigration officer for permission to hire a non-national. But there are ways around it. Not enough is being done.

Some critics talk about tourism as the
new slavery. What do you say to that?

Ask them to look at the industry in other parts of the world and you'll see not black people but white people serving. Here people need to feed their families, people need a home. So what other course is there? In Barbados, tourism drives the economy. Where would all these people work if it weren't for tourism?

What would happen if tourism was to decline in Barbados?

It would have serious repercussions on the economy. It's a very sensitive industry and—God forbid—if something were to happen on the island, such as a major crime or a major incident, we would see a drop-off in tourism. And you'd see a lot of people out of work, a lot of people struggling to feed their families. So we all need to be aware that a single act of misbehavior could have a great effect on the whole economy. Everything is interconnected; when some people stopped traveling because of the fear of terrorism, we felt it badly down here.

Epilogue

One year after this interview, the Coconut Creek and Crystal Cove hotels were sold. The new owners felt that the hotel management was too close to the old owners and asked Martin to step down. Shortly afterward, he was hired to manage a new all-inclusive hotel, the Tropical Escape.

5 THE BEACH

It is the clichéd sun, sand, and sea that still draw the most visitors to the Caribbean, though there is increasing interest in alternatives to the beach, such as adventure and heritage tourism. Few places have been more inspirational in our leisure life than the beach, note Lena Lencek and Gideon Bosker in *The Beach: The History of Paradise on Earth* (1998). These sandy stretches capture our imaginations with more directness, and in the industrialized world, beaches have served as places of retreat and relaxation.

The beach is a playground. The opportunities for recreation range from the active (swimming or snorkeling in the warm turquoise sea, diving the coral reefs, parasailing, water-skiing, and jet-skiing) to the passive (relaxing in a lounge chair, reading, sunbathing, and people-watching). The possibilities of romance and sex are also part of the allure. Barbados's travel brochures, like those for most tropical destinations, portray the island's beaches as sites for sexual adventures. The brochures feature color photographs of bikini-clad bronzed women lying on the sand or frolicking in the sea or beautiful, anatomically perfect couples holding hands while strolling on the beach at sunset or gazing at night into the velvety horizon, drinks in hand (Lencek and Bosker 1998). The language of the brochures appeals to our fantasies; they talk of "romantic interludes" and "tropical escapades" (Chambers 2000).

In Barbados, the workday on the beaches begins at 7 A.M, when hotel employees hand-rake the sand and pick up chunks of coral rock and litter washed ashore during the night. Once the beach has been manicured, they set out lounge chairs and umbrellas. Guests eager to claim the best locations get there early and place their beach towels on chairs and then retreat to their rooms or to break-fast. By 9 o'clock the hotel water-sports staff begins to arrive to put ski-boats in the water, rig the sailboats, and get other gear ready for the day. Meanwhile, the private water-sports operators launch their jet-skis and watercraft. Beach vendors begin to appear around 10 o'clock, waiting until most of the guests have finished breakfast and have made their way to the beach. The work slows down at mid-day, when the sun's heat is intense and guests retreat from the beach for lunch and often a short nap. Activity picks up again in the midafternoon and then winds down for the day after 5 o'clock, when the jet-skis, boats, and beach chairs are hauled up the sand and stowed away for the night.

In this section are interviews with a beach vendor, a jet-ski op-erator, a hotel water-sports director, and a diving instructor.

BEACH VENDOR | Rosco Roach

Rosco Roach, 28, cut sugarcane, unloaded barges, and caddied golf clubs before going on the beach to sell jewelry to tourists. Beach vending is part of a larger tradition of hawkers and mobile sellers of goods. In town, hawkers have long sold pigeon peas, coconuts, bananas, and other fruits and vegetables on the street. And rural Barbados has always been served by vendors, who once traveled by donkey carts selling produce and fish. Many villagers still purchase household goods, fabric, and clothing from traveling Indian salesmen, known derogatively as "coolie men." Rosco is quick to point out that he is a vendor, not a hustler. A vendor, he says, is someone who sets up his goods on the beach and lets the customers come to him. A hustler forces himself on the tourists. Rosco lives at home with his mother and several of his eight siblings in the St. Lucy village of Husbands.

I do about five beaches each day. I leave the house around 8 A.M. and get back around sundown. I start at Almond Beach in the morning, and from there I go south to Cobbler's Cove, King's Beach, Mullens Beach, Sandridge. Then I turn back up the coast in the afternoon and hit the same beaches, finishing up at Almond Beach. I don't spend too much time at King's Beach because you get mostly Germans there. Germans don't really understand the language we speak, so it's tough to sell to them.

I have a piece of white cloth, about six-by-six, that I spread on the sand. I put rocks on each corner to hold it down if there's much breeze. Then I put out the jewelry—all the hematite together, the pearls together, the leather lace together with the shark's teeth, the bracelets together, and the anklets together. I try to make the display look pretty. My best seller is hematite. That's a volcanic stone that comes from St. Lucia and St. Vincent. My next best are anklets, then the freshwater pearls (they're not real pearls, they come from England and the United States), and then the coral. People like coral stuff that comes from the Caribbean.

When I'm making jewelry, after I lay my stuff out, some people come over and watch and ask questions. And when people walk by I say, "Hello, how are you? How is your day? Is there anything you want to get? Anything that you like? Anything for the kids or

Rosco Roach. *Photo by George Gmelch.*

maybe your wife?" You tell them about what you're making while they look at your stuff. And some will buy something.

If there isn't much interest, I move on to the next beach. You can tell when the business is going to be slow by how many people are walking up and down the beach. If it's rainy or if the sea is breaking rough like today, most people are going to be lying down, not moving about. You want to see people walking on the beach, looking around, because only then are they going to stop and spend money.

The mornings and evenings are the best times to sell. During the middle of the day people go to lunch, and after they eat they're full, so they take a nap or they go back to their rooms and watch television. They'll come back outside later in the afternoon and stay until the sun sets and maybe have a little cocktail or something.

Sundays and Mondays are usually good days. Lots of visitors arrive on weekends. During the week the hotels have lots of activities scheduled for them, like an island tour or a bus to Bridgetown to shop, so there are fewer people on the beach then. After April, things slow down and they really don't pick up again until late November, when the winter tourists start coming back. In the summer season, when things are slow, I try to get a little job on the side, what we call a "pick." But most evenings, when I finish work, I come down to the beach and try to sell a little jewelry.

Most vendors sell the necklaces for 50 Barbados dollars, the anklets for 30 dollars [$2 BDS = $1 U.S.]. Those are my asking prices. I'll come down 5 or 10 dollars if I have to. A lot of tourists want to bargain, especially Canadians. Man, do they love bargaining. If you have an item that sells for 50 Barbados dollars, they'll want to give you 25, or maybe as low as 20. They'll say they can get it cheaper from another vendor, or sometimes they'll say they've seen it cheaper on another island. I find that the English don't normally bargain as hard as the Americans and Canadians. If you say to the Englishman that the necklace costs 50 Barbados dollars, that's only like 15 English pounds. It's a smaller number in pounds. When you say to the Canadian that the necklace costs 50 Barbados dollars, that's about 35 Canadian dollars. That's a big number, so the Canadians will try to bargain you down to the lowest degree.

But once they start to bargain, there's a good chance that you're going to make a sale. Bargaining is no problem for me. It's part of the business; you see it everywhere you go. If they offer too low of a price I say, "Okay, you don't want to pay the price. Go to the next fellow over there and see if you can get that price." I know there's no way they're gonna find the price they want. Sometimes you get really frustrated with them. But you tell yourself that you've got to control your temper. To have patience. Over the years I've learned a lot of patience. Overall it's best to sell to a rich person no matter where he comes from. Because if you say a price, and the rich person wants that necklace, he's gonna pay it. He won't bargain as much.

Lately it's been hard to make money on the beach. Too many guys are out here selling jewelry, too many guys trying to take the sale away from you. Like if I'm making a sale with a lady, and I give her a price, and she's about to say okay, then maybe this other vendor over there is telling her, "He's gonna rip you off. I can give it to you for 10 dollars less." Well, that's not nice. That's not fair. I'd never do that to him because I'm a reasonable guy. The woman is either gonna buy it from him or she's going to want it from me for less money. I had her at 40 Barbados dollars and now I've got to sell it to her for 30 or lose the sale. I want to make a sale, so I agree to the lower price.

Do vendors ever get together and talk prices? Do you ever try to eliminate competition with one another?

No. You'd never get the guys down here meeting to decide the price on a necklace. It might be a good idea, but Bajans don't care if you make a dollar. And I don't care if they make a dollar. It all boils down to everyone wanting to make money but no one agreeing to stick to one price. To sit down and make a fixed price for selling jewelry would never work.

Some days I go up and down the sand like a madman hoping to make maybe 100 dollars. Usually I don't get past 50, and I sweat all day. Sometimes when I go home I can't even sleep. The sun is so hot and the heat is still in my skin and my body. The best day I ever had was 300 dollars. But you have days where you don't make anything. Nothing. And when the rain falls, you get no work. Everybody is inside. The rain may fall for a whole week. We aren't like the people that work at the hotel that have a sure salary. To them it don't make no difference if the rain falls or if the guests don't come; they still get paid. The beach ain't like that.

But it ain't all bad. If I don't feel like working hard today I can relax. I can take it easy. And I love to look at women, for real. Every day I get to see them in bikinis, and some of them do be beautiful people. The guys working on construction sites don't get to see that. They only see people who have clothes on. I get to see people half naked every day [chuckle].

I like working with tourists. They are friendly. They are nice people. Sure, you meet some that are bad, that don't show their true colors. But most are good people. Also, being on the beach, you're close to the water. You get the fresh breeze off the ocean. Makes you feel good. And when you go home at night you sleep good, even if you do be hot.

Working the beach is a lot better than cutting sugarcane. I did that for a while. Cutting cane is very hard. Hot and sticky. You cook out there. And the sharp [cane] blades makes your skin very ugly. You've got to wear a long-sleeve shirt, long pants, boots and socks, gloves, and your head covered. You got to do that to protect yourself from the blades. And man, it's hot. Your blood gets hot and you're sweating all over. Sometimes when you get home you've got to sit down for two hours to let your skin cool off. Sometimes you can't eat your food, can't do nothing. You drink ice water all the time to cool you down. And just when you cool down, you got to go back out there and do the same, sweating all over again. No, I'd rather be on the beach anytime.

But if I had an opportunity to go someplace and make more money, I would leave the beach. I could still come down here and see people in bikinis if I want. I'd like to have a job working on a cruise ship. I know the guy that has the agency that hires workers. He organizes everything for you, but you've got to pay him. He gets a fee for himself. And you've got to buy a plane ticket because all the ships go from Miami. I'd like to save enough money to do that. But right now it's very hard to put away any money. I haven't been to the bank to make a deposit for three months. And now that my mother is building a wall house I have to chip in money to help her out.

How often do women tourists suggest they would
like something more than just your jewelry?

Well, I'm not that fortunate that they would want to approach me [chuckle]. But you do get some who come over and talk nice and friendly. Some might ask a question like, "Where are you going tonight?" If we go out, I'll take her to someplace far away, like St. Lawrence Gap. A place where people will leave you alone when you are out with a nice-looking white girl. If I take her to the Coach House [restaurant] there will be a lot of blacks coming around wanting to hustle her, forcing themselves on you.[1] So I try to get away from that and take her to a place where there are white tourists, like on the south coast. She pays, but I'll buy a round of drinks or two.

Do they usually want to sleep with you?

You got some tourist girls that don't know what's going to happen. She don't know what she wants for her holiday. Then you got some tourist women who know just what they want. They're down here to be with a black guy. Like she might say, "Do you want to come to my room for a cup of coffee?" or "Do you want to spend the night in my room?" She knows what her game is all about. She knows what she's doing. Some of them are married women, and some of them just break up with their husbands or they have problems back home. They're simply trying to get away from all that and come down here and want to have sex with you.

Some of them go back home and write to you. Some of them ask if you want to come for a holiday and spend some time with them. I was invited to England and to Montreal, but I didn't go. To me, a tourist woman is not an easy woman to get involved with. It's

---

1. Coach House is a popular, moderately priced restaurant in St. James.

like they want to spread their wings all the time. But they are easy to go to bed with if you have the right talk. They're not like black women that way. Bajan women are more difficult. They will talk to you for months and still not give you any business.

Of every ten white women that you take out,
about how many do you sleep with?

I don't know, maybe half. But if ten women go out with ten Barbadian guys and get drunk, then all ten will have sex. When a woman gets drunk, guys are gonna take advantage of that situation. But maybe that's what the women want.

Does it make a difference to you how good-looking the woman is?

I won't go out with any woman. I'd like it if she was pretty, if she has a good body. But she doesn't have to be good-looking, not if she has a sense of humor. If she has a good sense of humor and invites me out, I'll go.

When was the last time you took out a tourist woman?

Actually yesterday. She was staying at the Almond Beach in St. James with her parents. She went home today. She wants to keep in touch, to write. I'll try, but sometimes I don't have time to write letters. I don't think it will last. She says she'll come back, but she is getting married when she gets back home. She say that she likes me a lot, you know, she tell me blah, blah, blah. I don't know how much of it to accept. But that is life, isn't it?

Epilogue

Rosco has stopped drinking and smoking and has joined the Pentecostal church that his family attends in Speightstown. Rosco is still selling jewelry on the beach; he hasn't yet been able to save any of the money needed to get a job on a cruise ship.

HOTEL WATER SPORTS | Zerphyl Greaves

Zerphyl Greaves, 41, is supervisor of water sports at Almond Beach Resort, one of the largest hotels in Barbados. His staff of eleven men and one woman provides hotel guests with water-skiing, sailing, fishing, wind-surfing, snorkeling, water-bikes, and banana-boat rides. A competitive runner, Zerphyl rises at 4:30 to put in 6 to 10 miles before coming to work. A Seventh-Day Adventist, he drinks neither alcohol nor caffeine and spends Saturdays in worship.

I learned welding at Samuel Jackman Technical School, but when I finished the course I couldn't get a job. They wanted welders with more experience, and I was just an apprentice. So I started hanging out on the beach with guys who ran water-ski boats. I learned how to drive ski-boats. Somebody else owned the boats and you operated them for him, getting a commission or a share of what you took in each day from the tourists.

After about a year I bought a glass-bottom boat with another guy. The glass-bottom boat goes across a reef, like snorkeling, but with an even wider view of the reef. As captain you need knowledge of the reef and the fish that the customers see through the glass bottom. We'd explain to the tourists the coral, the sponges, and the fish they were seeing as we moved along. I'd read a lot about the reef and I watched a lot of Jacques Cousteau documentaries on TV to help me explain the things that we saw.

We'd get customers by walking along the beach, from hotel to hotel, soliciting. You'd never get a lot of people, maybe five at most, but you'd make about ten trips a day. So at 10 dollars Barbados per person, if you worked hard you could do okay. Most of our customers were older people who couldn't swim too well, didn't snorkel, but who wanted a view of the reef. It was mostly Canadians, because a lot of them stayed near where we operated. The ladies were the most eager.

We did that for about five years until a tractor working at one of the new hotels backed into our boat and crushed it. But it was a good time to get out of glass-bottom boats because the beach was dying. Most of the hotels had gone all-inclusive and had their own water sports. And other customers were channeled off by the big operators Atlantic Submarines and Explorer Sub It was very difficult for the small operators like us to survive.

When I got out of the glass-bottom boat business, I came to the hotel to work in water sports. In the last ten or fifteen years, water sports have really boomed. Most hotels now offer water sports as part of their package. Visitors want that sort of thing, so if a hotel doesn't have water sports they'll lose a lot of business. But it's hard to find good people because a lot of Bajans can't swim, even though we're surrounded by the sea. If you put an ad in the paper for a barber and one for a water-sports operator, you'll get 200 people applying for the barber and just a few for the water-sports job. Most of the Bajans that have experience with wind-surfing, sailing, or water-skiing are already working for a hotel. So you get young people who can swim and you train them yourself. Right now we're training two guys; one was a lifeguard, so he's got a good background, and the other was in the army. He doesn't have any water-sports experience, but he's strong and he learns fast.

I like teaching people. It's exciting to see a beginner who's never water-skied before get up and actually do it. He knows and you know that he's really achieved something. Some beginners learn in the first two tries, but others never get it. But some of them will come back the next day and be able to do it. If people sleep on it, their brain works it over, and the next day they're much better. I find that ladies learn quicker than men. Men put too much muscle into it instead of letting the boat pull them up. Ladies just hold on and don't try to force their way up out of the water. I find the Germans catch on to water-skiing very quick. Yes, a lot of water-sports operators say that the Germans are up in no time.

Wind-surfing is a lot trickier. A beginner can get up and fall in the water hundreds of times before he'll get the hang of it. The west coast is a difficult place to learn because we've got an offshore wind which makes it difficult for the beginner to get back to shore. We always have a guy with binoculars looking out for the wind-surfers. If we see a guy fall and he doesn't pull the sail up in three minutes, we send somebody out to see what's happening. You can get blown out to sea here and not get back. One day I was out fishing and I saw an object about a half-mile down the sea. I said to my friend, "It looks like a boat turned upside down." He thought it was just a log. I thought we'd better check it out to be sure. We drove for about fifteen minutes and when we got about 100 yards off, we could see one arm waving. It was an English guy who had rented a

Sunfish [sailboat] from one of the hotels and tipped it over in the strong wind. He couldn't flip the boat back over and was just holding on, hoping that somebody would see him. He was lucky because he was on his way out to sea.

We also take people out on the Hobie Cat for a half-hour sail. It's very relaxing, and if the wind conditions are right you can really get up some speed, twenty-five or thirty miles an hour. On the Hobie Cat, you're sitting right next to the guest, and since you're not having to teach them anything, you can talk. It's important to make conversation with them. You can't just sit there and not say anything. You need to make them feel relaxed. I often tell them about the coastline and how this side of the island is different from the Atlantic side. I talk with them about sports a lot, too. With Americans you can always talk about football and basketball, and with the British you can always talk about soccer and cricket. Being a runner, I like to find a tourist who runs a lot, especially marathons. I try to stay away from politics, because you never know what you're going to get into and people may not share your views. I find people are more relaxed talking about sports or the weather than about politics. Sometimes you get people that don't want to talk, though. You ask them a question and they'll just answer with a yes or no. I can find 101 things to talk about, but if they don't want to, then that's their business.

Some of the guests you get on well with will give you their addresses and you'll hear from them. Some will send a Christmas card. One family knew I liked Rod Stewart and sent me a Rod Stewart CD when they got home. Another guy sent me a running magazine so I could order some New Balance running shoes. I used to write back, but I've drifted away from that. Writing is very taxing, and I'm busy with my family. Sometimes they invite you to come visit them; I've been to Toronto twice to see friends I met down here. Another guy has invited me to Germany, but I didn't go; you know, finances, and I have a family to support.

I enjoy talking to tourists. I used to be a little shy, but with the years that have gone by it comes naturally to me now. I think all the talking that I do has made my voice a lot stronger, too. Before I had a soft voice, but not anymore. A lot of girls tell me I have a nice strong voice.

You learn a lot about the different countries, the different people—like the British tend to be reserved, the Americans and Latin Americans like to party, and you can tell the Germans by their appearance, they have a very sturdy structure. I like getting to know individuals from different places, getting to know what people do. They share things with you that normally you would only see on television.

Although I love working with tourists, I have to tell you that some can be very demanding. If they don't get what they want, they go crazy. We're a big resort, with 700 people staying here every day, and you can only serve maybe 200 per day in water sports. So what happens to the other 500 that want to go out and don't get to? It can be tricky. For instance, this morning, we had two boats lying up on the beach; one was getting painted and the other had a breakdown. This guy wanted to go out and was getting very agitated. I told him we already had two boats in the water with tourists on them and a mechanic on the way to fix the boat on the beach. I said the boat would be available in a couple of hours. But that wasn't good enough for him. Sometimes things just break down and there's nothing you can do about it. But that doesn't mean anything to the tourist who's paid a lot of money to be here and wants to go out whenever he wishes. With people like that you've got to take your time, you've gotta be careful what you say. You gotta make sure you let them know you're doing everything possible for them. You've gotta always be friendly. If he thinks you're not friendly, it's just going to make things worse. Over the years working with people like that has taught me to be patient. And I try to remind myself that they paid a lot for their vacation and they have a right to expect a lot. I'm not against that; I believe that if you pay for a service you should get it, and sometimes it takes some complaining. But you don't have to be angry.

Sometimes you get the feeling that maybe they don't like you because you're a different color. Not often, but it does happen. Sometimes you hear comments like, "These black people don't really know how to do things right." If guests have to wait in line for a long time to go skiing, they get frustrated and you might hear comments like that. But then some of the other guests who overhear those comments will say to me, "That wasn't nice what he said," or "That was wrong what he said." I just say it's okay and smile them along their way. In this industry you can't let prejudice bother you. You have to let color disappear from your way of thinking. You don't ever want a guest saying, "That guy over there in water sports doesn't like me because I'm white."

Sometimes the tourists don't mix too well themselves. It mostly happens on the speedboats because you've got to take four persons

Hotel water-sports employees interact with guests at
Almond Beach Resort. *Photo by George Gmelch.*

out at a time to ski. So you may have two British and two Germans.
Well, the British may not want to go out with the Germans. So one
group says, "Okay, we'll wait for the next boat." Last week some
Jewish people from New York were on the boat along with two
British. I could see that neither group was happy being there with
the other. Sometimes I'll try and get them both in a conversation,
but it doesn't always work.

I think water sports has been a good choice for me, because I
always wanted to be in the sea. You know, a lot of Bajan parents
caution their children not to go into the sea. My grandmother never
wanted me to go near the beach, so I learned to swim on my own.

Some parents would beat you for going to the beach because
they'd be afraid you might drown. Bajans have a saying: "The sea
has no back door." Most adults around my age still can't swim. Even
today a lot of kids never swim. In a country surrounded by the sea,
I think the schools should teach kids how to swim and to snorkel,
too.

Epilogue

In 2010, Zerphyl was still supervisor of water sports at Almond
Beach.

JET-SKI OPERATOR | Ricky Hinds

Ricky Hinds, in his mid-30s, has been working on the beach and attracting the attention of female tourists most of his adult life with a handsome face, a well-muscled body, and a friendly come-on. Although he sometimes fishes and does carpentry, his preferred occupation and primary source of income is from operating jet-skis and ski-boats. Growing up in the west coast village of Checker Hall, he was exposed to tourists from an early age.

When I was a kid we used to go down to Heywoods Beach a lot to relax and swim. You'd be around white people who'd ask you questions and talk to you. I got to like talking to them. The visitors would speak to me more often because I could put my words in a way where they could understand what I was saying. The other native kids spoke more in dialect. I was also exposed to foreign people by my sister, who used to baby-sit for them. When I was just 9 or 10, she used to take me around with her. When you're around these people you learn to speak better English, so that you can be understood. Sure, I speak dialect with my own kind, but when I'm with a guest I speak their English.

When I was a kid I always wanted to be a pilot. Maybe it was because I knew about planes and travel from the tourists. But I never had any of the certificates [diplomas] that you'd need to get a job like that. So I did masonry. I did carpentry. I did fishing. I did landscaping. I cooked, washed, and even baby-sat. But most of all I do water sports—ski-boats and jet-skis.

I've always liked jet-skiing. It's a guy's thing, like road bikes, but I don't like driving on roads. I'm a water person. The water excites me. I come down here in the morning with my jet-ski, put it in the water, fire it up, and take it out for a run. A nice ride early in the morning clears my head. Then I come in to the beach and I'm ready to do business.

To do business you've got to be nice. That's number one. I approach the person and say, "Good morning sir." Or, "Good morning ma'am. Would you like to have a ride on the machine today?" I might take them over to the machine and ask them if they've ever done it before.

"No."

"Well, let me show you how to do it. It's quite easy."

Then I give them the rules. "Sir, pay very good attention to what I'm saying because it's very important." Maybe they're going to take their kid or their wife with them on the jet-ski. "You don't want to hurt your kid, you love your kid. You don't want to waste your time on a holiday with a broken leg or a dead kid or a dead wife, so keep the machine away from the other machines and boats." Now you think these guests are smart people or they wouldn't have the money to be here on vacation. But often they don't know how to listen. And then they go and crash into one another. That shouldn't happen because it's a big ocean.

What happens when they do crash and damage your jet-ski?

The best way to deal with that is not lose your temper. Losing your temper is not only embarrassing, it will give you a reputation. Not with the visitors, because they're going home, but with the locals. Those who aren't going anywhere. You don't want them saying about you, "Oh, he beat up a tourist guy because he crashed his machine." A better way of dealing with this stuff is to explain to the guy that these machines don't have insurance to cover damages and repairs. We only have third-party insurance. I'll try to get him to pay, and if he doesn't I'll just have to take it home and try to fix it as best I can. The last time my machine got hit, it cost me 500 dollars. The guy who did the damage said his company had paid for his vacation and he didn't have the money. He only had a couple of more days to go on his holiday and he didn't have any money left. Well, that's what he said.

On a good day you might get six rides, but sometimes you only get one, sometimes you burn half a tank of gas cruising up and down the coast looking for customers and you don't get any. The rate is 50 U.S. dollars for a half-hour of riding. But most of the time you give them a deal and do it for 40, sometimes you come down to 35. Or you'll give them twenty minutes for 25 dollars. I have a stopwatch and I tell them to look for me and I'll wave them in when their time is up.

"Sir, you overstayed your time. You will have to pay for that time."

"Oh, my watch must be a little slow." Or, "My watch says I came in on time."

"Well, I've got a stopwatch and it works pretty accurately."

But most of the time you don't have any problems. People take care of your machines and most come in on time.

Have you ever had a serious accident?

Not on my machine. But a few years ago we sold a 500-dollar machine to this American family. Their 16-year-old kid took it out to sea and never came back. They found him weeks later off the coast of Florida. Died from dehydration and sunstroke. He was still on the machine when they found him. I think he went so far out that he got lost. Or maybe he had a breakdown, then the currents took him away.

There's competition among the guys on the beach to see who can earn the most. Sometimes they'll say things to tourists to take away your business and get it for themselves. "Oh, be careful around Ricky; he went to prison." And folks will believe them, because they don't know any better. They think if a local said it, it must be true. I don't do much with those guys unless it's necessary. Sometimes two can be a crowd. Sometimes you can be dealing with guests and if one guy screws up everything, it will be like all of you are the same. You get where I'm coming from? Like, to some people one black person's face is the same as another. Or, "God, they look like brothers."

Jet-ski riding is like fishing. You have days where you make some money, and you have days where you hardly do anything. Like fishermen, you must have patience. If you don't have patience, you'll always be stressed out, worrying where the next meal is coming from. I don't worry about it because there's always food around. There's more than one way of skinning a cat. You have a relative that will give you a meal, and if not you can go mount a breadfruit tree. Grab a breadfruit, cook it up, get a fork in it, and a little butter and there you go. Get some limes and sugar and you got your drink.

The jet-ski I'm using now, this other guy owns. I keep a third of what I take in and he gets the rest. It works out okay for me because I don't have to pay for maintenance or insurance. On a good day you've got money in your pocket and you pay your bills, buy some provisions, go to the rum shop and have a few drinks. I try to put money away. Maybe this month I'll put away 500 dollars. But the way the work fluctuates, I might have to spend it next month. The money never grows to the amount that you want, because there's always bills coming in. If I could save 800 dollars, I'd go buy a fridge to put in my house. And next I'd buy a stove.

Ricky sold his refrigerator, stove, and other household appliances before moving to Canada with a woman he had met on the beach. He spent seven months living near Thunder Bay, Ontario. Ricky explains why it didn't work out.

She asked me to come up. I went for a holiday to start, but then she got me a job. An under-the-table thing working for a guy who was designing molds and making fiberglass boats. They were making better stuff in the United States and he couldn't match them. His company was going down, so the work wasn't steady. Then things didn't work out with the woman. As soon as I got there I knew that it was different with us. When she was here in Barbados, she didn't mind me being around other women. She couldn't mind because she wasn't just my woman. But when I got down there she got very jealous-minded.[2] The women up there found me attractive, like all women, old and young. I'd walk the street and a car would pull up. "Hi [he imitates a high-pitched voice], where are you going, would you like a ride?" It was a small town, everybody got to know me quick. Well, the woman got very bitchy. She wasn't nice anymore so I told her that I was leaving. She figured that I was hers, that she had got me the job, and that if I wasn't going to be with her then she would destroy whatever reputation I had in the town. When I left her home and moved in somewhere else, she called Immigration. They wouldn't extend my visitor's visa because it was alleged that I was working. I had to leave the country.

Can you talk about the women you meet on the beach?

Some women come down here with this fantasy of screwing a guy of my color. Some of the women have a feeling that black men have bigger dicks than white guys. When I was in Canada, one woman came right up to me and asked me if it was true that we have bigger dicks. I told her I wouldn't know because I don't walk around examining dicks. Besides, I haven't seen many white dicks.

There are some women that look at me and I can tell that fantasy enters their minds. They want you just because they want to have sex with you. Like they call it, "humping your bone." They want to screw your head silly. Some are very bold about it. Some

---

2. Barbadians, like most West Indians, refer to going north to North America as going "down," not "up," as northerners would say.

will walk up to you and say something like, "Looking at you, you get my pussy wet." Stuff like that. I've had women say, "If I weren't with my husband, I'd have to take you to bed." They think you, being a black man, are gonna give them that feeling, that explosion that they're looking for. For some ladies this is the fun of going on holiday. I met one woman who said she had to have sex with a black guy in every Caribbean country she went to because she gets so horny seeing us. I guess if our black girls go to your country and see a lot of white guys that are appealing to them, they might want to do the same thing.

Is there a nationality that is particularly attracted to Bajan men?

I think Canadian women are more horny. They'll have sex with a guy faster. I guess it's because they spend so much time in the cold. And a lot of the men down there in Canada are outdoors working and then spend a lot of time in bars drinking, especially in winter. Their women don't get enough. So they come down here on holiday and see these nice-looking black guys, with their bodies so fit, and it turns them on.

The American woman might want to have sex with you too, but she only wants to do it at the end of her stay, a day or two before she leaves. Just to try it out. The Canadian wants to do it the whole time. The American just once, she doesn't want memories of it. She doesn't want any loving. Like this woman said to me, "It's just another fuck." When she's done, she's going home to her husband or boyfriend. He probably doesn't like sex. He's probably one of those guys that likes to go to the bar and get drunk. Or one of them that drinks wine all night.

Now there are some Bajan men who won't sleep with a tourist woman. They hate it; they like black women. Myself, I like white women. I can't remember the last time I had sex with a local girl. Sexually, white women turn me on. They're more efficient, sufficient, and satisfying. They make me feel really good about myself. That's important. It's nice to have your brain telling you that you are perfect, that you're doing a good job. And it's fun. I mean you don't walk down the beach and go up to her and say, "Let's do it." Although they sometimes do say that. No, you court the woman for a day or two and she finds you more and more attractive. Then suddenly it happens. It builds up until the two of you have the same feeling, and you can't wait any longer.

Does the woman have to be attractive to you?

If she's not, I still chat with her. But what she comes looking for she might not get. Sometimes I'll tell her where she's going wrong. Like she might come over and say, "I want you to fuck me." Well, that's not so good. I tell her I don't find that attractive, I don't find that sexy. I tell her to take her time and try to be friends and work her way in. Then I might see something nice in her and take her on.

What about HIV? Do you take precautions?

They say the best protection is not to have sex. Maybe. But I love having sex. So my alternative is to make sure I have a wide supply of condoms. And a lot of the women insist that I wear a condom. I like that. There are some women that don't like condoms. But I let them know straight: no condom, no sex. I don't know how many guys they have slept with and how many of them have it [HIV].

Do you ever get attached to the women?
Does that make it hard when they leave?

Yeah, sure. But if she's really attached to you, she'll come back. I have some women that return here every year. One woman went home and three weeks later she was back because she couldn't live without it. She wanted more. She wanted to be here in the sun and to live with me. Years ago there was a girl from France. She was studying at the University of South Carolina. Her parents kept her in school all the time because she was so brainy. Well, she came here and fell in love with me. Sex and the whole thing. She wanted to come back on her holidays and see me. But her mom and dad were prejudiced and wouldn't let her come back. They threatened to cut her out of their will if she even attempted to come back to Barbados. She used to phone me and she would cry and cry. She wrote me all these sad letters. We had talked about getting married, but the parents didn't want that.

Ricky married an English tourist who moved into his small house in the village of Checker Hall. They had a child and lived together for five years. After they married, Ricky left the beach for a while because, he says, his wife was jealous. "She thought I was on the beach with tons of beautiful women and that I would take off with one of them." Neigh-

bors say they had a stormy relationship, "loving" for a while but then, usually after Ricky had been drinking, abusive. One day after a violent argument, she left, taking their daughter with her back to England. She has never returned.

"Harassment" of tourists by vendors selling goods (jewelry, aloe, wire sculptures, shells), drugs, and services, such as jet-ski rides, has been a chronic problem in Barbados. It is of great concern to the tourism industry. The government has tried to reduce harassment by cracking down on beach vendors and others who solicit guests. Many Bajans who make their living on the beach feel the government and the hotels have gone too far in their efforts to curb harassment. Some, like Ricky, now feel harassed themselves.

The hotel security and the beach rangers won't even let you sit on one of the beach chairs. Say some guests invite me to sit on a chair next to them because they want to chat, because they want to know about my island. They don't want me to sit on the sand, they want me to sit with them. Boom, here comes hotel security. Boom, here comes the beach ranger. "Get off that chair." You set one foot on the hotel property and boom, "Get back on the beach, you don't belong here." To them, we are pests, rodents, bloodsuckers, leeches. They'll do everything in their power to get rid of us.

We don't need all that tight security. It freaks people out. Our country was never like that. It's getting out of hand. Too many rules. You've got to have a license to sell this, a license to sell that. You can't go here, you can't go there. If you're selling something, you've got to sit under one of those little kiosks and you can't set up anywhere else. Now when the guests walk down to the beach, they look at you like dirt because they've been warned to stay away from you. Well, how are those people going to learn about the island if they're discouraged from talking to us?

On TV all the time they say, "Tourism is our business." Well, tourism is my business, too, and they're trying to stop me from doing it. The visitors aren't going to see sea turtles unless I take them. The hotel doesn't tell them anything about sea turtles; that's something I do. And when I show guests the turtles, they come alive, they're really excited, it makes their holiday. I take them by boat and I show them all the luxury houses along the beach that they would never see if they just sat in the hotel. Without me, some of these visitors would never see Barbados. It would just be airport, hotel, beach, airport. Maybe they see sugarcane because they drove by some fields going to the airport, but they will never know what sugarcane is if I don't tell them.

I tell you there will come a day when black people are not going to be able to walk down this beach. I tell you they will try to privatize these beaches. Big rich people from overseas will come in here and want to buy the beach and the government will sell it to them. They'll leave a little strip for black people to pass on, and security's gonna be so tight that you won't be able to go anywhere else. The big people are already buying up all the houses on the coastline. Just look around you. Buy land and build, build, build. Just look at all the land they took away for them big golf courses. They're pushing black people inland, right back into the bush. If you just look down this coast you'll see that hotels have taken all the land where black people once lived. The west coast is already gone, and soon they'll be starting up north, first beach houses and then hotels, all the way around the coast to Pie Corner. I tell you, there will come a time when I would rather live in a foreign country.

Epilogue

In 2010, ten years after this interview, Ricky was still working on the beach.

DIVE SHOP | Brian Rock

Brian Rock, 40, has worked in tourism for fifteen years, first as a jet-ski operator, then teaching wind-surfing and water-skiing. For the last five years, he has been a diving instructor and operated a dive shop that he co-owns with his father. Brian's mother is Swiss, his father Bajan, his wife Jamaican, and he grew up in Trinidad. His family moved back to Barbados when he was 13, and he fell in love with the water, first surfing and later water-skiing, sailing, and scuba-diving. The dive shop is international, with one employee from Ireland, another from England, and another mixed German-Barbadian. They operate like a family and often socialize together at night. An accomplished water-skier, Brian nearly joined the American professional circuit, but because he was from a small island he was unable to line up a sponsor.

I did jet-skis for three years. I'd go from beach to beach, asking people if they wanted to ride. Fifteen minutes for 30 dollars. On a good day you might get twenty rides, on a bad day maybe five. You'd be busiest in winter, but summers could be okay when the kids were out of school. But it's a crazy way to make a living. The people who rent the jet-skis just don't listen, and that's basically why I got out of it. Too many people doing wild, crazy things. You tell people what to do, where not to ride, and they just wouldn't listen to you. They'd ride over the reef and smash up, they wouldn't come in when you called them, when their fifteen minutes were up, and sometimes they'd crash into big boats right in front of your face. And of course they never paid for the damage. I lost one jet-ski when a guy drove into a rock and crashed it. He had lots of money, he could have bought me ten jet-skis, but he didn't have a word to tell me. Didn't pay me 1 dollar. In those days you couldn't get insurance for jet-skis, but you can now, thank God!

I taught wind-surfing for a while on the south coast. Wind-surfing is the hardest thing I've ever taught. It's just not an easy sport to learn. But once you do learn, it's a great feeling because it's all wind-driven. Fresh and healthy and exciting. You teach them on the beach first, then when they're ready you take them in the water with a long board and a small sail. Pulling up the sail is the hardest part, so you want to start them with a small sail. They have to learn where the wind is coming from. If you pull the sail down you go into the wind, if you let the sail out you'll go downwind. Sounds simple, but it's tricky for someone who hasn't done much sailing. With an average person it takes about a week to learn. It helps if you have a nice shallow area where they can stand up when they fall off and where it's easier to climb back on the board.

I also taught water-skiing for three years. Teaching water sports teaches you a lot about people. Teaches you that everybody is different. You have to understand that every person has a breaking point, a point where they can't take any more. You can't pressure people. You can't force them to do things they're not prepared to do. You get a sense pretty quickly whether they're going to be a quick learner or a slow learner. Some people you can tell them just one time and they can do it. With others it takes five or maybe ten times before they get it. A lot of it comes down to how well they listen. Common sense is part of it, and coordination can be important, too. Overall I find that people who are introduced to the water at an early age pick up water sports quicker. Usually young people catch on quicker than older people. But it's not always true. I remember teaching Senator Leahy and his wife from Vermont, and they caught on really quick.

You don't want to ever get angry with them. When someone's not catching on, when they're getting frustrated, it's time to stop and let them rest. I think I've learned to be more soft-spoken and relaxed with people by working in this industry and by dealing with people from all over the world. Westerners are very aggressive people, and they sometimes forget that a lot of other people aren't like that. To do this job well, you've got to be able to deal with all kinds of people.

My day is like this: I get here in the morning and open the shop, get everything ready, bring the boat in, go pick up the divers from the hotels and bring them back here, get them their gear, brief them on where we're going to dive, load the boat, and then take them out. The first dive is usually about 80 feet. They're down for thirty minutes. We come up and do a surface interval for forty minutes, then do a second dive to about 50 feet for another forty minutes. Then I bring them back to the base and we wash off the equipment. All the time we're out, the shop's been open and people have been coming in looking for courses, dives, certifications. Something is always going on.

By that time, the resort divers [beginners] are ready to go. With the beginners we first do a lecture and a video session that shows them what they're going to feel and goes over the skills and what they'll need to do when they get into the swimming pool with the gear. And finally we take them into the sea. We usually start them in about 8 feet of water before swimming out to 20 feet of water.

Breathing is the main problem with beginners. Right now we're all breathing through our noses, but underwater you can only breathe through your mouth, and people aren't used to that. That's the most difficult part to get the hang of. Sometimes they panic, or they'll worry about water going into their mouth and choking. But once they get over that, they realize it's easy.

I think diving would be good for handicapped people. I've taken a blind woman diving. I had to hold her hand throughout the entire dive, but it was amazing. She wanted to feel what it was like on her body, and she wanted to touch things like sponges. Our clients are a mixture, but more male than female and a high percentage of young people. We get both people off the cruise ships and land people. On the whole, cruise-ship people are harder to deal with. Maybe it's because they're all Americans, if you don't mind me saying that. But it's also because they're pampered on the ships. Everything is done for them on board, and if they complain about something the staff will give them a bottle of wine or champagne or something. So when they come here they expect to be pampered a bit, too.

About 60 percent of our divers eventually get certified, which takes three to four days. There are different levels of certification —open water, advanced, medic, rescue, dive master, assistant instructor, and, finally, instructor. All of us in the shop here are divers—instructors and dive masters.

Barbados has very good diving. We have a barrier reef that runs north to south and two ledges—an eastern ledge and a western ledge. The reef starts at 60 feet and drops away to 130 feet on either side. It makes for a very pleasant dive. You go down to 80 feet, cruise for about twenty minutes, then go up to 60 feet and finish your last ten minutes there. The barrier reef doesn't have the big drop like you have in wall diving, like in Jamaica and the Caymans.

Usually we're diving with the current, letting it take you along. But one time we got caught; we were on the barrier reef in 60 feet of water when the current pulled us down to 200 feet and we couldn't see the bottom. I had the group form a circle and hold hands so that nobody would get disoriented. We came up together, and nobody panicked. Sometimes in that situation people will panic and fly to the surface. You can only ascend so fast, just 10 feet per minute, or you'll be in trouble.

The visibility is usually pretty good, between 60 and 80 feet. Our reefs have a lot of color, a lot of nice sponges, sea fans, sea whips, and a lot of growth, a lot of small stuff. We don't have the big stuff like some islands do, but then we have a lot of turtles. You'll see a turtle nearly every dive in Barbados.

We have six wrecks. The *Stavronikita*, a Greek freighter, is a real gem to dive. Her front mast is 20 feet below the surface and she extends down to 130 feet on the bottom. Everyone that goes down there is amazed. She's been rated one of the ten best wrecks in the world to dive. There's also an island schooner wreck off of Almond Beach Resort, and there are a couple of wrecks in Carlisle Bay, like the *Berywn,* a French tug boat, and the *Friar Craig,* which rests in 50 feet of water. But it can be tricky because it is broken into three pieces. One of them has a lot of old history and on certain days we find old bottles from the sixteenth century. There is another wreck around the bend by Astor.

Our diving is not too far off what you get in the Caymans and Tobago, which are the best in the Caribbean. Ours could be a whole lot better if more was done to protect the reefs. We're trying to do that now with the Coastal Conservation Commission, but we need the government to get involved and recognize the value of diving. It could be a tremendous asset to the country and to tourism. But it's taken the government a long time to realize that every time you throw an anchor down it damages the reef. Damage that takes centuries to repair, for the coral to grow back again. I think the older generation of politicians don't relate to diving, don't think there's any money in it. In all the tourist literature that the government puts out you hardly see anything about diving. But the new minister of tourism is trying very hard, so we may see some improvement.

I've been doing this for five years and I haven't gotten bored yet. Sure, some days are less fun than others, but when you go out you almost always see something different. Today I might see some sea horses and tomorrow stingrays or big barracudas. Not every day is exciting, but most days are exciting enough. Right now I love it. Maybe in the future, I'll get into setting up or owning accommodations for divers. But even when I'm 50 or 55 I'd still like to be diving, though when you are older you can't put as much pressure on your body, so maybe I won't be in the water quite as much.

6 THE ATTRACTIONS

Tourist attractions are the activities, things to do, and places to see that occupy and entertain tourists away from the hotel and beach. The Barbados Tourism Authority lists seven categories of attractions: *Activities at sea* are cruises above the sea, snorkeling tours on the sea surface, and submarine dives beneath the sea. *Activities on land* are visits to parks, botanical gardens, and limestone caves. *Historical attractions* involve visits to museums, plantation houses, and sugar mills. *Ecological attractions* are horse treks, cycling tours, scenic hikes, and a walk through a wildlife reserve. *Tours by air* are by helicopter or light airplane. *Dinner shows* and *rum tours* are visits to the Mount Gay or Malibu rum distilleries and visitor centers.

The wide range of activities Barbados offers today is a response to the many tourists who now want something more than just the beach. A survey of U.S. tourists found that 40 percent now desire "life-enhancing" travel, while only 20 percent seek the sun (Honey 1999). They want personal development along with relaxation, and consequently the Barbados Ministry of Tourism, like many Caribbean governments, is now actively encouraging and subsidizing alternative tourist attractions. Its efforts are bolstered by private foundations, such as the Barbados National Trust, which, in an effort to preserve the island's rich heritage, has opened former plantation houses for tours. They also offer weekly guided hikes in different parts of the island.

In this section are interviews with individuals who work at the island's most popular attractions—Harrison's Cave, the Jolly Roger

Pirate Cruise, the *Atlantis* submarine—and also the narratives of the owner-operators of a tour bus and an adventure-cycling tour company.

CRUISE-SHIP SHORE EXCURSIONS
Rosie Hartmann

Rosie Hartmann grew up in the suburbs of London, studied humanities at the University of Surrey, and worked with children in day care and residential children's homes before immigrating to Barbados in her late 20s. Now in her late 50s, she has worked in tourism most of her adult life and today is a marketing executive for Cruise Management Ltd., where she arranges catamaran and boat excursions for cruise-ship passengers. With Rosie's easy laugh and a gregarious personality, it is not difficult to understand why she has won several major tourism awards, including Tour Rep of the Year. All of her children are involved with tourism: one child is married to the culinary executive of a large hotel in Dubai, another is a food and beverage manager at a boutique hotel in St. Lucia, and her third is a chef in Barbados.

I was raised in England and came to Barbados when I was 28 after I had married my husband, now ex-husband. I was a housewife and a young mother with two small children and my husband was in export sales and traveled a lot. He was raised in Majorca and wanted to relocate to an island and a warmer climate than the UK. He loved the Caribbean, so we moved first to Trinidad, an experience we both really loved, but his work situation there was not successful so we came to Barbados. The government then had an open-door policy for people founding light industries with employment potential for Barbadians.

The first few years here I was not able to work due to not being entitled to a work permit. I became terribly bored. I didn't have any of my family or friends from home, and my marriage wasn't perfect, and it is not easy to find friendship in this society if you do not have reason, like a job, to interact with local people. I wasn't sure I liked living in Barbados at that point. But that changed when I was finally able to work.

I took a job with Air Canada Vacations as a tour guide on their newly started island tours. I'm the type of person that if I'm going to do a job, I'm going to do it as well as I can. So, to get up to speed for the job I started to read about the background of Barbados—the botany, the economy, the heritage, and so on—all so that I could field questions from visitors. Well, I became fascinated with the whole development of the culture and of the island. I started to do the tours for Air Canada, and they became very, very successful. Some people actually used to come back the following year for another tour; they'd say, "It was so much fun last time that I couldn't miss it, and I want to do it again."

On the tours I used to play up the funny little anecdotes and the stories and the folklore, the things that people wouldn't so easily find out for themselves, like showing them the Shak Shak trees, which are locally known as Women's Tongue due to their incessant chattering sound made by their seed pods clattering in the wind. And I always involved my bus driver, a red-skinned man named Michael. He was always an integral part of my tours. He wasn't just a functionary on the tour; he became a character and I would ask his opinion on some things. People would ask me a question that I wasn't 100 percent certain of and I would turn to Michael—"Say Mike, what do you think of this question? What's your take on it?" It worked very well. We used to get some great tips at the end of the tour, which I would divide right down the middle with Michael. He was happy to tour with me and I was happy to tour with him. In the process of telling the people all the good and interesting stuff about Barbados, I began to fall in love with the island. And in doing the tours and explaining things to visitors, it became clear to me, for example, why the architecture was the way it was and how it represented the way people thought about their lives and so on. The other thing I loved about island tours was at the end of the day everybody said, "Thank you very much. We really enjoyed that." And then you'd go home and didn't have to think about work until the next day—no homework. Not like in the job I am in now. It was wonderful.

But unfortunately my husband and I split up, and I got thrown into the deep end. I could see that being an island tour guide was not going to pay the bills, so I left and took a full-time job as a tour rep for a destination management company that had won the contract to represent a company called Airtours. That was 1987 and it was the first year that Airtours came on the island. It was a revolution for Barbados's tourism sector because it was the first time Barbados had experienced low-budget, charter visitors. It was the lower end of the scale of tour packages. Airtours was run by hard-nosed businesspeople from the North Country [England]. At the end of the first year with Airtours the two British managers, a husband and wife team, told the local agent that they were thinking of getting rid of me because, they said, "I cared too much about the guests." I had to laugh when I heard that. The managers said that with the small amount of money our clients [visitors] paid for their travel packages, they were lucky if they got a tent on the beach, and that anything extra that I did for them was more than they had paid for. That was probably true as some were paying just 299 pounds for their entire holiday package including airfare from the UK. Anyway, I wasn't fired and not long after I won a Barbados Tourism Authority's award for best tour rep. I was quite amazed that I had won because as a foreign-born person and as a white woman I did not expect that I could ever have won. One result of having won the award was that I was head-hunted by a newly started attraction, Bajan Helicopters. They had begun operations and although everything was in place they weren't marketing themselves very successfully. It was mostly due to personality problems with the person who was managing. He was a bit pushy and since the helicopter tours were already pricey, people in the tourism sector weren't giving him much business. I took the job and we soon started getting business. It really came down to personality and touching base with people, making relationships of trust and following through, and making sure people had information. Early on we also did a rep familiarization day—a whole series of short flights to introduce the reps to helicopter tours. It was a huge event, and because helicopter time is so valuable and expensive it was like organizing a military operation.

Was there resistance to helicopters buzzing up and down the coastline?

No. It was regarded as a sign of growth, sort of Barbados becoming part of the First World and all that. You think back to Barbados 20 years ago when we were starting up and it was a time when many people didn't have cars, and often if they did it was a tiny Suzuki, so I think people were quite proud of their island having helicopters flying visitors around.

While I liked working at Bajan Helicopters, I had several other job offers. I was then divorced and a single parent raising children with nobody to help me. I went to my boss and I said, "Look, let me be straightforward with you, I have several offers, I'd like to stay here if we could just straighten out a few things. You promised me health insurance and I don't yet have it, and is there any way you could give me a small increase in wages?" I only asked for a modest increase. Well, he took the opportunity to let me go and to promote a young girl who was working under me and that I had trained. I felt it was really unfair, especially since I had literally gotten the company off the ground. He was a cut-and-dried type of business-person. He felt that he could manage now that I had put everything in place. [Bajan Helicopters went out of business in 2008.]

What is it like being white in a predominately black society?

It's been a great education living and working here. I'm still very intrigued by the cultural differences. Even after all these years I'm still learning, still cottoning on to stuff. [Being a minority] you need to be very careful, very diplomatic in your dealings, because the Bajan expectations are that you, the white person, is going to win and they are going to lose, and that's tough. Even if I was win-ning, I would underplay it because it won't do me much good—the knives will come out. Yes, there is jealousy around, and if you think back to slavery you can understand why. But please don't come to me and tell me that it's all my fault personally; because I'm going to tell you that I wasn't here during colonial times and I would never have done what those early settlers did. I think people know that about me. At this stage of my time in Barbados, which is 30 years, they know me and they know that I mean well.

What did you do after Bajan Helicopters?

I went through a period of time where I was out of tourism, I went into sales and marketing, and I managed a plant, patio, and garden store. As a single parent and not having any extended fam-ily here in Barbados who might've helped out with the children, I needed a job with regular hours, where I had some time for my kids. In tourism you don't have weekends or summer holidays, bank holidays, or school holidays to be with your kids. In tourism, often the job doesn't stop. So, I did other jobs for a while. But I did come back to tourism seven years ago with this company, Tall Ships [Cruise Management Ltd.]. We have three subdivisions: MV *Har-bour Master*, a big coastal cruiser four decks high and 100 feet long that does both day and night cruises; then we have five luxury cata-marans; and finally, there is the *Jolly Roger*, the pirate ship, my fa-vorite old girl, which is not operating right now; the last vessel was sold and unfortunately is currently resting on the bottom of the ocean.[1] As a tour representative I used to tell visitors that there are a few things they absolutely must do before they leave the island. One, you should not leave Barbados without eating flying fish. Two, you must see the east coast because it is so beautiful and unspoilt. And finally, you can't go home and tell people that you did not sail on the *Jolly Roger* because they'll laugh at you if you missed it.

Can you describe the work you do and what your daily routine is like?

I am one of three people who do all the marketing legwork for Tall Ships. My job is to facilitate and organize the cruise-ship business by liaising with the cruise lines, set up the schedules, and then meet and dispatch their passengers when they are in port and coming on our tours. I am on e-mail at 6 in the morning checking things; get to the office no later than 7:45; dispatch the early tours and then the lunch cruise tours. That means organizing the buses, meeting and greeting the shore teams and the guests, making sure everybody is scooped up and arrives on time for their tours. Nobody wants complaints, so you try hard to make sure all the visitors understand and feel secure about what is going on and that the bus operations are timely. Most people are pretty good, but there are also people out there who are miserable, and they're upset about everything. I love it when I can turn somebody around and make them into a happy camper. I'm very lucky in a way because I get to deal with them in very short spurts. When you work in a hotel and you've got them for a week or two and you can't stand them, it's more challenging.

Then, I come back to the office to deal with communications with the ships, upcoming calls, fine-tuning. A major part of my job is to maximize our business by being proactive and finding ways to fill our space [on the various tours] on any day. In the afternoon, after lunch, I am again dealing with communications, reconciling tickets, and making sure everybody's on the same page as to what business we did that day. Some cruise lines also expect detailed reports of how the day went, timings, weather, sea conditions, and any incidents or issues you may have encountered so that they

---

1. The *Jolly Roger,* described in detail in Dwayne Parry's narrative, was a wooden island schooner or cargo boat, painted and made up to look like a pirate ship with red sails, cannons, etc.

have a heads-up prior to their dealing with the guests back on the ship. So basically I am on duty from early in the day until the ships leave in the evening and then some. I try to leave here at 5 or 6 o'clock in the evening. But when I get home I will spend an hour or more with e-mails, reconfirmations, getting numbers for the next day, and making phone calls to transport and anybody else that needs information about operations for the following day. It is a 24/7 job because if you're going to get their trust and respect you must be available within a couple of hours on any matter. And when the ships come in almost every day during the season, you more or less have to put your personal life on hold for six months.

I don't really have much downtime. I have a beef about this and I feel that I can't carry on forever in this way. I don't get many days off. And even when you're off you can't really check out in your head because you have to monitor the business, you are always thinking about the business. It's important to the business that your clients know they can count on you to respond to them in a timely fashion. Like, a cruise director saying, "We have this wheelchair person, can you take them on this tour?" They need an answer because that wheelchair person is going to come back to the desk [on the cruise ship] and want an answer. It may not take much to respond, but you can't be away from your computer for too long. I was really fed up in March; I only had four days off the entire month and none of the holidays or Easter. I love my job but I am just too overworked; I feel if I don't have someone else who will back me up I may become ill, and this has happened already despite being a generally very well person.

Most of the interviewees for this book deal with stay-over tourism; can you compare that to cruise tourism?

Caribbean cruise tourism is very much on the up compared to land or stay-over tourism. I think people like having multidestination holidays without changing hotels. The all-inclusive package has become much more attractive in the last ten years, whether it be on land or on cruise ships. People like knowing how much their whole holiday is going to cost up front. I also think all-inclusive holidays have become more attractive as people have become more fearful. It's a worldwide phenomenon where people have become nervous, and for them the cruise is more comforting than negotiating their own holiday on the land.

How do you find cruise passengers to be different from stay-over tourists?

Well the cruise passenger is very spoiled. There is a great deal of competition between the cruise lines, which has allowed some cruise passengers to be unreasonable and petulant. They've become accustomed to getting things—all they have to do is squeak and someone is going to oil their wheel. They've learned that all they have to do is yip and someone will give them something. This is not good, and it's not fair. It comes down to the fact that there's lots of competition in the cruise market and that the lines all want to have great service comments from people.

Most of the cruise guests are perfectly well behaved and honest, but there is a criminal fringe who will take advantage of this bias toward the guest. I heard of eight people, four couples, who used to go on holiday on Princess Cruise Line and were overheard talking about who was going to do what this year to get them a freebie of some kind. Apparently, they were drawing lots to see who was going to be the one to make a complaint to see what they could get. On this particular cruise all of them were sailing for free over some complaint they had fabricated in the past. This type of con is infrequent, but it happens. It's appalling and the cruise lines should not tolerate it. I always say, you train your market how to behave.

At Tall Ships we don't get many complaints, but I must say this year it has been more niggling than usual. We've gotten comments like, "They only served us beer and punch and I couldn't get anything else. I couldn't get what I wanted to drink." Well, this is patently untrue. I say to my shore excursion teams that if they have the policy of getting rid of people by giving them something they don't deserve, in the end it will come back to bite everybody. We are all dealing with the fact that some people have become unreasonable in their expectations, in their hopes for gifts or money back. We've even had people say they didn't do the tour in order to get a full refund, when in fact they actually were on the tour. This is a story that came from Carnival Victory where a chap said he didn't do a tour, that he never booked it, and that it needed to come off his account. He said somebody else must have put it on his bill. So they looked it up and yes it was on his bill and yes the ticket was issued. Funnily enough there was a videographer on that tour and when they looked at the video, wouldn't you know there he was, caught on video having a great time. When he came back to get his account sorted out, he started out very antsy, then the staff person said, "Excuse me a moment, sir. We'd like to play this video for you." When he saw himself on the video, caught red-handed, he just chupsed [sucked his teeth] and walked off, just left without a word of apology. People like him are more common today.

Anybody who works in tourism should have a natural desire to please people, to make sure that people are happy. To me it's huge that people have a good day. So when somebody does something like that, something so dishonest, and then tries to make out that you were cheating them, well it is a big discouragement for the staff. It really affects you, seriously, because it's so unjust. These are the kinds of things that really beat up the shore excursion personnel on the cruise ships. These people really have a tough job to begin with; they have four- to six-month contracts with the ships, seven days a week, and when they come off they are fit to die. Some of them say that they are so wiped out that they sleep for five days when they get home.

Regarding cruise visitors, the hope is always that we can convert them into stay-overs who will come back to Barbados. As you know, stay-over visitors contribute far more to the economy. There is some conversion but I think we need to work harder at it. Visitors feel really safe with us and we are very friendly. Generally cruise people love to be in Barbados, they tell us so all the time. But our welcome needs to be 100 percent throughout all the people the guests meet. The people involved in the attractions, like Tall Ships, are a higher-qualified group of people with a good attitude toward service, but that isn't always true in other sectors that visitors encounter, such as customs, or security, or the port staff. Sometimes it's pitiful the way they handle situations. They can leave such a bad impression on a visitor. If they had a better attitude, we'd get even more cruise visitors wanting to come back to Barbados [as stay-over visitors].

Why is it that people working in tourism like to
stereotype the different nationalities they deal with?

They have their sayings about all of us—you know, the English are mad, the Americans have money, and the Canadians are tight. All people make generalizations to a certain degree. It's a shortcut to dealing with people. When you don't understand people thoroughly, it helps if you can put them in a particular box. I suppose it helps people know how to deal with them. There is usually some truth to the sayings. There are always reasons why people come to those conclusions about other people, but obviously they are not always accurate. For example, I don't think the English are mad. I think the English are eccentric; the English revere eccentricity. I enjoy them for it and I get a smile on my face when they are eccentric. Nor do I think that all Americans have money, and I don't think those that do always flash it around either. But they do usually have a short holiday and therefore will spend their money faster perhaps than Canadians or others. The English have longer holidays, and although they also like to have a good time they are going to make their holiday money stretch. And, honestly, many Canadians have longer stays and can be tight, but there are always exceptions to the rule.

A lot of times you hear locals make the comment about visitors, regardless of where they're from, that, "They come here on holiday, but they leave their brains at home." Well, not really. Just imagine all the new aspects that a new visitor has to take in—from the climate to the people to the language to the customs. Everything is new, so they are adjusting to much more than you think they are. If they appear to be stupid, it's not that they don't have any brains, rather they are adjusting to many new things. So we need to give them advice and help, ease them in. People are unbelieveably grateful when you do, when you help them to find their feet. So yes we do make assumptions and stereotypes; however, I personally don't like the one that most visitors left their brains at home.

Now, sometimes visitors are a bit fearful because they are not used to being surrounded by a sea of black faces. It's a 95-percent-black country and there's some real culture shock for some visitors in dealing with that. I remember when I was a tour rep all those years ago, somebody saying to me, "We wandered up the beach and there was a family there having a barbecue and they invited us to come and have a drink. And we didn't know if it was safe, so we said 'No.' They said, 'Never mind, we're doing something else on Saturday and would you like to come along?' What do you think we should do?" I said, "They offered you a genuine invitation and you should go and not be afraid. Keep your head on like you normally do at home and don't worry about it. They are people just like you and me, they're not out to trick you." Barbadians are friendly like that. They say good morning to everybody. When I come to work in the morning I have to go through and give everybody a hug, and if they don't get it they tell me off. But in other places that is far from the norm. When my girlfriend came to visit from New York, we parked the car down by the Careenage and walked into town, into Broad Street. She said, "You just said 'good morning' to more people walking from the car to here than I do in an entire month in New York." Well, that's Barbados.

What do you think of the notion that
tourism can be a form of neocolonialism?

Well, I think there is a hangover from colonialism, all that stuff about service and servitude. Personally, as a white person I have no hang-ups at all about delivering wonderful service. It's not part of my heritage to feel like I am put upon. But for others [black Bajans] it can be different when you are coming from a background of slavery. I think we white people don't really understand how it could possibly feel to not have the freedom to do what you want, to have no personal power, even down to the fact that when you had a relationship with a loved one—husband or wife— they [slave owners] could split you up, and take your children away from you and put them in different places, sell them to other plantations. I don't think that we white people can even imagine what slavery meant to these people. How dreadful that experience must have been. It's very hard to eradicate that residual bitterness. People [black Bajans] just assume that white people think less of them, that they are not as worthy, not as smart.

I come from a society where there weren't a lot of black people in my upbringing, and there weren't any in my school. I was surrounded by white people when I was growing up. Of course, it's certainly not like that today; it's a completely different society in the UK today. But even though I grew up being surrounded by white people, I do understand why they [black Bajans] get bent out of shape. They imagine that white people think they are inferior, that they're more like animals, that they are like monkeys. I don't think we white people can conceive how bad that makes people feel. They have to overcome that, they have to get past that. So it's not surprising that some get a chip on the shoulder. But many Bajans do get over it, or at least they have learned to manage it. They realize that it's not intentional. However, I should add that we still have some visitors who are colonial in their attitudes, who assume that somebody should be punkah wallering—the Indian servant who fans the white people with a huge palm leaf fan—and waiting on them hand and foot. They assume that other people don't have the same feelings as white people. There are still prejudiced, racist people in the world and they sometimes come to Barbados on holiday.

*What does Barbados need to do to maintain
its place as a premier tourist destination?*

I think Barbados has done tourism well over the years. I'm very proud that we get a huge amount of repeat visitors here. However, we are in danger of losing our edge right now. I'm really worried about the overdevelopment of the island, and I wonder if the powers that be realize that once the golden goose is strangled you're not gonna get it back too easily. But right now the tourism product we deliver is still excellent, excellent. If I've heard it once I've heard it a million times from guests, "Your tour was wonderful! The day was wonderful! Your staff is wonderful!" We see that all the time on the comment forms. It all stems from providing great service and that is something that we need to foster and keep going. A lot of tourist professionals need a pat on the back; they need encouragement, to be told how important it is that they keep putting out that extra effort.

What are the big threats to the future of tourism in Barbados?

We have to be very careful of the marine environment. It's under some serious threat. If you want to boil it down to the basics, it is our beaches and our water that are intrinsic to our offering, to what makes Barbados appealing to visitors. I don't think the government has the money, no matter which party is in power, nor the will or vision to understand that if we allow the reefs to die the whole thing goes to hell in a handbasket very quickly. The reef is the barrier that protects our beaches. Climate change is also a factor. Because of high sea temperatures we are expecting a major bleach [killing off of coral] this year. We've never had sea temperatures as high as this; high sea temperatures also contribute to more severe hurricanes. And hurricanes don't encourage tourism; they can bring a lot of destruction.

Also there has been some uglification of the island by building tall condominiums; that has really affected the tourism plant in a very obvious negative way. This has happened while allowing heritage buildings to decay and crumble away. The government has allowed property and buildings that have been sold to just sit there for years, ill-maintained, falling apart and looking ugly without anything being done to them. They are an eyesore. About twenty years ago we had an environmental levy of 1 percent put on every imported item to deal with the environment and the disposal of waste and so forth. I don't know what's happened to that money. It certainly doesn't go to the environment. The levy is still there, 1 percent on every imported good, but it has never been used for the environment. Never.

ISLAND BUS TOURS | Anderson Hughes

There are fifty-six private tour buses on the island of Barbados. Anderson Hughes, 55, operates two of them. The tour buses are used to transfer arriving passengers from the airport to hotels and cruise ships and to take visitors on tours of the island. Anderson and his wife, Arlette, live in the parish of St. Lucy, in one of the most remote villages in Barbados. They have a daughter who teaches at a high school in New York.

I left Barbados in 1964 when I was 21 years old. At that time I was a fisherman and I thought there wasn't much of a future in fishing, that it was better to go to a developed country to gain some experiences. There were companies over here from England looking for people willing to go over there to work. Quite a few of my friends went ahead of me. So I went into Bridgetown and had an interview with London Transport. About one month later I was in London working on the double-decker buses. For the first four years I was a conductor, and then I became a driver. I spent twenty-four years in England, all that time working on the buses.

I always had it in my mind that I would like to return to Barbados someday before I reached the age of 50 to contribute some of the experiences I had gained from living in England to my own country. I had a friend who returned home ahead of me. He decided to go into the minibus operation. I was thinking of doing the same thing until my brother told me that the minibuses didn't last long because of all the rushing and carrying around and the bad roads. They had lots of expensive repairs. He advised me to get into tour buses instead, and that's what I did. I applied for a permit to run a tour bus and my application was successful.

So I came back in '88, and the bus I'd bought arrived from Japan the following year. When we left England I sold our house and used the money as collateral for the bus. It was a twenty-eight-seater. A few years later I bought a second bus, a thirty-three-seater, also from Japan.

Unlike with the first vehicle, all the dials and instructions for the second bus were in Japanese. Anderson was having a difficult time under-

standing the Japanese characters when he saw me walking with my Japanese anthropology student Akiko Tsuda, who was living in Anderson's village. Anderson was thrilled that Akiko not only spoke Japanese but offered to translate for him. He rushed inside, returning with notebook and pen. The two of them worked their way from front to back of the bus translating the Japanese symbols and instructions. Several days later, Anderson came to Akiko's house with the Japanese instruction manual and hired her to translate it.

Most of our work is with the cruise ships. I depend on five tour operators who subcontract tours for the passengers to me. I have just one employee, who drives the other bus. The different tour operators call before the arrival of the ship. The passengers can go up to a desk on the ship and see what tours are available before they get to the island. They have to prebook. The ship then calls the tour operators the night before to let them know how many people are coming the next day for each tour. Then the tour operators call us. It's all first come, first serve, so you go down early in the morning to get a position in line. I leave home at 5 A.M. to get to the harbor by 6 A.M. even though the tours don't start until between 8:30 and 9:00. If you get an early start, you can do a morning tour and then make it back in time to get a second group for an afternoon tour. So to get the maximum out of your day, you go early, line up, and wait.

The tours are normally a half-day, about three to four hours. There are different kinds of tours: factory tour, photo tour, two-stop tour, lunch tour. If you have an English-speaking group, some tour operators don't bother to hire a guide because they know that you're capable of handling the commentary. It's a way they save some money.

A popular tour is Harrison's Cave: it's about twenty-five minutes from the harbor. After they tour the cave, I take them to St. John's parish church. I talk to them the whole way. At the church they spend twenty minutes on their own walking around. Then it's a thirty-five minute run back to the harbor.

Then there's the rum tour. You leave the ship and take them to the rum refinery, where they see a video and then go on the tour. They get to sample the different rums and can make purchases. There's also the photo tour, but my other driver does it. He takes the group to different scenic spots and lets them get out and take photographs. The tour includes stopping at a local rum shop to buy rum punches or whatever. Then he passes by the sugar factory and

Visitors chance upon a wedding at St. John's parish church.
Photo by George Gmelch.

finally comes back to his photography studio, where he shows them some of the shots that he's taken. Some people will buy photos from him.

I've always enjoyed driving, though I do get a little nervous changing gears coming up the hills in St. Joseph. I feel relief when I get out of those hills. And I really enjoy talking, giving a commentary, especially when people are a good audience—when they're listening and everything is flowing well.

I start off the tour by telling people that Barbados has been settled since 4000 B.C., when the Arawak Indians first came here. And then the Portuguese arrived in 1536, but they didn't stay. They left some pigs and other animals in case other settlers were to come, so that they would have some sort of food. The British came in 1625, liked what they saw, and came back two years later to settle. On their way over, they captured some African slaves. The Africans and the British worked alongside each other to get Barbados going. I tell them the Africans seem to have adapted better to the conditions than the Europeans. The Europeans came wearing their kilts from Scotland and the sun was so hot that it burned their legs. I tell them that at one time there were a lot more Europeans than African slaves, but that lots of those whites migrated to North America.

After the end of slavery, that gave Africans more chances to expand. That is how we have come to outnumber the Europeans. That is why whites are only 5 or 6 percent of the population and those of African origin are over 90 percent today. But I tell them that the whites, more or less, still control the economy because they were able to hold on to their wealth over time. But that gradually you have blacks coming into wealth today.

When a question arises I always try to find the answer. If I don't know it, when we stop I'll make some inquiries and try and give them an answer. I try to feel the pulse of what the passengers want to hear. If they ask questions and I get a feeling that they want me to veer off in that direction, then I do. If you have black Americans on board they may ask, "How come I don't see many blacks in managerial positions?" Then I'll tell them what I know. But actually, I'd rather not have a black American on board. I find it's too taxing. American blacks seem to think that we Barbadians, as black people, are not doing enough. They think we should be putting up a stiffer fight to claim what is ours. Maybe, but I'd rather not talk about it too much because I feel I can't do anything about it.

I think having lived abroad helps me speak in a way that other visitors can understand better. I drop my Bajan accent. You have to speak slowly to visitors. And that's what happens to your speech when you're living abroad. I find a lot of visitors comment on the way I speak. They'll say something like, "This morning I was on a different tour and I didn't understand a word. But with you, I can understand every word you say." When you go outside it's a whole education on its own. Living away widens your scope, gives you an appreciation for other people and how they live. When you're just here in Barbados you're in a little nutshell—limited resources, limited vision, and things like that. There are a lot of locals who resent people like me who come back from overseas because they think that we think we are better than them for having lived abroad. I tell my friends in England who are thinking of coming back that they have to be prepared to take a lot of criticism. I tell them to be careful about comparing Barbados with England, that people here don't want to hear it. I was fortunate when I came back to have a lot of my relatives around here.

What kind of silly questions do you get?

They won't usually say it directly to me, but some people are surprised to see so many black people. "This place is so good [developed], how come so many blacks are living here?" I heard one person ask a white tour guide that. I wasn't angry, I just laughed at how ignorant people can be.

Showing visitors your island makes you proud of how far Barbados has come. Of course there are also things that you don't like. The roads are very bad. Too many potholes. And in some places the trees are overgrown on the sides of the roads. Litter is another thing that gets me. There's way too much litter on the island, and a lot of local people don't concern themselves with keeping their immediate area clean. I keep a trash bag on the bus because in a lot of places there are no trash cans. Another thing I don't like are the boys in some areas who jump in the tourists' cars. The boys tell them they'll give them a tour or that they'll take them to the destination they're looking for. A lot of tourists don't want to offend them and will let them stay and then have to give them money just to get rid of them. They're afraid they'll get robbed or mugged if they don't. I know some of the tourists bring it on themselves. They think they're on vacation in a little paradise, where nothing bad happens. Well, it's not, and you have to keep a good eye and your wits about you.

Like in every job, not everything always goes smoothly. If there are a lot of cruise ships in the harbor, you get your group up to Harrison's Cave and then they have to wait a long time for the tour. These tourists have less than a day on your island and they don't want to be sitting around one place waiting for a thirty-five-minute tour of the caves.

The other day I was doing a morning tour and I had thirty-two people on board. I left without realizing that two people were missing. I always do a head count, but this time there was some confusion. I had only driven five minutes down the road when I realized they were missing. I turned back and found them about to board another bus. I apologized to them but they weren't too happy, and when they got back to the ship they reported it. Well, the next tour I took was from the same ship. As soon as everyone got on the bus, I told them my name and the bus number. As soon as I said it a man stood up and said, "Oh, you're Anderson, the man that left people at St. John's church. I hope you don't leave us behind." The fellow was ripping me all day but in a joking way. By the time the tour ended we were best of friends.

Having lived abroad makes me want to help people because I know how it is, especially when somebody is lost. You reach out to help people, because you hope they would do the same for you.

Some of the passengers like to joke with you. The English will tease you about cricket, tell you that their country is gonna thrash the West Indies team. The main thing I want is to have my passengers happy. I hate to see a miserable face.

For me, a bad day is a rainy day, or when there is an accident up ahead and I can't get through, or when I don't make it back to the harbor in time to get a second tour. And every once in a while when you get a passenger who makes trouble. Like the other day I had this American gentleman who wouldn't put out his cigar. I have "no smoking" signs up. I said to him, "Please, I don't want any smoking." He was trying to hold his cigar out the window but the smoke was coming inside. He was one determined man to have his cigar. Sometimes you have people talking while you're giving your commentary. That annoys me. Once I actually stopped the bus and asked this fellow to stop talking. Most people are glad when you ask others to stop talking, because they do want to hear.

When we get to Harrison's Cave, I always tell people that they have restrooms and I say the same when we get to St. John's parish church. Still, you have people who never seem to remember that they have to go to the bathroom until you're in the middle of nowhere. Then they want to go. Especially when they're coming from the *Jolly Roger* cruise and have been doing a lot of drinking. I had a young girl, no more than 25, ask me over and over "how much farther." Finally she couldn't wait any longer and I had to stop the bus and let her squat down in front of the bus outside of everybody's view.

You get some people who want you to stop so they can sample some sugarcane. That's illegal unless you get permission from the owner, so I don't do it. I even had a Barbadian who was living in Germany working for the tourist board. He came back with a group who wanted to go break off the cane. I said no, I'm not doing it. So he did it himself. And I had a French-speaking fellow who asked me to stop. I thought it was something he wanted to show to people. But instead he jumped out and broke off a cane stalk. If I had known I would have left him behind. My bus number can easily be seen, so if the owner was around he could have taken down my number and brought a case against me. And I never let people go pick mangos and fruits unless the owner's around and they offer to pay for it. People need to know that this is someone's livelihood, that they rely on selling those fruits for an income.

One day I worked this ship and when I got my load to Harrison's Cave, I realized that they were all men. Then the other bus came down and I saw that he had all men as well. Then we realized there were all men on all of the buses. We didn't realize this ship had all queers on board until we saw some of them holding hands. There was a lot of controversy that day; they even talked about it on the news. That same ship was refused entrance to one of the other islands after it left Barbados. The next time it came to Barbados it had both men and women on it.

A lot of people comment on the driving in Barbados—that it's really fast and that the roads are much narrower than at home. And for those coming from America, we're driving on the other side of the road, which takes some getting used to. I tell the people to have confidence, that because the roads are narrow and the cars pass much closer to one another it seems like we're going faster than we really are. I tell them, "Take your foot off the brakes and let me do the driving." And I slip in that I was in New York a couple of years and was terrified by the speed up there but after a couple of days I got used to it, and I'm sure they'll get used to the driving here.

If you have to change the route on prearranged tours, a lot of people don't like that. You can't just take them to another spot. Sometimes when there's been a lot of rain the water in Harrison's Cave reaches a level where they have to close it down. There are other good places to go, but people are very strange. They will say, "Well I didn't book for that tour, so we're not taking it." Many of them will say no and will want their money back.

People can be pretty rigid. Even the captain of the cruise ship can't just change things. Like one day this captain came and another ship was in his spot, and the sea was rough. When the other ship couldn't move, the captain headed off for some other island. Well, some of the people on board called the head office in Miami and they ordered the captain back to Barbados. I had just gotten home, a forty-five-minute drive, when the tour operator called me and said come back, the ship is on its way back and we'll do the afternoon tour.

We are paid 80 dollars Barbados for every four persons. They call that a "car" because that's how many people a taxi can carry. It goes back to the days when most people were taken around in taxis and not buses. So if I have thirty-two people on board, I have eight cars, and that's good for 640 dollars Barbados. If you look at what we're getting for each person, it's only 20 dollars Barbados, and the passengers are paying more than three times that for the tour. Most of that money goes to the ship and to the tour operator.

The ship collects the money from the tourists on board. The ship then passes on some of the money to the tour operator, who then subcontracts the actual tour to us. The tour operators began with the government trying to give the poor man an opportunity to get into the business. That's fine but some of those fellas are now better off than us, and we're the ones who own and operate the vehicles. I know one tour operator who bought out a couple of people who had buses. He has four buses himself; you know that when the work is small, when there aren't many passengers, his buses are always working. And they're always full. Well, that's unfair. And now he's trying to buy up even more buses.

At the port, taxis go in one lane and buses go in another. Each sticks to his own. The taximen get annoyed with us because most passengers would rather ride in a van or a bus. The visitors think that the bus is bigger and there is less chance of having an accident. And some feel that if they sit up higher they get a better view. So when people have a choice, they move to the vans and buses. The taximen don't like that. You see, when the harbor first opened it was just taxis and only one or two buses. So as the buses increased—there are now fifty-six—and their seating capacity got bigger and bigger, they took more and more business away from the taxis. Taximen are now complaining that they're not getting enough work. The taximen got together with the port authority people and they now put a charge on buses to go into the port. I have to pay 128 Barbados dollars a month just to get into the port. Taximen don't pay anything.

What differences have you noticed in tourists in terms of nationality?

I find that Germans don't like air-conditioning. And they don't like the windows open. They'd rather sweat than have an open window or have the AC on. So when you get down the road you begin to feel pretty warm and you look back and see all the windows are still closed. I explain, "Please open the windows." But they don't understand. They'll lean forward with deaf ears. So I put on the AC. And then you look back and see the windows open. So they're a mystery to me. A lot of Americans think they can get whatever they want. They don't seem to understand that when you go to another country you have to comply with their regulations. For instance, you can't pull the bus up alongside the ship to load passengers unless you have special permission. People have to walk to get to the buses. One day, this American guy was quarreling, saying that I made him walk all this way when I should have driven the bus up to the ship. I said, "Excuse me, sir, but I'm not allowed to go there." He said, "Oh, you can do that. They always say that you're not allowed. I hear that word all the time." I think the English are more satisfied, more content with what you offer. I like working with the English, maybe because I spent a long time in England. And I find the English don't talk while you are talking the way some Americans do.

Since I've come back I've thought about getting a fishing boat. My brothers put me off the idea, though. They say, "You're not going back to that." Maybe I won't go back to sea, but I'd like to own a boat. They think it's not good for me, a bad investment, not safe. Even when some friends wanted to take me out just for the day, my brothers heard about it and said I shouldn't go. You see, years ago we didn't have radios, and sometimes boats were lost at sea. But today boats have all the latest equipment. They're much safer today.

When you drive through rural districts how do local people react to the tourists looking at them from the bus?

When I go through villages I often slow down to show people the old wooden houses. Most local people don't mind, but a lot don't want you to take their photographs. If you pass a cane field during the harvest, for instance, some people will shout, "You have to pay me for my photograph." Or they just say, "Don't take my photograph." Most of the tourists have been told on board ship that if they want a photograph they should ask politely for it.

I first heard of Anderson Hughes in 1990, eight years before doing this interview. I was then living in the nearby community of Josey Hill, a mile from Anderson's home. He had a large flock of sheep, and instead of staking them out on the land like all the villagers did, he enclosed them with fences. It was a novel idea and the source of some gossip.

When I came back in '88 I didn't know how long I'd have to wait to get a permit for the bus. I was told that it could be over a year, and since I had a fair amount of land I thought I could keep myself going with sheep. Barbados was exporting sheep to other countries at the time and sheep farmers were doing quite well. At one time I had ninety-three sheep. Even after I got the buses going I kept the sheep. I got a lot of joy coming back after a long day and just leaning over the fence and watching them. But when the second bus came along, I realized it was too much work looking after them. Now I'm down to fifteen. But I like having the animals to look after, especially when the tourist season finishes. I like knowing I still have something to do.

We finish doing tours in May. In June, the travel agents come around to see the island, and the Tourist Board asks us to take them on tours so they can go back home and sell Barbados. July and August are virtually dead. You don't have anything to do, and you can get very bored. If you plan on making a trip, that's the time to do it.

Epilogue

One year after this interview, Anderson had overcome the suspicions of some bus owners and the laid-back attitude of others to organize the Coach Owners Association of Barbados, Inc. Anderson wrote to me, "With this Association, we can now fight for a fair share of business and not be exploited any longer. We intend to send our own representatives abroad to meetings with tour companies and travel agents." When I returned to Barbados in 2010, Anderson had sold his business because of illness and retired.

CO-PILOT, ATLANTIS SUBMARINES
Michael Walcott

Michael Walcott, 32, grew up in Bridgetown and spent much of his youth on the beach. He did well in school and graduated top in his class in electronics at the polytechnic. He worked at repairing computers until he answered a newspaper ad for submarine co-pilots. Michael has been a co-pilot on the Atlantis *submarine for eight years. The tourist brochure for Atlantis Submarines reads like this: "Get set for an experience of a lifetime. An exciting journey through the natural undersea world of Barbados. You'll cruise along at depths of up to 150 feet . . . You'll gasp as you enter this breathtaking world of coral reefs, sea flora and fauna in a kaleidoscope of living color. Your experienced co-pilot will narrate your unforgettable journey."*

We take the people out to the submarine by boat. The submarine is about a mile offshore. When you get out to the dive site you don't see the sub at first. I tell them to look down in the water for the light-blue patch coming up. When the sub pops to the surface it's really magnificent stuff. People say it reminds them of scenes in the movies when military subs break the surface.

The passengers board by climbing down the ladder and sitting along each side of the sub. Sometimes you get someone who's claustrophobic. Usually being able to look out the windows, or viewports, calms them down. Being able to look out lets them concentrate on something outside and takes their mind off their environment and doesn't make them feel trapped inside. But for some it's still a problem, at least on the daytime dives. Oddly, no one ever seems bothered by it on the night dives.

On the last dive I had a guy say to me, "What happens if you're claustrophobic?" He was laughing. I said, "Hey, are you serious?" He was serious but didn't want to just admit it, so he tried to make a joke of it. Usually I tell people, "This is your choice, if you want to try it then go ahead, but it's okay if you want to go back." Even if we've started the dive, we'll come back to the surface if someone starts to panic. But the best thing is find out if they're going to have a problem before you get under way.

Atlantis submarine. *Courtesy of Barbados Tourism Authority.*

You get a few people who worry about what might happen if the submarine broke down, would they be trapped on the bottom. Well, if the submarine loses power it will automatically float back to the surface. Even if, God forbid, the sub was to get tangled on the bottom, there are trained scuba-divers on the surface in the tender and they'd be able to go down and free the sub. And even if something really weird happened, like both the pilot and co-pilot were incapacitated, we have methods for hauling the vessel to the surface.

The submarine is 65 feet long and takes forty-eight passengers and two crew—the pilot and co-pilot. Large viewports line each side of the submarine, so that every passenger can look out. At the front of the sub is a large bubble where the pilot sits. I sit in the back to narrate but also to let the pilot know what's happening to the rear, because the sub doesn't have rearview mirrors.

We descend about 130 feet and follow the barrier reef for about a mile and a half round-trip. Schools of fish, like jacks, swim right up to the viewports. If the glass wasn't there they'd probably come in and kiss you; they're that close. We see a lot of big fish as well, like snappers, margate, and barracudas. A lot of people want to see a shark. Last month we saw a 20-foot whale shark, and everyone said it was unbelievable. One of our best experiences was seeing a manta ray with a 14-foot wingspan. He put on a show for the passengers; he flapped along the starboard side, then disappeared behind the sub before coming around the port side. At night you see a lot of different fish, some of the big predators like groupers, octopus, squid, and moray eels. At night the external lights from the sub introduce a lot of color that is lost during the day. Night dives are a whole different experience, and it's very quiet and people really mellow down.

I've had passengers who were filming their vacation who were so excited about the tour that they sent me a copy of the video when they got back home. One of the highlights of the tour is seeing an old shipwreck. For a lot of people, going down in the sub is the closest they'll ever get to scuba-diving. I think a lot of people would really like to scuba-dive but never will. They've been scared off by some friend or neighbor, who probably has never been himself but who's warned them about the danger.

My job as co-pilot is to interact with passengers and to narrate—to tell them about the underwater environment and the fish and sea life they are seeing out the viewports. When you start out as a co-pilot, the company gives you a script with the basic information. But each co-pilot has his own style and branches off. If you want to talk about currents, you talk about currents. If you want to talk about sponges, you talk about sponges. A lot of the information I use comes from the marine biologist who used to be on our staff, and he got his information off the Internet. I do some research on my own, too, like watching the Discovery Channel and on the Internet. And I get some information from books. My training was in microelectronics, not marine biology, so there are things I don't know. And once in a while I get a professor on the tour who will correct me on something. A few weeks ago I had a professor of physics and his wife, who is also a professor. After the tour he was telling me, "Well, Michael, I heard you say blah, blah, blah, but that's not necessarily the case." What he said made a lot of sense. I don't have any problem with someone coming up and saying, "Okay Michael, what you said was really great but maybe you might also look into this." If I have a professor on board, usually what I say to him is, "Look I'm going to tell them some stuff; if I say something that you might not agree with, you can see me at the end of the tour."

Every group is a little different, and to some extent you tailor your narration to the passengers you have. For example, not all passengers want to hear jokes. When I say hello or good morning to them as they board the launch and begin to interact with them I can tell what type of group I have—a lively group, a foreign group that might not understand much English, or whatever. If they don't speak a lot of English, I know that they just want to hear the information and not my jokes. Like if there are a lot of Germans, they are very serious, at least they have a very serious look on their faces, and you say to yourself, "Okay, let me work my way into this slowly." The English are reserved, but after the tour they'll give you accolades: "Oh, that was a smashing tour, we really enjoyed that." But you wouldn't be sure during the tour. But if you have a lot of Americans you think to yourself, "Great," because they show their excitement. Those from Latin America can also get very excited. I think what tells you best about the group is whether many of them are smiling. If they're already smiling they'll be open to you and you'll have a better time with them. Humor is important and makes the trip more fun for everyone.

One joke that usually works for me goes like this, "Ladies and gentlemen, please look out your viewports. Do you see that long, slender, stick-like fish?" Everybody always says, "Yeah, yeah, I see the fish." Then I say, "Do you know what they are called?" They say, "No, no, no." I say they are called "long, slender, stick-like fish." Then after they've stopped laughing I tell them they're actually called trumpet fish.

Another joke I tell is about angelfish, how they pair off and stay together for life. Then I ask, "How many of you on board would do that? Stay with your mate for life?" They say, "Yeah, yeah, yeah!" Then I tell them that angelfish take their relationships very seriously, so seriously, that if their mate dies, the surviving angelfish will starve itself to death. It will literally commit "sushi-cide." Then I ask for a show of hands for how many of the passengers would do that for their mates. Anyway, that's true about angelfish living in pairs, and because you made a joke out of it, people won't forget it.

Sometimes we have long days, sometimes we make four trips. It can get tiring but it never gets boring. You don't see the same fish every time, and the big thing is that the passengers change. A different group every time. It sure beats having a real job. I get paid to talk to people, to laugh, to smile, to do stuff. Before, when I was repairing computers, I had to wear a tie and a long-sleeve shirt and work in an air-conditioned office all day. Now I wear shorts, work outdoors in the fresh air, and deal with people from all over the world. Seems like a good trade to me; and some days instead of co-piloting, I'm in the water scuba-diving next to the submarine. That's recreation for me, real stress relief, because the sea is an entirely different world—you leave your land world behind and you explore another. I forget everything when I'm on a dive. And I'm getting paid to do it.

Has doing this job changed you?

I'm a lot bolder now. Being in this job has made me much more extroverted, more of a people person. Five years ago, I wouldn't have been able to sit here and speak to you into a microphone [tape recorder] like I'm doing now. When I was in computers I was dealing with people but usually only with irritated people who wanted their computer fixed, and as soon as possible. "Why isn't my computer working, I just bought it last year!" I think doing that kind of work made me shy, because I never knew how to handle irritated people. Now I'm working with people who are in a happy mood because they're on vacation. I look people in the eyes now; I used to always look down. I was very insecure about looking people in the eyes.

Speaking to visitors all day has forced me to speak standard English so that people can understand me, not mixing it with my Bajan dialect. Even when I go home, I talk to my wife and child in proper English. I want my daughter to talk to me in proper English rather than the dialect she picks up from the other kids that she hangs around. If I were to speak in dialect on the submarine, people wouldn't understand me and they would just close their minds to what I had to say. I've learned Swedish as well, learned it from my wife, who I met on the submarine. She was working for a Swedish tour company when we met. Outside of *Atlantis,* I've read a lot of books too, inspirational books, about how to interact with people, the power of the subconscious mind, personality, and stuff like that. The books have helped me grow and helped me in work as well. This job teaches you how to handle all sorts of situations because of all the different people and different problems you meet.

Being around people of different cultures opens up your mind. It brings you a lot of new information, it makes you want to see and experience some of the places they come from and the things they've done. I've discovered there's a whole world out there waiting to be seen. And even if you can't travel to where the visitors are from, just meeting them and hearing something about their country, their way of life, makes you more interested.

Doing this job has also made me more aware of the marine environment. Now toward the end of my tour I like to talk about conservation, how we have to protect the underwater environment. It upsets me when I see plastic bags and stuff floating in the water. Plastic bags end up on the reef and kill turtles who eat them, thinking they are jellyfish. If people would just take the time to drop their bags and candy wrappers in a garbage can, they wouldn't wind up in the sea. I can't educate everybody, but I can start here in the submarine. A lot of visitors come up after the tour and thank me for talking about that.

Epilogue

Two years after this interview, Michael, believing his potential for personal growth was limited at Atlantis Submarines, moved to Sweden with his wife, Annika, and now works as an IT network engineer.

TOUR GUIDE, HARRISON'S CAVE
Malika Marshall

The coral limestone cap that covers much of Barbados is permeated by underground streams, creating an extensive system of caves. The most spectacular is Harrison's Cave, now the most popular attraction in Barbados. Although the cave has long been known to locals, it was not until Danish speleologist Ole Sorensen saw its potential when exploring the cave in 1970 that the Barbadian government considered developing it as an attraction. Malika Marshall, 28, is one of eight guides who take visitors on battery-operated trams through the cavern. She was raised by her grandparents in Bridgetown. Malika taught math for five years in a primary school in Bellplaine, St. Andrew, before becoming a tour guide.

Each tram holds thirty-two passengers and three staff members—a driver, a security guard, and a tour guide. All of the drivers are men, all of us tour guides are women, and the security personnel are mixed. There is one lady tour guide who is thinking about becoming a driver, but most women are not brave enough to drive through the narrow passages in the cave. There is a script that the tour guides are supposed to follow, which talks about the history of the cave and all the places of interest you see as we move along in the tram. Like we say, the cave is 78 degrees year-round because we're close enough to the equator that temperatures do not fluctuate much. We can add to the script if we want. Sometimes I tell the visitors when Barbados became independent from England and what our main source of income is and maybe something about the free education offered to all Barbadians. But a lot of the guides just stick to the text.

To be a good tour guide, I think, you have to have a friendly personality, be a people person. And you have to have good diction. You can't speak in dialect, and with Americans you have to slow down your speech. With Canadians you can talk faster. If I have both Americans and Canadians on the trip, the Canadians will sometimes ask, "Why are you talking so slow?"

You can get pretty tired saying the same thing eight times a day, especially when the people are not responsive. You can tell when they are not being very attentive because they will ask you questions about things you have just finished telling them. Overall, women are the most interested in what you have to say, especially older women. Older men are jovial but not as interested in learning. Boys, especially if they are in a group, are just not very open.

In terms of nationality, I'd say that Americans and Canadians are probably the most enthusiastic, maybe because you have lots of caves in North America. A lot of Americans compare Harrison's with the caves they have seen at home, like Mammoth and Carlsbad. They like to tell you the difference between the caves. The British don't seem to have caves, or at least they don't ever talk about them.

When I first started this job, even though I had good diction and my English was good, I was very nervous. I would look at the people in the tram and say, "Good morning," and then quickly turn and sit down so they wouldn't look at me. I was thinking, "I can't do it, I can't do it." You think everyone is looking at you and thinking, "Is she going to be able to do it?" But you gradually get over it, and after three days I was okay.

I know what I am saying so well and I have said it so many times that I don't even think about it. The only time I forget something seems to be when I am very hungry. And if I do leave something out or make a mistake, I've learned it is best not to correct it. Unless it is really a stupid mistake, the patrons don't know any better. So I don't draw attention to my errors. Often I ask the driver at the end of the day how I did: "Was I my usual self today?" He might say, "No, you were sounding low, you slipped once or twice."

I do a lot of reflection on my performance. Even though it is all pretty routine, you don't always perform the same. Sometimes you have a cold or sore throat or you have something on your mind. It affects how you do. If I have just done a tour and I've been flat, I think, "Hey, these people have never been here before and they deserve better. So let me deal with my problems outside of work." Usually I can snap out of it. When you are really good, it's because you are really in tune with your job. You leave everything else behind, and you just give it your all. Of course you should do that every day, but it's not always possible. Sometimes you just wake up and you are not in that happy-go-lucky mood, and it's hard to get yourself into it.

The job itself is not very challenging, because you're doing the same thing over and over again. It really can become monotonous.

Three months after I started working at the cave, I told my boss that I really needed something more to do. Not only is the talk scripted, but there are a lot of slow days where you don't make many trips into the cave. You're sitting around on top for five hours doing nothing. My boss tried to find some projects to keep me occupied, like I set up a display of letters and pictures that kids who had visited the cave sent back to us.

The other cave staff spend the downtime with gossip. They talk about everybody, and it can be quite malicious at times. But it does occupy them. I'd rather do constructive things, so now I'm reading a lot. But I'd rather be busy working. I strive for Wednesdays when we have lots of cruise-ship passengers and we're busy all day. It can be hectic and it can get very wild at times, but you're always busy.

Also, the day is more interesting if I have a chance to speak French or Spanish. In the summer I get to use my French a lot because we have students from Martinique and Guadeloupe here on student exchanges. I've always been interested in languages; I think it runs in my blood. My great-grandmother was Portuguese, my great-grandfather was from Africa, and my grandparents, who raised me, always encouraged me to study languages. I get looks sometimes when the visitors overhear me speaking French or Spanish. It puzzles them. Some will ask if there is another language on the island. I say, "No, we learn other languages at school." Actually, I learned it in school, but I used to go to Martinique on student exchanges every year. There is a lot of satisfaction in seeing native French or Spanish speakers be so surprised when they come to this place and meet someone who is actually able to respond to them in their own language. It also makes them more relaxed in the cave, knowing that somebody can understand them if something should happen.

Some visitors are shocked just to hear me speak proper English. They ask, "Did you go to school here?"

"Yes."

"But you speak so well."

Then I explain that we have a very good educational system. Sometimes they ask which school on the island, as if there is only one school that could provide such a standard. You even get some visitors who arrive thinking we all live in grass huts. Actually, it's a little amusing that people can be so narrow-minded and so ill-informed. I mean, if they are coming all this way for a holiday, you'd think they would know something about Barbados. You'd think they'd learn something about the place before they got here.

Some people seem disappointed to see that we are not primitive. It's as if they can't deal with it; the island isn't what they expected. Some are complimentary but others are shocked, and some can get very aggressive. And some of them believe that if you have tourist attractions, the country must be run by white people. One lady even said to me, "I didn't expect you to have colored people here." I said, "Well, most Barbadians are of African descent, so wouldn't you expect there to be a lot of dark people here?" She said, "No, because it's a tourist attraction." Sometimes it's not just ignorance but racism.

For me personally, I try not to be bothered by prejudice. But I know it happens. Like in the waiting hall, darker people will come in and sit up front. But when we call everybody to board the tram, they remain seated and let the white people go ahead. I don't know why it happens. If you sense that there is prejudice you try to put one group together at the front and the other group at the back, so they won't be facing one another. Usually you can't tell that someone's prejudiced until something really happens. For instance, one day I almost had to have this white man and this dark man taken off the tram because they didn't want to sit opposite one another. The white person didn't like the dark man talking. The black guy said, "Who are you to tell me that I can't talk?" They were both Americans.

No matter how many times you tell them, you still have some people who don't listen to you. I ask them not to touch the rock formations. Your hands have natural body oils on them that don't mix well with the calcium deposits. It retards their growth, so if you want a nice cave, you can't have people touching. Even though you tell them over and over, you still get people asking, "Why can't we touch?" There is always a certain percentage that don't want to obey the rules. Like this man from Puerto Rico. When the driver told him not to touch, he said, "Who do you think you are to tell me not to touch anything?" He was so aggressive that we had to call the supervisor and the warden to come down. And then he pretended he didn't speak English. We've had such a problem with people touching the formations that we now have a guard on every tram.

Sometimes we have a problem with people wanting to stand up on the tram. We tell them it's for their own safety. And once in a while we get a person that doesn't want to wear the hard hat that we require everyone to wear. One guy just refused to put it on. I told him it's no different than getting on an airplane and having the hostess tell you to buckle your seat belt. Here we ask you to wear a hard hat in case something falls from the roof of the cave. He said, "If you have a rule it should be printed on the ticket." I said, "If you print every rule there would be no room for the ticket." We went back and forth. By the end of the tour he had calmed down, and actually he was complimentary when he left.

Once in a while you get someone who is claustrophobic. I often ask in advance if anyone is claustrophobic but no one ever says anything. Then, once you're in the cave a person will whisper to you, "I'm claustrophobic." It's best to get them out of the cave because they will only get worse. If there is another tram heading to the exit, we'll put the person on it. If not, we'll off-load the people and take the person out and then come back. It's annoying because you had asked in advance if anyone had a problem. But I think it's human nature for people not to admit that they have a problem. A couple weeks ago I had a lady who was frantic, really frightened. I didn't tell the others what was wrong, I just said that we had to get her out because she wasn't feeling well. You don't want to scare the others.

Some people have trouble with the darkness when we turn the lights off. Some will even yell, "Turn the lights back on, turn the lights on!" I let the parents know that at some point we are going to turn the lights off, and if it's a problem for their child to let me know now. They say, "Oh, it's okay, he's not afraid of the dark," and then you hear the kids screaming.

The visitors are on holiday, so they expect the best from you. They expect everything to go smoothly, no mix-ups. They're here to relax, so they want you to do everything for them. You have to treat them very, very kindly. No matter how angry you get with them sometimes, you have to keep it in. A few of them come here with a world of problems on their shoulders, and they try to take it out on you, but you're not to resort to that type of behavior. In the training course for guides, they tell you over and over that the customer is always right.

If the tram breaks down or if there is a long wait and people aren't able to wait because their cruise ship is leaving, that's bad for business. The same is true if one of the staff is rude. Every visitor who has a negative experience is going to tell others. The guest leaves here unhappy, tells his friends, who tell their friends, and on and on. It's the domino effect. "I heard Harrison's Cave is the pits!" They are not going to say that it was just one tour guide or one driver that was unpleasant. No, they'll say, "The cave is the pits," and that bothers me. I've seen some of my co-workers treat the guests badly and they don't think of the repercussions.

To be honest, some of the staff shouldn't be working at Harrison's Cave at all. They are only here because a politician got them the job. Otherwise they would have never been hired. Some of them have been so lackadaisical for so long that they're never going to change.

Epilogue

While still working at Harrison's Cave and raising her 6-year-old son, Malika is now pursuing a degree in French and Spanish at the University of the West Indies and trying to discover "How [she] can best reach [her] full potential." She now uses the downtime on the job to do her homework. She was a nominee for Tour Guide of the Year, an award given by the Barbados Tourism Authority.

CAPTAIN, JOLLY ROGER PIRATE CRUISES
Dwayne Parry

The Jolly Roger *is an old inter-island cargo schooner enjoying a second life as a pirate-themed cruise boat. At 10 o'clock each morning it leaves its Bridgetown berth and travels under full sail along the west coast, carrying 8 crew and up to 250 passengers. It drops anchor near Holetown for two hours to allow its passengers to swim, snorkel, eat lunch, dance, and party on deck. Dwayne Parry, 41, has been a captain of the* Jolly Roger *for fourteen years. He grew up in Black Rock, near Bridgetown. Athletic and active, he played soccer and beach cricket and was one of the top runners for his secondary school. Fond of animals, he owned ten cows until he began to work on the* Jolly Roger. *Like most Barbadians, Dwayne left secondary school at 16 and entered the workforce, first with his stepfather on the shuttle bus that took tourists to the* Jolly Roger. *As a child he was often among tourists at the beach he frequented.*

When I was a kid, I thought the tourists were the best people in the world. I mean, I always looked up to them because they were white, they were better off, and they were friendly. I always had a good impression of them. Now, I know better than to think in terms of anybody being better off than anybody else.

I started working on the *Jolly Roger* in 1977 as a deckhand, primarily doing maintenance in the bathroom area. I worked alongside some experienced guys who taught me a lot about sailing the ship and how to deal with people. It was the first experience I'd ever had working with boats. In fact, my first exposure to the *Jolly Roger* was driving the shuttle bus bringing tourists to the boat. We had some good conversations with tourists before and after their cruise, and I got to thinking I'd like to work on board. When there was an opening for a deckhand in 1977, I grabbed it. I worked in different positions—barman, lifeguard, and so on—and management saw that I had some potential as a leader. In August 1986 they made me a captain.

As captain I'm in charge of everything on board the ship, overseeing everything that is done for the safety of the passengers and ensuring that they have a good time on board. At 8 o'clock in the

The *Jolly Roger* sailing along the west coast with a full load of visitors. *Courtesy of Barbados Tourism Authority.*

morning I come in and make sure the crew is reporting to work, and I check to see how many passengers I'm going to carry. I go over the vessel to make sure that it is clean, that the food and drink are on board, that the engineer has checked out the ship, and that my staff is in position to welcome the guests as they arrive on board. At 10 A.M. we depart, and as we sail along the island, I make a speech about safety, life jackets, and so on. I tell them about the places of interest along the coastline.

There are two captains on every cruise. One stays at the wheel, while the other moves around the ship to mix with the guests. One is an entertainer, and the other watches the ship. You talk to the people and find out how they feel, if they're enjoying themselves. One conversation leads to another. You relax people by telling them where you are from and asking them how it is in Canada or England or wherever they're from. People tell you basic things, like it's very cold down there. You might ask them what kind of work they do. If it's their first time in Barbados, they might ask you a lot of questions, like what the main resources here are. You tell them sugar and tourism. Sometimes they have a misconception about where Barbados is located. People who don't know the region well believe the West Indian islands are very close together. So you'll set them straight and tell them where Barbados is in comparison to Jamaica and Trinidad. A lot of conversations involve comparing Barbados to the places they come from—governments, resources, education, that sort of thing.

I like a balance, where you give me your experience and I give you my experience. I tell you what things in Barbados are like and you tell me what things in Canada are like. For instance, when I tell people that education and medical are free in Barbados, they are like, "Wow." That blows their minds because people think that in a small country like Barbados that doesn't have a lot of resources, people would have to pay for schooling and health services. When you talk about schooling, a lot of tourists who have traveled around the country mention that our schoolkids dress very well. A lot of tourists like the fact that they wear school uniforms. We think that it's the big things that tourists look at, but it's often the small things that they find interesting, like school uniforms.

Steering the boat is the easiest job. It's just a matter of running down the coastline and knowing the depth and where the reefs are located. You don't need a lot of navigation or radar experience. It's a simple straight course down the west coast and then a simple straight course back again to Bridgetown.

We get to Sunset Crest around 11 A.M. and drop anchor. We announce the things that people can do, like snorkeling or taking the barge ashore to the beach. Then we start preparing the lunch. The captains help out with cooking the steaks and chicken on the barbeque. Once lunch is completed, we try to create a little more atmosphere on board the ship, like seeing how many people we can get on the rope swing at once. There's a large rope attached to the mast that swings from the deck out over the sea, and people hang onto it and then drop off into the water. At 1 o'clock we pull up anchor and head back toward Bridgetown. On the way we do a pirate wedding on the top deck. It's a takeoff of a regular wedding to which we add entertaining lines to make it funny, like, "Did you bring a ring for this occasion?" The person says no because we've just picked these two people out of the crowd. Then you say something like, "Well, you cheap son-of-a-gun." That gets a laugh every time. Years ago a pirate captain had the power to marry people on board ship or he could hang them, either way. That's what we try to imitate.

The pirate wedding only takes about fifteen minutes, and after that people party all the way back to Bridgetown. We get back around 2 o'clock and make sure the passengers get off the ship safely. Then we come back to the office to report anything that needs to be reported, like problems or repairs.

When I move around the ship, I try and get a feeling for the people, try to get their pulse. If they're into a partying atmosphere, I adjust the music accordingly, depending on the group. If I have a lot of middle-aged people, they probably like rock-and-roll music from the '60s. If I've got a lot of English people, some of them like Bob Marley and some like calypso. With black Americans, I know that they like to party from the time they board the ship until they get back. Sometimes I start playing normal music and I see that people aren't responding, not getting out there and dancing, so I switch to rock-and-roll or disco. Once I see people coming to the dance floor, then I know this is the music they like.

When I approach a passenger, I can tell from the level of their vocal cords whether they're interested in speaking to me or not. Some people just want to say hi and go on without rubbing shoulders. Others want to sit down and talk. I can tell whether this person wants to talk to me or not. I find that women often like to go into depth, to go really far down to understand things, whereas men would rather debate. Women are more interested in how people are. Women hardly ever get into hard-core politics; they'd rather talk about health services, children, and education. The men are often more interested in what kind of government you have, what kind of systems. And they like to make suggestions for how to do things. To be honest, I find that Americans tend to be the better debaters, more outspoken than the English or other Europeans. The English are more easygoing, more accepting. If I mention Tony Blair to English people, they won't really get into it a lot, they kind of let the subject go. Whereas if I mention George Bush to American people, they like to get into it, at least the men. The people from Sweden, Germany, and Holland are not very fluent in English, so our conversations are shorter and I get less information from them. But I know for a fact that I've learned something about Americans, Canadians, and the English from talking to guests.

Most of our passengers are young, 20 to 35. And I'd say about 60 percent are British. Years ago we had mostly Canadians and Americans, but the North American market has dropped tremendously, while the UK market has really picked up. Wherever they're from, the people have changed, too. They're now more safety-conscious, and they don't drink as much. Everything—food and drink is free on board. But we're only serving half as much alcohol as we were years ago. Back then you'd have people who drank until they were drunk and stumbled off the boat or had to be lifted off. You don't see much of that today.

We have very few problems. If it starts to rain when the cruise is already well under way, it has no effect. Often people party better when it's wet than when the sun is out and it's hot. I'd say the best parties we ever had were in the rain, after a few rum punches and people had a chance to get into the water. If they're already wet on the outside, it doesn't make any difference if it's raining. But if the rain starts early, before people have started to party, then a lot of them will take shelter and not party much. The only real problems we've had relate to alcohol. Alcohol is something that changes people; they act differently after a few drinks. Years ago we had people who jumped off the boat while it was traveling after they'd had too much to drink. But like I said, today you don't see many people doing stupid or foolish or ignorant things because of drink.

I think the *Jolly Roger* appeals to people because it's a package. It's a combination of things—a sight-seeing tour on the way down, plus swimming, snorkeling, the rope swing, the deck wedding, the meal, the music, and the party atmosphere. It's the total package that makes people have a good time. Right now we're trying to bring back more of the piracy theme. The original owners of the *Jolly Roger* sold the company in 1991, and the new owners toned down the piracy stuff. Now that the original owners have repurchased the company, they're trying to bring back the piracy.

Being around tourists all day has killed my social life. After all the talking to people and partying, the last thing I want to do is be around anybody when I get home. I just want to be by myself. When I get home, I get the newspaper and put my feet in the air and relax. I take the rest of the day off. I need that time alone to recuperate and to recharge for the next day. My girlfriend understands what I do, so if she wants to go out someplace she'll invite a friend or one of my cousins to accompany her. They'll go out as a team rather than putting me on the spot.

I think talking to tourists has widened my knowledge of people and the world. It has led me to think that all people are under the same struggle. A lot of Bajans think that tourists have a lot of money, a lot of privileges, and this and that. I used to think that too when I was young, and even when driving the shuttle. But getting to know visitors on the boat has led me to a different level of thinking. Whatever their nationality, whatever their standard of living, all people are basically similar. Our customs may be different but deep down we're all the same. We might think that because they're white or American or Canadian that they're better off, but often they're not. All people, whether they are black or white or yellow, have the same problems.

I never get tired of the job because every day I meet somebody different. People are the motivators in this line of work. There are so many different people and so many different things being said that it carries you into a different world when you sit or stand there and talk to them. It's a whole lot better than sitting in front of a computer in an office. I'd much rather look at people's faces than at a screen.

Epilogue

The *Jolly Roger* was sold to a Trinidadian company a few years after this interview. After returning from an evening cruise, it sprang a leak during the night and sank in its berth. The company, Tall Ships, has plans to build a new *Jolly Roger* in Canada, made of fiberglass but with the appearance of wood. Meanwhile, Dwayne is a captain on the MV *Harbour Master,* and, in the words of his colleague Rosie Hartmann, "He is a huge asset to the company. He is a natural and knows the business inside out . . . a tremendous personality who has made tourism his career."

OWNER-OPERATOR, CYCLING TOURS
Robert Quintyne

Robert Quintyne, 32, was raised in a middle-class Bridgetown household. His mother was headmistress at Queens College, an elite secondary school; his father an agronomist. I first met Robert in 1990 when he was the activities coordinator at Heywoods Resort. I lost contact with him for some years until 1998, when I chanced upon him in a distant corner of the island leading six young Germans across an exposed reef before huge crashing waves. He was showing them one of the most spectacular coastal settings on the island in an area unknown to most tourists.

When I was at school, I really wanted to be a marine biologist. I spent one summer helping out at Bellairs Research Institute, collecting samples, to see if it was for me. I really liked it, but everybody said, "Look, if you do marine biology in school you'll either end up teaching biology or working for the Fisheries Department." I wasn't going to be doing new important studies that would actually be of use, so I forgot about marine biology.

By chance I got into tourism, first with a travel company called Sun Link Inc. We organized itineraries and activities for large groups, like 250 people, from companies like General Electric and Ford Motor. They would send their people down for a week in Barbados, and we'd organize everything from the time they landed till the time they left. I left Sun Link after a year and started doing things on my own, like making jewelry out of clay, and for a while my sister and I did hand-painted greeting cards.

I only got back into tourism when I went overseas. My mother was in England, and I was looking around for things to do. I saw a degree program in tourism and leisure management in Luton, outside of London. I thought it would be pretty cool, and what drew me was that they went on field trips and got to travel. When I finished their two-year course I came back to Barbados and got a job at Heywoods Resort as their activities coordinator. I really wanted a job in sales and marketing, but there were none around. Bajans have this mindset that when you mention tourism they automatically think hotel. If you've studied tourism, they immediately think that you know how to run the front desk, do rooms, or whatever. But that wasn't at all what I'd learned in England.

Heywoods had something called a "kids club," which to their credit was the only one in any of the hotels on the island. Basically, we organized activities for the kids staying on the property, everything from little arts and crafts to water sports to just taking them around the island. I got to know a lot about foreign kids. For example, the American kids were a lot more outspoken than any of the others. They weren't shy; they spoke their minds. Bajan children of the same age are much more reserved in what they say. But American kids would even talk back to the parents. Wow, we couldn't get away with that. The English and European kids weren't nearly as brash. English children were curious, questioned things more, while the American kids had more confidence. When they spoke, they spoke with authority whether they were right or wrong.

We also organized activities for the adults, like fashion shows, calypso dancing sessions, and a Bajan taste test where they could sample Bajan delicacies like turnovers and coconut bread. One of the favorites was a beer-drinking contest. You had to drink three bottles of beer nonstop. The European men did very well; it was always an Englishman or a German that won. But there was one time when an American woman beat everybody. Everybody was totally blown away by it. It was a doss [easy] job, but when Heywoods switched ownership and became the Almond Beach Resort I left. By then I knew that I didn't want to work in a hotel unless it was in sales and marketing.

In 1995, myself and an American guy started a mountain-bike rental and touring company called Irie Mountain Bikes. I had six planned routes, ranging from on-road stuff for beginners to rugged, hilly off-road riding for the advanced. I'd always have a vehicle following, meeting us at points along the way carrying food and at the end to transport the bikes and people home. The riders were surprised at the diversity of the terrain on the island. If you're staying on the south coast you're only seeing one side of the island, which is all beaches, hotels, and lots of people. But when you take them up to the north or to the east they're like, "Wow! This is a different environment." Small villages, lots of open space, cane fields, chicken farms, and steep cliffs. Sometimes we'd tour with six to eight riders, other times just two. And there were a few times we took out just one person because you don't want to say no. When you're starting a new business, it looks bad when someone calls and you say, "Sorry, we can't do just one person."

A lot of our bike rentals were to Europeans. They'd rather go off on their own than do a tour. North Americans and some British were more interested in having a guided tour, where you pick them up at their hotel, go ride for the day, and then take them back. It has to do with the lifestyle the people are coming from. The whole cycling, outdoor thing is big in Europe. We even had Europeans in their 50s and 60s renting a bike and going out on their own. Europeans are not so worried that the sun is going to be too hot or the trail too difficult.

Bajans, in general, aren't interested in going out on a bike for a day. Cycling is something people did years ago when they were poor. Today this is a car society. Everything is based around the car. Bajans will pay to work out and ride an exercise bike at a gym, but most won't ride a bike on the road.

A big problem selling cycling tours is that you're competing with so many other activities and services. Also, tourists depend a lot on what the tour reps recommend to them. Some tourists are independent enough to do their own thing, but most believe whatever the tour reps tell them, like, "You should go on the *Jolly Roger.*" "Okay, we'll go on the *Jolly Roger.*" The tour reps weren't any help to us because they don't know much about cycling and therefore don't push it to their guests. So unless a visitor had a prior interest in cycling and inquired about it on his own, he didn't come our way.

Our partnership went sour after a while. My American partner was really looking at Barbados as a kind of holiday home, and he wasn't into the business as much as he should have been. He put up the money in the beginning and I did the work. But when he came down he lived the good life, and the bills ran up. He was paying $2,000 a month for a house, which really wasn't necessary because the business could be run from one bedroom, since it was mostly done by telephone. But he wanted the huge house and lifestyle he was accustomed to in the United States. And he was running up huge phone bills. We were losing money, and after a while I got angry and said, "Enough is enough." Then all of our bikes got stolen. I was stashing them in my sister's garage and somebody came in and took them. So we shut down.

A few years ago I set up a new company called Caribbean Cycling. I'm doing the same active adventure travel I did before, but now I do the marketing outside of Barbados, with direct mailings to mountain-bike and outdoor clubs in North America. I'm trying to get people who are actually involved in the sport. I've also made it a multi-island company. Our tours take place in both Barbados and Tobago.

You need to offer your riders a certain level of service—like offering them drinks and food at the right time—if they are to really enjoy themselves. At the same time you don't want to crowd them. A lot of times I found that by the end of the tour, when it came time to have a picnic lunch, they'd be serving me drinks and serving me lunch. That used to blow me away because as far as I'm concerned that's what I'm supposed to be doing. But they'd say, "Hey, sit down, you relax, you've been working hard."

That's the kind of thing that's never going to happen on a tour bus. You can be sure of that. There the tour guide has a sheep-herding mentality. It's follow, follow, follow. But when you have small groups of people, like you do in cycling, you can have one-on-one conversations. Pretty soon you begin to bond with them. Then they want to come back on their next holiday and do it again. Like right now there's a 35-year-old woman from New York who works in the fashion industry who's come back every year since '95. Whenever she gets here, she calls: "Robert, I'm here, we need to go riding." Whether she comes for one week or two, every day I take her riding. Every single day. Mostly early in the morning before the sun gets hot. I take her out for two hours and she pays me $45 U.S. Part of me says, "You know, you don't have to pay me because it's something I would do on my own anyway." She says, "No, it's your business."

On the rides you get a range of people, from the very wealthy to those who came down on a charter flight. But usually by the end of the ride everybody will have bonded because they're all doing the same thing, all facing the same challenges. Even where people might be standoffish at the beginning of the tour, by the end they're exchanging addresses. Even though I personally don't have a lot to do with that, it's nice being a catalyst for that kind of experience.

And once I know that people are happy that makes me happy. I can usually tell by the comments they make or leave in the guest book. So most days I feel pretty good. I'd like to be making more money, but doing this is a lot better than working in an office, wearing a collar and tie all day. I know a lot of those jobs pay well and you have all the nice creature comforts, but they don't make you happy. A lot of office workers don't get their happiness until Friday night when they go to the Boat Yard [nightclub] to drink. I know a lot of people like that, and basically they get old before their years. They're trapped. They're not willing to risk leaving their job because they've put in x number of years and they don't want to lose that pension. A lot of them wish they could leave and do something else, but they're not prepared to take the risk.

Here I'm doing it for me, not working for someone else. And I'm outdoors. I'm not looking to get rich, I just want to make enough money to get by. And I like the idea of providing people with an experience they really enjoy, something they can look back on: "Yeah, I had a really good time in Barbados and I saw places that most visitors never see."

What do you learn from having so much exposure to tourists?

I am not sure, but it makes me want to see some of the places that they've been, places like Colorado with its mountain biking and outdoor lifestyle. I'd like to go to Norway and see the fjords, based on what people have told me. I'm not interested in New York or California because I'd rather go somewhere quiet, small town–type places.

I've learned that how you're raised and the kind of education you get make a big difference in how you think about things. Knowledge has a lot to do with it. Some people come here not really knowing anything about Barbados. Not a clue. Some of them come here thinking we're really poor and backward and then they're surprised to see the level of development and the education here. They have this vision of a little paradise where the natives are running around half-dressed.

I think this job has taught me a lot about other peoples, too. Like I find the Germans to be very, very rigid. They're very authoritarian when they say things, even if they don't mean it. They just come across that way. They're a very disciplined people. If they put their mind to do something, they do it. The Swiss and the Austrians are also very, very disciplined. I find Europeans overall are more independent, more willing to go out on their own, while Americans tend to prefer organized activities, organized tours—they're more inclined to do what the tour guide tells them. Europeans might listen to the guide but then make up their own minds. Even when Europeans are staying in a really nice hotel, they still want to get out on their own. But I've been impressed with some American teens who ask a lot of questions about rock formations and how the island was developed. Wow, I didn't expect that from them. We get questions from them that you expect older people to ask. But maybe that's because they're cyclists.

But overall it's the English who are probably most interested in Barbados because they already know a little bit about it. They've heard of Barbados as "Little England." A lot of them come here because of our English history and colonization. Also, they feel very safe here. It's almost like they're home in a way. So I find them very curious. They want to get into the actual heartbeat of the island, as opposed to the tourist side of things. Like they want to know about the politics.

How do your clients hear about you?

Most are referred. Like I know a German guy who brings in a new group every two weeks, and he pushes for me because he knows that a lot of his clients would rather go cycling than sit on a tour bus. A lot of his clients are young people—wind-surfers—and some days when there is no wind, he'll suggest that they go cycling.

I also do a little business with cyclists from cruise ships. A lot of them bring their bikes onboard, though some ships now supply bikes as well. When they get off, they don't know where to go, so I go down to the port to meet the ships and try to sell the cyclists a ride. Sometimes that's difficult, because if they've been to Mexico and places like that they're used to paying next to nothing. They find Barbados very expensive. I had an incident last year where a guy had thirty-six cyclists from a bike club in Minnesota. I offered my service as a guide for the day, leading them around the island. When the leader asked me how much I was charging, I offered him a group price of $200 U.S. My price was very reasonable. I'd have responsibility for thirty-six cyclists for the whole day and I'd provide a van to trail the group. But he thought that was way too much, my fee was going to cut too deep into his profits. He was thinking $200 is a lot for a guy from the Caribbean to be making in one day. He offered me less. I finally said, "Forget it," and went home. You have to feel badly for the thirty-six cyclists because this guy didn't have a clue where to lead them.

It's been an uphill struggle getting the Barbados tourism people interested in what I'm doing. I get all the usual lip service—ya, ya, ya—send me information. I send the information but never hear from them. Barbados is the kind of society where if you know the right people things will get done for you. Obviously I don't know the right people. But a lot of it is that they have a narrow notion of tourism. They don't have the vision to see that cycling tours are something new and different and really can work.

Right now I'm developing my cycling tours in Tobago. Tobago is like Barbados twenty-five years ago, before this island became so developed. Unless you've been coming here for many years, you don't realize how much Barbados has changed. It used to have a niche as a "little paradise." Now that the whole world has become tourist-oriented, there are lots of places where you can have the same sun, sea, and sand and for a lot cheaper than here. Like the islands of the South Pacific, and I hear the service is a whole lot better there.

I think you can already see that we're losing some of our tourists to other places. And our reefs aren't what they used to be. I remember growing up and going snorkeling off Heywoods and you'd see a tremendous amount of fish and marine life. Tons of black coral. Today there isn't any black coral because everybody pulled it up to make jewelry or to take home as a souvenir. And the way the island is developing, it's becoming more difficult for mountain biking. A lot of the trails I used to ride are now gone. Up in St. Thomas [parish] where we actually staged a race earlier this year, the whole area has now been bulldozed for new housing. So I now find myself looking to other islands to ride.

I just hope Tobago doesn't make the same mistakes. They need a lot of education about their environment and the effects of tourism on it. Like they let fishermen put out seine nets on the reef at night, nets that trap fish of all sizes and shapes. When they pull them onto the beach in the morning they leave the fish they don't want to rot on the sand. In Barbados those nets are banned, as they should be. When I was first down in Tobago it would take a whole village to pull in a net, they'd be bursting with fish. No longer. And they're not doing much to protect their reefs, either. They're letting tourists get out of the boat, put on water shoes, and walk on the reef. It damages the corals, and now you can see huge areas where the reef is dead. Tobago also has lots of turtles that nest there, but they let the fishermen slaughter them and take the eggs. I know it's hard to tell old men who have been fishing all their lives that they can no longer hunt turtles. It's hard to change old habits, but something has to be done.

7 THE RESEARCH AND PROMOTION OF TOURISM

In 1958, as tourism to the Caribbean region was beginning to take off, the Barbadian government created the Barbados Tourist Board as the authority responsible for marketing and promoting the island. In 1993, the name was changed to the Barbados Tourism Authority (BTA); however, its mission remained the same: "to position Barbados as a premier globally competitive year-round warm-weather destination contributing to a sustainable quality of life for all Barbadians." To do this, the BTA has offices or representatives in many overseas cities, including New York, Los Angeles, Miami, Toronto, London, Munich, Stockholm, and Paris. In Europe and North America, BTA employees travel from city to city presenting audiovisual shows, giving speeches, running question-and-answer sessions, and distributing promotional materials to trade, business, and airline personnel and anyone else who can influence people to travel to and/or holiday in Barbados.

Back at the head office in Barbados, familiarization trips are arranged for travel agents, journalists, authors, television crews, and photographic groups. They are shown a sampling of hotels and attractions; in exchange for the BTA's hospitality, it is hoped they will create favorable publicity for the island. The other important area under the BTA's jurisdiction is the education of the Barbadian people regarding tourism. There is no point in advertising the attractions of the island if the hosts are not going to make the visitors feel welcome. In the private sector, the Barbados Hotel and Tourism Association (BHTA) is also actively involved in promoting and marketing Barbados's tourism product, and it has been doing so since the 1950s. The BHTA is a 300-member association of tourism-related businesses, notably hotels and resorts, whose mission is to bring people, research, and technology together in the tourism arena "to stage a world-class experience and performance." The association was established in 1952 and it was then called the Barbados Hotel Association, reflecting the focus of tourism at that time on hotels and resorts. As the tourism industry matured and expanded with everything from the *Jolly Roger* and Atlantis Submarines to hiking and biking tours, its name was revised in 1994 to the more inclusive Barbados Hotel and Tourism Association. In this chapter, the president of the BHTA, Colin Jordan, talks about his life and work in promoting tourism and in educating Barbadians about its importance. Then, in the final narrative, Everton Gill, the chief research officer of the Ministry of Tourism and International Transport, the other government body that deals with tourism policy and research, explains his research, most of which is concerned with gathering data on tourist arrivals, length of stay, and expenditures and how the information is used.

BARBADOS HOTEL AND TOURISM ASSOCIATION
Colin Jordan

Beginning his career as an accountant, Colin Jordan developed an interest in human resource management and rapidly rose to become the CEO of a hotel group. In 2009, he was elected president of the Barbados Hotel and Tourism Association, a nonprofit trade association whose members promote sustainable growth and development of Barbados's tourism product. Intellectual and curious, Colin, age 41, is married to a schoolteacher and has two young daughters. He is passionate about the development of his island homeland.

When I was growing up the feeling was that tourists were people who had a lot of money. I remember very clearly that if a vendor was selling, say, mangos for 1 dollar, it was understood that the price would be 1 Barbados dollar for locals and 1 U.S. dollar for tourists. Twice as much. It wasn't done out of any malice; rather people felt that tourists could afford to pay more because their money was worth twice what ours was worth, and they were coming from a rich country. But beyond being aware of that, I wasn't really interested in tourists, even though we often saw them traveling through the countryside and walking the streets in Bridgetown.

While growing up, my grandfather had an over-the-counter shop in Rose Hill, St. Peter, and my dad had a small wholesale business in which he would buy items in quantity from large merchants in Bridgetown and then sell smaller quantities to the shops in St. Lucy and St. Peter. Barbados has lots of small shops and their owners and operators must buy in small quantities due to cash flow constraints. I did deliveries to small shops around St. Peter and St. Lucy for my father. When my grandfather grew old and decided he'd had enough of the shop, my dad took it over and turned it into a mini-mart [a small supermarket]. I worked there all through my childhood and teens and had to work very hard—mornings before school, after school, and during school vacations. It was work, work, work. So you can see that I grew up in a business environment, and I believe it prepared me for the future. I left Harrison College so that I could study business subjects at the advanced level.

When I went to university [University of the West Indies] here at Cave Hill I registered to study economics. My dad said that it was not going to be very easy getting a job in Barbados as an economist, and that I should also think about doing accounting where there were more opportunities. He suggested doing a double major, economics and accounting. I listened to him, and he was right. For one, the accounting courses were a lot easier for me than economics. My best grades were always in accounting and I became known as a relatively strong accounting student. When I was leaving [graduating from] the university I told one of my accounting lecturers, Dr. Robertine Chadderton, that I wanted to be a consultant business advisor. She said okay but suggested that I spend three years in an audit firm and then branch off into that area. That was 1990. I finished my exams in May and by the first of July I was working for KPMG, one of the big international accounting firms. Dr. Chadderton had said to spend three years there and that's exactly what I did, to the very day. I then went into tourism.

I was thinking that tourism is what fuels our economy in Barbados and that it will be the last industry that the government would ever allow to collapse. Sugar was on the way out and I didn't think other types of agriculture had very good prospects. As a country we just didn't seem to be able to get our heads around what we were going to do post-sugar, after the inevitable decline of the sugar industry. Were we still going to produce enough sugar to satisfy domestic consumption? Were we going to get into the export of cotton? And with regard to fruits and vegetables, were we going to grow them to satisfy domestic demand or grow for export? These questions still haven't been answered. Successive governments have not been able to make a decision on what we're going to do with our agriculture, or even decide on what the focus is going to be—domestic demand versus export. So I decided that tourism was going to be the industry with the best future.

At first, I was thinking of looking for a job with the airlines because I knew that airline employees could fly around for very little money, but then I applied and got a job with the St. James Beach Hotel Group, which is now called Elegant Hotels Group. I became the senior accountant at their Tamarind Cove Hotel, which was the largest hotel in the group. But before I left KPMG a senior partner cautioned me that tourism was fickle, that it was subject to natural disasters, global recession, and other uncertainties that made it very vulnerable. Well, I had already made up my mind that tourism was the place to be and that the government was dependent on tourism for the country's success. At that time many of my colleagues who left accounting firms were going into international business because it paid very well, but I still thought tourism was a better choice.

I stayed with the company for over four years and while I was there I became good friends with the director of human resources at our hotel group. I would spend a great deal of time talking to him about procedures and management. I would assist the HR staff with things that were accounts-related. I think because of my background working in the family business I had learned the importance of managing people and that it was the hardest part of business. In my fourth year at Tamarind Cove, the company changed hands. New ownership came in and I didn't like the new direction of the company, so I thought it would be better to try something new. I applied for the position of chief accountant at Asta Beach Hotel and was successful. Before I took the job my old supervisor advised me that based on my experience I should request the job title of "financial controller." Asta agreed—it wasn't going to cost them any more money. Also, when I was about to take the job, I told them I wanted to start an HR department and received permission to do so. I began to compile records for the staff, deal with issues like absenteeism, and I got involved in counseling, industrial relations, and dealing with the union—things that really interested me. After a few years doing these things I became director of finance and administration. That was a very rewarding segment of my life. Later on, Asta became Amaryllis Beach Resort and part of the Palm Beach Hotel Group, and I became the chief executive officer.

As financial officer and later CEO did you
have much contact with tourists at the hotels?

Yes, more than you would expect. I think my upbringing in the family business and my father's influence made me always think of the bigger picture, so even though I was an accountant I would go out and talk to the guests and try to get to know them a bit. When I saw them in the corridor I would stop and speak to them and ask them how they were doing. I was sort of doing the general hospitality stuff that is expected of hotel managers. When our offices were moved inland into an office complex and I was no longer on the hotel property, I still often went down to the hotel to talk with the staff and the guests and to observe them. I attended the weekly cocktail parties for the hotel guests. I learned how to talk to them and get information about where they lived, what they did for a living, what they liked or didn't like about their trip to Barbados. When you do that you get to realize that most tourists are regular people—nurses, teachers, builders, roofers, farmers—and not just movie stars and sports figures like Tiger Woods, Simon Cowell, and others who visit Barbados and are written up in the newspaper. It was something that I also encouraged my accounting colleagues to do because I strongly believe that it's important for accountants, actually for all people who work behind the scenes, to understand and become familiar with the people who generate our tourism revenue. It's important to know where the money comes from.

Accountants by their nature are not very people-oriented. Many believe that we like to sit in front of the computer all day crunching numbers. We are not like the food and beverage managers or the wait staff who just naturally enjoy interacting with people. Accountants are not very chatty. You have to coax accountants to get out there and talk. Plus I recognized that it was a weakness in my own character, that my interactions with people were not great. It was just more natural for me to sit at my desk and do my work than to get up and go out and interact with guests. That was one of the reasons I started going out to meet the guests, and a reason why I decided to study and practice HR.

Has that interaction noticeably improved your social skills?

Yes, I believe so. It has enabled me to form conversations with people I don't know. It has also developed my listening skills. The demographic for visitors to Barbados tends to be slightly older than for some other islands, especially among our English visitors. People who are older have lots of experiences that they want to share, and if they find a good listener they can talk all night. I became very sensitive to older people because when they are talking you realize that they are enjoying the conversation so much, that they enjoy telling you their stories. I learned how to ask the appropriate questions to keep them going, and to let them know that I was interested in hearing their stories. So, yes, conversing with guests has bettered my own social skills. And I have learned much from listening to their experiences.

What led you to become president of Barbados Hotel
and Tourism Association at such a young age?

When I was at Amaryllis I wanted to get more involved in the industry, and so I volunteered with the BHTA and indicated that I'd

like to serve on the HR committee. I was really loving human resource management. On the HR committee I got to know many
people in the industry outside of my hotel. During this time I was
also very involved in church leadership [Seventh-Day Adventist
church] as an elder and evangelism leader. Between the hotel, the
BHTA, and the church I was easily working twelve-hour days,
about sixty hours a week. I had been on the BHTA board about
seven years when a former president of the BHTA, Peter Odle,
asked me if I'd ever thought of running for president. As I thought
it over, my mind went back to a conversation I'd had with an attor-
ney and former magistrate from St. Lucy by the name of Emerson
Graham. Emerson was lamenting the fact that many young Bajan
males were uninvolved in civic society. As a former magistrate, he'd
had a lot of experience with young males, and he liked that I was a
board member of the BHTA and also involved in church administration. So when Peter Odle asked if I was interested in becoming president that conversation with Emerson came back to me and I said
yes. To make a long story short, I was elected over two more experienced candidates.

What is it about young Bajan males not being engaged in society?

This is not limited to Barbados, but it is certainly evident here.
Our young males are not going after leadership roles in society. It is
the women who are trying to further their education, trying to
move ahead, trying to get a career, trying to get a house. It is the
women who do better in school. Our young men are very laid-back;
they like to lime [hang out] on the block, and often they get into
trouble. Not many of them seem to be trying to make a mark for
themselves. Not many of them are seen to be contributing to society. Of course that's a generalization and there are exceptions. Emerson Graham saw this up close in the court system, as a magistrate.
There are several reasons people put forward for this state of affairs.
One is the struggle of past generations of Barbadians to earn a living. It started with slavery of course, but long after that you had so
many Barbadians emigrating to find work and having to work hard
in the United States, England, or Canada just to get by. Among
them, who sacrificed so much, there is the feeling that their children should not have to work as hard as they did. Secondly, there is
also the influence of the U.S. culture on our thinking, with its ma-
terialism and emphasis on acquiring wealth and possessions and
wanting to do it quickly and often not without the hard work. We

Barbadians have been exposed to your consumer society through the media, especially TV shows and the movies. At the same time there has been a breakdown in discipline. This is certainly not limited to Barbados, as I think it's also become common in the United States and elsewhere in the world as well. There's a pretty strongly held view in Barbados that the social movement away from corporal punishment, away from tough punishment, to more talk and negotiation has not worked well. Because of all this we have a lot of young people who have become wayward, undisciplined, and not very ambitious. And that is very unfortunate.

As president of the BHTA, what are your concerns about the future of tourism in Barbados?

I grew up hearing the slogan "Tourism is our business, let's play our part." But I am convinced that hardly any of us growing up knew what that slogan meant. As I said before, I am very aware that tourism is critical to our economy and given the social changes in our society, like the decline of discipline, it would be very easy for people who are not aware of tourism's importance to destroy it. So a big concern of mine is to see that all Barbadians become aware of the contribution of tourism to our economy. As a society we have not educated people enough about the role of tourism. I believe Barbadians are intelligent people and that once they have information they make right decisions. As a small country we've weathered a lot of storms that have severely impacted larger countries with far more resources than us, and we have been able to do that because Barbadians are sensible people. So I think that once the information is out there, Barbadians will make the right choices. That is the overarching theme in what I do here at the BHTA.

How do you go about educating Barbadians to the importance of tourism?

I have met with all the media houses and have tried to enlist their assistance in getting our message out to the public. And I have promised to work with them by being accessible, even giving them my cell phone number. People in similar positions are usually advised not to give their cell number to reporters. I have promised reporters that I will never say "no comment" to their questions, no matter what the question is. I will never brush them off. As a result the BHTA is developing a good relationship with the media and it's paying off as people are saying that they now hear a lot more about tourism from us. When we at the BHTA speak today, we try to put forward things that are educational and better inform Barbadians about tourism.

We also meet with the Ministry of Education and Human Resources to get our message across to children. Children are our most impressionable citizens and can be reached much more easily than older people. In the back of our heads, we wanted tourism to be a subject in the school curriculum. But the ministry was not amenable to that because the curriculum is already full and they can't think of anything they could drop to make room for tourism. With my wife, Charmaine, being a teacher and with my parents having been teachers, I am aware of that reality. When I first met with the ministry they expected that I was going to push for tourism to be a full-fledged subject. I said, "No, that's not it at all." I told them that my wife had given me a social studies syllabus in which tourism is one component. I said I wanted to work with the ministry to help them bring that component alive, to make it something that will really engage students. And we've had good response from them, especially since the education officer in charge of curricula is a relative of my wife. Because of that relationship, along with the importance of the awareness we were proposing, we are getting some movement and cooperation from the ministry on this.

We also launched an essay competition in primary and secondary schools in which children write about tourism. The subject this year was "Tourism is key for all of us—let's treat it with the respect it deserves," and the students wrote what that meant to them. Over seventy essays were submitted for judging, and we have just given out the winning prizes. Also, to help the tourism component come alive we are having industry practitioners—hotel managers, food and beverage people, even those who work back-of-house—go into the schools and give lectures about their work in the industry and tourism in general. And we are trying to expose teachers to tourism by inviting them to stay in a resort hotel for free, to eat in one of our restaurants, to go on tours, and to experience the other attractions for free. We want them to experience firsthand our tourism product—we want to immerse them in the industry so that they will then go back to the classroom well informed and hopefully excited about what tourism has to offer.

Another thing we are planning is to have hotels and other tourism businesses adopt particular schools and develop a relationship with that school. This will involve inviting the students down to the sponsoring hotel and tourism attraction. They are letting the children know that tourism businesses are not something that just rich, white people or foreigners enjoy but are there for all members of the community. Something else we are working on is to reach out to that segment of society, mostly young guys but some girls, who are not interested in news and academic stuff and who just listen to music, just listen to their iPods all the time and don't read a newspaper or magazine. They generally don't pay attention to what's going on in society. We need to reach these people, and since they are no longer at school we decided to place thirty- to sixty-second spots on the popular radio music stations, so that when they're listening to their music they will also be getting some information. We have to do it in short segments, because they're not going to listen to a five-minute spiel at one time. But by doing it often enough, even for thirty seconds at a time, we can get tourism into their subconscious.

What is a typical workday like for you, as head of the BHTA?

As we are talking, I have my computer on and I am constantly getting all kinds of questions such as how to respond to an industrial relations matter, what is our official position on this or that, or questions about developing a marketing package for Barbados. I'm always responding to these queries. And then I write several pieces each month about tourism and the work of the BHTA for our newsletter and for a page that we do in the *Barbados Advocate* newspaper. At the moment I am also writing a welcome piece for the next issue of the *Barbados Trident* magazine [a publication of the Barbados Tourism Authority] and an article for a special tourism issue on a business website. And then I have to write an assessment of the new proposed budget. And then there are invitations to all kinds of cocktail parties, lunches, and dinners that you're expected to go to as president. So it's crazy. Some days during the Christmas period you have two or three invitations. Peter Odle told me before I took the job that I was going to be running from meeting to meeting to meeting and that's exactly how it's been. But actually I enjoy doing it, even the meetings as long as they are meaningful and I feel that I'm contributing something to moving some project forward. I've always believed that if you have an opinion or a view on something, then you need to put yourself in a position where you can have influence on decisions.

What do you do with what little free time you have outside of work?

Outside of work there is my involvement in the administration of my church. I also spend the free time I have with my family, especially my wife, Charmaine. I sometimes leave the children with their grandparents, and go out with Charmaine and spend as much time as possible with her. The reason for that is I've seen too many instances where men get so focused on their professions that they don't spend enough time with their wives and they lose touch. Then when the children are grown, the couple files for divorce. I want to make sure that doesn't happen to us.

I love current affairs and read widely and watch television channels that tell me what is happening in the world. I also love theatre and attend as many plays as I can with Charmaine and when appropriate with our daughters.

What do you think are the major threats to tourism in Barbados?

Societal indifference is one; that is where people don't treat the industry or our visitors as important. The world economic situation is obviously another threat, not just to tourism but to just about every kind of business. Natural and man-made disasters are also threats, such as climate change with changes in sea level that will affect coastal development and increase tropical cyclone activity. There is also the issue of our now having much hotter days in summer, leading to increased air-conditioning costs. We are really beginning to see that. War and terrorism, such as 9/11 when many Americans basically stopped traveling, are also threats. 9/11 impacted every destination that was dependent on U.S. tourism and it hit us hard, but it was even tougher on countries like the Bahamas, where some hotels closed.

A new threat for us is the airline passenger duty which the British are adding to all air tickets. The duty is supposed to compensate for the carbon emissions of the flights. It's supposed to be an environmental tax. The problem is that the size of the tax is much larger than what is really called for to offset the carbon emissions. We are of the view that it is simply a way for the British government to raise additional revenue to help address the problem of their deficit. The tax is supposed to be structured so that the farther you fly the more you pay, which sounds okay. But they calculate it from capital to capital. So you can fly from London to Hawaii and actually pay much less in taxes than if you were to fly from London to Barbados, which is half the distance. The reason is the tax is calculated on a trip from London to the U.S. capital of Washington, D.C., rather than the actual distance you fly. It's just not fair. And if it's really meant to be an environmental tax, they should use the real distance of the flights. This tax has hiked up airfares such that if you're flying premium economy from London to Barbados you will pay an extra 150 pounds per person, and even if you're flying economy it's still 75 pounds more per person in tax. That's a lot of money, enough to keep some people from coming to Barbados. The majority of people surveyed say that this tax will impact their decision on where they travel and some will be more inclined to go to southern Europe, to the Mediterranean, for vacation because the duty is so much less.

What do you think of the notion of tourism as a form of neocolonialism?

I will explain it this way: because tourism today is so broad, including leisure, sports, romance, traveling to get married, culinary, etc., it's become a medium by which small countries share their culture with the people from larger countries. Let me give you an example—the number-two attraction after Harrison's Cave for tourists in Barbados is Oistins [an outdoor fish fry on the south coast]. This is a place where visitors get to mingle with locals and sample authentic, local food, like fried and grilled fish, fish cakes, sweet potato, macaroni pie—as opposed to going to a fine-dining restaurant with a four-course dinner and wine. Because of the advances in the Internet and media technology there is no longer a need for people to travel to small countries like Barbados to indoctrinate us into their culture. We know all about the big metropolitan countries from the Internet and from the media in general. That old indoctrination now happens in reverse—when people from the metropolitan countries come to islands like Barbados they learn something about our life and culture. Just look at all the young white girls on the beach having their hair braided and with beads added for style and color. They do that because they want to identify with the place they are visiting. Today people travel to experience different things. They want to see how the locals operate, they want to swim with the turtles, and they want to try our food. This is quite different than coming to Barbados and saying, okay, in England this is how we do things, this is how we live, and implying that their way is a lot better than what we have here. In neocolonialism it is the values of the larger countries that are transmitted to the smaller developing countries, and I don't see that so much today in our tourism.

In fact, I don't hear many Bajans talk about tourism as neocolonialism today. I think they are giving up on that idea. Just look around the world and you will see that almost every country wants to get into tourism. Just recently the UK, for the first time in history, appointed a minister of tourism. Their prime minister, David Cameron, gave a speech on tourism; that's unusual for the head of state of a large power, but it shows how important tourism has become. Even the oil- and gas-producing countries in the Middle East are plowing time and money into developing tourism, because they see tourism as a serious alternative industry, as their oil and gas are not going to last forever. Most of the countries in Africa are building out their tourism infrastructure, and the same is taking place in South America—Colombia, Peru, Chile, Argentina. They're all doing it—Cuba and China as well! Now, if tourism really was a form of neocolonialism I don't think they'd be doing that.

Is there anything else you'd like to add?

The single biggest influence in my life has been my father, especially in terms of work ethic and a love for business. He's the one who told me when I began to study for a degree to think about doing accounting as well as economics. My dad looks at things from a broader perspective and does not rely on listening to everything people say. He believes in assessing decisions in your own mind and following it. All of that stuff comes from my dad. I keep telling him that my greatest love would be to carry on his business, the small supermarket and wholesale operation. He is from the generation that used the business to educate his children and to give us a decent life. My father will soon turn 75 and he knows there will come a time when he can't carry on running the mini-market. I told him that my sister, Andrea, and I will continue it after him. Wherever I go to work, I always tell my boss that if anything happens to my father I will have to take care of his business. The track record of black businesses in Barbados is not good: after one generation many of them disappear. Part of that is the original owner's fault because they use the business to get out of poverty, to make a better life for their children, and then they don't think it right for their children to have to get their own hands dirty in the business. They believe that their children should be professionals—lawyers, doctors, accountants—rather than doing the hard-core business. Well, they can't all be lawyers and doctors and accountants. With my father's business I would not be happy simply managing it as a mini-mart; no, I would expand it to a good, vibrant supermarket. Ideally, I would like to own or have some ownership stake in an accommodation (hotel) business because that's what I've been doing for the past seventeen years. You can make a good living running a small boutique property with twenty rooms. You don't need fifty or a hundred, and who wants the extra headache when you can be quite comfortable with a smaller property. There's more to life than money.

God has been good to me. I am leading a full life, I have a great family, and I have been entrusted with leadership responsibilities. I try to live the concept captured many years ago by George Washington Carver: "No individual has any right to come into this world and go out of it without leaving behind distinct and legitimate reasons for having passed through." I have been longtime friends of many people who are now also making their mark in the life of the country, and I hope I will follow them. For all that, I consider myself to be truly blessed.

CHIEF RESEARCH OFFICER, MINISTRY OF TOURISM
Everton Gill

As chief statistician, Everton Gill, 45, worked for ten years in Barbados's central statistics office on the country's census. In 1988, he moved over to the Ministry of Tourism as head of their new research unit. Everton was trained in sociology at the University of the West Indies in Barbados and at Georgetown University in Washington, D.C. He and his wife have three children; their eldest daughter is studying at the Hospitality Institute to be a pastry chef. His favorite pastimes are tennis, gardening, and playing the guitar.

Tourism is a very interesting area; a lot is happening, and as a research person I get to be involved in all sorts of things. I can be involved in the industry at any level, from giving guest lectures on tourism in the schools and at the Hospitality Institute to talking to the hoteliers. I also meet with visiting researchers and I'm able to help them design their studies and survey instruments. I also get to shape policy by advising the government on certain things—if you do this, that will happen. Sometimes the advice is taken, sometimes it's not. So as I say, it's a rewarding job.

Essentially I'm in charge of the Research and Development Unit. We have five people in the unit, and we collect, compile, and analyze key tourism indicators. A lot of our information comes from the Embarkation-Disembarkation cards [E-D cards] that all people arriving at the airport or seaport are required to fill out, and we process information that people can use.[1] The E-D card is primarily an immigration instrument to track people's movements, but since most people who come to the island are tourists, the information is very useful to us. The data from the cards produce detailed profiles of the tourists. For instance, we break down where our visitors come from—for the United States by each state, for Canada by province, and the United Kingdom by county.

---

1. The E-D card is the responsibility of the Central Statistical Office, with input from the Ministry of Tourism, the immigration office, and the Barbados Tourism Authority.

Do you get complaints from passengers about having to
fill out this information every time they arrive in Barbados?

Sometimes. But we try to strike a balance between getting the tourist to the beach in five minutes and getting as much information as possible. There are some tourism people who want to get the tourists out of the airport as fast as possible, but from the national security and research point of view we ask for this information so that we can get a better handle on who we have coming to Barbados and what they do here.

Our resources are very limited, so we only do a rough analysis. It's all quantitative. For example, we look at the arrival cards—the ones passengers fill out on the flight and submit when they pass through immigration—but we don't have the money to process the departure cards. If we were able to, we could match arrivals and departures and get more reliable data on length of stay. Right now our information is not on the *actual* length of stay but on the *intended* length of stay. A person will come and say they want to stay two weeks and then they might stay three, or they might go home early.[2]

We'd also like to be able to project trends more accurately, but it's difficult because there are so many variables that your predictions can be easily thrown off. If you can't make projections, you can't anticipate things. There are certain areas where if we had more intelligence, we'd be able to cushion ourselves from some of the overseas impacts. For example, it would be very useful to track economic conditions in America and the other tourist-generating areas in order to predict future tourist arrivals here. That information is important to our policy-makers and planners.

Also, if we could get reliable data from the hoteliers, we could do a better job. But it's often very difficult to get information from people in the industry. For example, we'd like to get some detailed financial information from them so that we can address issues like profitability. We get complaints all the time that even though our hotels are able to attract some of the best rates in the region, their profitability is low. That's what the hoteliers say, but they're not willing to give us the information. Even simple things like achievement rates—if we know they have one hundred rooms and their

---

2. Since many people come on package tours, with fixed arrivals and departures, the data are fairly accurate for most visitors.

achievement rate is, say, 150 dollars a night, then we can better estimate their profitability.[3] We just want ballpark figures. In requesting information from the hoteliers we tell them, "You help us to help you." But still the response is not always forthcoming. I think they figure we're another government department and that we will probably share the information with the income tax people.

Most of our surveys are done by the Central Statistical Office. We get the results and their reports and then we do a more detailed analysis. But with our limited resources, even that sometimes is difficult. There's definitely a need for more research, particularly when you remember that tourism is our number-one industry. It brings in about 50 percent of all foreign exchange, contributes about 14 percent of GDP, and employs 20 percent of the labor force directly and indirectly. It's not only the most important industry to Barbados but also to most of the island nations in the Caribbean. So we need to put more resources into understanding it.

What other kinds of data on tourists are available to you?

The statistical department does a Survey of Overnight Guests, which is sent to all hotels. But the response is not very good. They also do an Accommodations Survey, which solicits financial information. Here in the ministry we give out a survey to determine the occupancy of the hotels. And in collaboration with the Caribbean Tourism Organization (CTO) we survey visitors when they depart from the airport and seaport. The survey looks at everything from their reasons for coming to Barbados to their expenditures here. We break down how they spend their money—accommodation, meals and drinks, transportation, entertainment, recreation, souvenirs, and other shopping. We also ask if they are willing to return to Barbados and we ask them to rank on a scale of one to ten various aspects of the product—food, accommodations, attractions, facilities, etc. The information is published as a report, which we send out. Because a lot of people can't make sense of tables and crosstabs, we add a narrative. And we often do a comparison between one year and the next or bring in some historical information. It's sad to say, but like everything else it's the bad things, like beach harassment, that get pulled out of the reports, focused on, and sensationalized in the press.

---

3. Data required to calculate the achievement rate include such things as the ratios of money spent on food, rooms, and maintenance.

*Do you do any damage control with the media, such as asking them
to downplay negatives because of their potential impact on tourists?*

I don't think we're able to influence them. As a matter of fact,
sometimes we complain to the press that they're sensationalizing
certain things that are harming the country's image. For instance, if
there's a murder they'll put it on the front page. A murder is still big
news here and it scares some people.

Do you make use of the academic research done here on tourism?

We don't use it much because we're not aware of it. We don't
have an easy way of knowing what's being done out there. Scholars
come down here and we help them out, but when they go back
they usually don't send us copies of their publications. The ministry,
really, should be a clearinghouse for academic studies. It's quite
possible that a study someone's proposing might have already been
done, and we wouldn't know it. We need more collaboration between the academic community and government.

Does your research suggest that there is a problem with harassment?

Yes, but it's not as serious as some people make out. Harassment
is very subjective; what may be harassment to one person may not
be to another. I like to use the example of a nice friendly taximan at
the top of Broad Street, our main shopping street. Nice and friendly,
he says, "Good morning, sir, how are you doing? Hope you had a
nice flight. Do you want a taxi?" He is friendly and polite. But by
the time you walk 200 yards down Broad Street, ten nice friendly
taxi people ask you the same thing. If asked if you were harassed,
you'd probably say yes. Likewise, you go to the beach, take out
your favorite novel, stretch out on your towel, put on your suntan
lotion, and start to read. A nice friendly vendor comes up to you,
"Good morning, ma'am, you have a beautiful tan. How are you
doing? Could I interest you in some of this coral that I have?" You
look at it, you turn over and say, "Well, no thank you." No harassment there. But over the course of the next hour you get ten nice
friendly vendors doing that. After a while, yes, it's harassment.

But there's also another form of harassment that stems from
one type of tourist and the type of product they're looking for.
That's women looking for sex. And it doesn't have anything to do
with age, because some older women come looking for it, too. The

problem occurs when the guys [beach boys] see a single woman and just assume that if they proposition her that she might be interested in them. While very few women are here for that reason, a great many get propositioned. And that's harassment.

How does the ministry categorize tourists?

In the broad sense, we divide tourists into cruise tourism and long-stay tourism. Long-stay is anyone who stays over twenty-four hours, which excludes cruise passengers. There is an inherent conflict between land-based tourism and cruise tourism. The land-based operators see the cruise operators as having an unfair advantage. The land people figure they provide the facilities and everything else and they pay far more in taxes, while the cruise ships deposit their guests onto the island for less than a day and turn them loose. The hotel guests pay for their facilities and pay all sorts of taxes, while the cruise tourists use the beaches and facilities and pay next to nothing.

What do you think about cruise tourism?

We're still not sure what we want from cruise tourism. When we really analyze the figures, cruises contribute more than 50 percent of the arrivals on the island but less than 10 percent of the revenue. In some ways they are more of a burden to the infrastructure than an asset. But then there are locals who benefit from the cruise-ship visitors, such as taxi and coach owners and owners of other services. Overall, I don't think cruise visitors make enough of a contribution to offset their impact on the infrastructure. But governments in the region don't agree, and some spend a lot of money on infrastructure to accommodate cruise passengers.

As a researcher, what do you think Barbados
needs to do to attract more tourists?

In general, we need to give more value for money. If we are to be an upmarket destination, then we need to lift the general standard of the island in terms of the quality of our attractions. We have to recognize that we can't compete in price with some of the newer destinations. So then we have to focus on quality and cut a niche for ourselves in that way. If you're going for upmarket tourists who stay in villas and in four- and five-star properties, you have to make sure you offer them quality, that everything is well managed, well organized. You make sure that things work. You make sure that people pass through the airport as hassle-free as possible. You make sure there's good service in all the places they're going to stay and visit—hotel, restaurant, bank, wherever they go. You concentrate on service excellence. There's a market for Rolls-Royce and there's a market for Suzuki. If we can be a Rolls-Royce in the tourism business, people won't mind paying extra to come here. But you have to provide Rolls-Royce quality.

When you travel do you still wear your hat as a tourism researcher?

Yes. When I travel, I'm always looking to see how they do things. I invariably spend some time in the hotel lobby talking to the workers and the front-desk people to get a feel for what's happening. These are the people who deal with tourists more than anyone else. Usually I am able to draw a lot of conclusions based on what they say.

*To your mind, what are the negative
impacts of tourism for Barbadians?*

A high cost of living, for sure. Tourists not only stay in hotels but they eat in restaurants, go to fast-food places, and shop in supermarkets. That pushes up the prices of many items. Because of tourism you have lots of people purchasing property, especially along the coastline, and that pushes up the cost of real estate. And some say too much of our land has been taken up for tourism. As a sugar plantation, a plot of land can sell for, say, 1 or 2 million dollars; converted into a tourism project it might bring ten or twenty times that much. Tourism contributes to traffic congestion. And on days when cruise ships come in, Bridgetown is overrun with visitors.

Then you have the old question of male and female prostitution. And tourists create a market for drugs. And as long as there's a market, people will find ways to supply it, so tourism has encouraged drug peddling. And sometimes you have violence, which is often traced back to drugs. Of course there are also some environmental impacts. For instance, most hoteliers want to build as near as possible to the sea, and that obviously impacts the shoreline. Also, the more tourists we have, the more garbage and waste is generated, and we don't have room for it in our landfill. So yes, there are some negatives.

What do you think of the academic critique
of tourism as a new form of slavery?

I don't agree. Central government will get involved in any activity that will increase foreign exchange and provide employment. We need to increase foreign exchange in any way we can to fund our social services. In Barbados, health care is free for most people, education is free from primary through university, and so on. Government's social budget is very high, and tourism helps pay for a lot of it.

In terms of attracting the best brains, it's true that a lot of people still have not accepted working in the industry as a top priority. That's something we need to change. We need to sensitize people that working in tourism is rewarding. It is service, not servitude. It is true that coming from a plantation background, where certain classes of people were owners and others were slaves, there is a notion in some circles that tourism is simply new slavery in which the owners are the same and the workers are the same. But it's simply not true. Black Barbadians have been able to achieve better positions in tourism than they would ever have done on sugar plantations. A lot of them own businesses—taxis, water sports, etc.

How often do you come into contact with tourists yourself?

Very often. I live right in the midst of the main tourist belt on the west coast. I see them as they travel to the grocery store, to the gas station, and even in the church that I go to. Sometimes they even venture into the neighborhood where I live. When I go somewhere and I see a large number of tourists having a good time, I feel good and proud. After all, I'm with the Ministry of Tourism and these people are making a contribution to the economy. But when I see negative things that impact on tourists, I don't feel good.

Right now tourism in Barbados is at a very interesting stage in its development. Way back in 1992, we took a serious look at how our tourism is organized, and we recognized that we needed to do something about our product. So in '92 we started a tourism development program. The overall aim is to make tourism sustainable. Environmentally sustainable and financially sustainable. We recognize that there is a new type of tourist coming who is not only interested in sand, sea, and sun but is also interested in the culture and heritage of the country, and some in certain sports and activities. We looked at cruise tourism, its impact, and how we could enhance it. We looked at boating tourism, whether there's a market for it here. We looked at urban renewal because we recognized that some visitors like to go into the city and see restored period buildings. We did an inventory of nature-based sites as current and potential attractions. As part of the airport and seaport expansion, we looked at expanding duty-free shopping. Basically, we looked at enhancing our entire product, from the service side to the product side. Lots of recommendations have been made, and it will be important to carry them out if we are to remain attractive to tourists.

Sometimes it's frustrating. You hear all the time how tourism is the engine of our growth, the most important sector of the economy, yet it's not accorded the priority that it requires, especially in government budgets. A head tax on cruise passengers would help. We have provided an elaborate port infrastructure where the ships can come right up alongside, rather than passengers being ferried in from the harbor. And we've provided all the modern telecommunications services, banks, post offices right in the port. Somebody has to pay for that. When you go to a national park in Canada or the United States, you pay an entrance fee, when you go to Disney World you pay an entrance fee, and those fees are far more expensive than what Caribbean governments are asking the cruise lines to pay as a head tax. The cruise-ship companies have to realize that there must be partnership: they need us and we need them. Fifty percent of all cruises are to the Caribbean, and even though they play hard-nosed and say they'll leave if we insist on a head tax, where will they go? They should just cooperate and build the tax into their pricing structure. The region must act as a common voice to stand up to them.

I think that tourism is going to increase in the future. With the advent of the Internet, people are now able to sit down and visit any part of the world. It's hard to say exactly how it's going to affect tourism. Perhaps some will use the Internet to sample a destination and then get on a plane and travel to it to actually see it face-to-face. Maybe others won't feel the need to go there. In any case, the Caribbean generally and Barbados in particular has to position itself to benefit from these changes. For one, we must make sure we're on the leading edge of the new technology and that our product is competitive, not only with our Caribbean neighbors but with people as far away as Africa, Japan, and Indonesia. Every state in the United States is now promoting itself as a tourist destination and therefore is a potential competitor of the Caribbean. The same is true of the UK. The world is becoming one large global village, and we are now competing not only with our Caribbean neighbors but with the world as a whole. To succeed, we must be more focused, more aggressive, more organized, more price-conscious. If tourism was to seriously decline here, the bottom would fall out of our economy, and in the short run, it would leave us staggering.

8 CONCLUSION

As oral historians well know, it is difficult to generalize from a small number of narratives. The diversity of the work portrayed in the preceding pages makes the task even more complex, as the twenty-one narratives represent a range of jobs in a large industry—the largest in the world today. Nonetheless, some common threads are evident and some speak to important issues in our understanding of tourism.

Workers and Guests

The highly seasonal nature of Caribbean tourism, with the vast majority of its visitors arriving during the winter season, produces fluctuation in the economic fortunes of some workers. Hotels and other tourism-related businesses cut back their staffs during the slow summer season, causing layoffs or shorter work weeks among maids, bartenders, and waiters, for example. Some self-employed workers, such as beach vendor Rosco Roach, must seek alternative work outside of tourism during summer, or, like tour bus operator Anderson Hughes, go on vacation.

While interaction with visitors is said to be the most salient characteristic of work in tourism, the narratives show that the amount of contact with guests varies considerably, as does the character of that interaction. The upper echelon, like hotel manager Martin Barrow, director of guest services Marilyn Cooper, and BHTA president Colin Jordan, socialize with guests at hotel cocktail parties and freely converse with them around the hotel property at other times. The tour guides, bartenders, sea captains, and taxi and tour-bus drivers also freely interact but more strictly in a work environment. Taximan Trevor Mapp, for example, often talks with his passengers while driving, and Zerphyl Greaves chats with the hotel guests around the water-sports shack and on sailboats where there are no distractions. It is the beach boys who enjoy the most sustained interaction with guests. Ricky Hinds and Rosco Roach may know their guests better than all the others, going to dinner and sharing a bed, often over several days or more. In contrast, chefs working in the kitchen and maids cleaning hotel rooms after the guests have left for the day rarely meet the guests they serve.

Frequent interaction with guests has given many of the workers "confidence" and improved their social skills. Water-sports director Zerphyl Greaves said dealing with tourists helped him to overcome "shyness." "Working at the hotel made me braver," said room attendant Sheralyn O'Neale. "It made me feel freer to talk to people that I don't know." Before being employed by the hotel, she rarely spoke "about things" and didn't share her views with others.

Not all workers welcome contact with the visitors, however. Some shy away because they feel nervous or uncomfortable around them. "[Visitors] are so different, they act different . . . I just get a little shy sometimes," said one chef. A clerk in a souvenir shop said about visitors, "They don't talk like we and they don't walk like we. Sometimes I just don't know what to say to them." Fear that they won't understand what the tourists are saying also inhibits some Barbadians from interacting. Management may not want room attendants to chat too much with the guests because they have work to do.

Working among guests can be exhausting where there is frequent interaction. Some said that by the end of the day they are worn down and need time alone to "unwind." Hotel manager Martin Barrow and *Jolly Roger* captain Dwayne Parry needed "personal space" and time with no one else around after getting off work. Both men had "understandings" with their housemates that enabled them to do this. Barrow's girlfriend stayed away from him for an hour or two, while Parry's partner would invite a cousin or friend to go out rather than Dwayne.

Workers' Perceptions of Guests

Overall, the workers generally hold favorable opinions of visitors. Many clearly enjoy interacting with guests, and a few even develop friendships with them. On the other hand, the workers are critical of those tourists who are boorish and insensitive. A common complaint was their ignorance. "How can they come so far and know so little about us?" or similar words, was a common refrain. A hotel worker and village neighbor of mine said, "Tourists often say they've never heard of Barbados before they came here. They ask me about the size, what type of people live on the island, our language. Man, why they here?" A beach vendor said, "They think Barbados somethin' like de wilderness of Africa. They expect to see de people runnin' round with a cloth about de waist." Taxi driver Trevor Mapp was appalled when one visitor who had just arrived at the airport asked him if Barbados had television and running water. "How can people think we're so backward?" Anderson Hughes and Malika Marshall were dismayed by comments from tourists on how well they spoke—"My, but you speak well"—as if they expected Barbadians to be uneducated. A former hotel manager relished telling me stories about naive visitors:

> They'd come and ask where they can get stamps. I'd tell them, "There's a little shop around the corner that sells stamps." They'd come back, "Well, they don't sell American stamps and we want to post a letter to the States." I'm telling you, it's absolutely amazing. Any 5-year-old in the Caribbean would know that, and they [guests] don't because to them the U.S.A. is the whole world. . . . Some of these people have saved up a long time to come to the Caribbean and when they get here, they figure everybody here has to be more ignorant than they are. They're just the tops and aren't we glad they came!

In defense of the tourists, Rosie Hartmann noted that "If they appear to be stupid, it's [because] they are adjusting to many new things. So we need to give them advice and help, ease them in."

The workers, like many Barbadians, are annoyed with the attitude of many tourists that they should be able to do whatever they please because they are on "vacation." Vacation, they reason, is an escape from established routines, from the behavioral codes that rule ordinary daily life. Most Barbadians don't see it that way; while they are tolerant, they do expect visitors to be somewhat respectful of local custom. For example, Barbadians don't like tourists wearing skimpy beach attire in public places. "Even in supermarkets you see men walking around without shirts and the ladies in only their swimwear," commented one with distaste. "A Bajan would be arrested if caught walking around with the lack of clothing that tourists walk around in." About tourist women wearing bathing suits on the street, one local woman said with disgust: "They would tempt a man to rape she because it looks more naked than naked. You know they don't walk on the street at home that way." Anderson Hughes and Trevor Mapp objected to tourists getting in their bus and taxi, respectively, bare-chested. Barbadians are not prudish; rather, they think that businesses and town streets are not the proper place for beach dress.

Reminders to tourists to dress appropriately are now found in advertisements in the free newspapers for tourists, the *Visitor* and the *Sun Seeker.* One reads, "When you're in town or just shopping around don't be confused, you may be a peach but leave your swimwear for the beach." Another says, "We value your business and we know that you're cool, but please leave exposed tummies around the pool" (Wirthlin 2000). Some store owners have put up signs informing tourists "No bare backs" and "No scantily dressed persons allowed in the store." And on the beach, rangers enforce the code by clapping their hands loudly in disapproval whenever they see a naked breast.

The difference in the pace of life between the metropolitan countries the guests come from and the Caribbean is sometimes a source of irritation for both guests and hosts. Some guests are un-happy with "slow service," while some workers are annoyed with guests who hurry them. "Some of them want everything done yes-terday," said Malcolm Bovell. "Man, this is a laid-back island, this not McDonald's. You don't get a fantastic meal cooked here in five minutes." Another cook who had trained at a hotel school in Eng-land said, "I know where they are coming from. It's a high-tech, fast-paced world they live in, but you'd think that when they got here on holiday they'd ease up." Such complaints are often directed at American visitors. The slow pace at which many Bajan employ-ees work, however, can also create friction with their own hotel managers who themselves come from high-tech, efficiency-ob-sessed metropolitan cultures with different attitudes toward time and work.

Some workers had no patience for visitors who complained about rain. "They can come down very heavily on you when the rain is falling," said an entertainment director at Almond Beach Re-sort. "They figure they're here for a week and it shouldn't rain and God should curse Barbados if it does," said Trevor Mapp. "That's the hardest thing for me to understand." Certainly the way Barbados is portrayed in the travel brochures, in which nearly every image has bright sunny skies, contributes to the visitors' expectations that the sun will always shine. The photos and captions in the brochures also invariably exaggerate the friendliness of the natives, creating another set of unrealistic expectations.

The insensitivity of some tourists negates some of the goodwill that tourism workers might otherwise have for them. But rarely do the workers retaliate directly, in part because their employers have drummed into them the code of "the customer is always right." There is the awareness that the business of tourism depends on keeping visitors happy. Many Barbadians excuse some tourist misbehavior with an indulgent "They're just here to have fun." Many of the workers stressed the importance of being patient and not losing their tempers. Only Trevor Mapp admitted to having an altercation with a guest (who was hanging out the window of his taxi), but even his response was muted. What little verbal confrontation there is with tourists often takes place on the beach. It mostly derives from the frustrations jet-ski operators experience when their clients do not obey the rules and vendors experience in trying to communicate with and make a sale to tourists, especially non–English speakers, and from the aggressive bargain-hunting of some visitors.

One way workers deal with the boorish behavior of visitors is through gossip and ridicule. I have listened to taxi drivers sitting around a taxi stand and water-sports employees at the water-sports shack parody the mannerisms and things tourists had said to them. Some like to toy with tourists, especially visitors who are ignorant of local conditions, by telling them tall tales. Parody, gossip, ridicule, and stereotyping tourists in unflattering ways are often forms of "covert resistance," explains Jeremy Boissevain (1996), who edited a book titled *Coping with Tourists* that examines how local Europeans deal with mass tourism. Such burlesquing of guests not only enables workers to retaliate against boorish visitors but helps locals, who are always in a subordinate position, to maintain their self-respect. Displays of rudeness, such as the behavior of the clerk behind the American Airlines counter described in chapter 2, may accomplish the same objective. Similarly, obstruction, such as village boys misdirecting visitors seeking directions, is sometimes a reaction of locals who object to tourists invading their communities. Such resistance illustrates that workers are not mere pawns in their interactions with guests. Though relationships between guests and hosts are inherently asymmetrical, the workers are not defenseless.

Work Satisfaction

Although the workers generally find the hours long, all spoke favorably about their jobs. Some, like Michael Walcott and Robert Quintyne, compared their jobs in tourism to the office jobs they had previously held. They especially liked being outside and working with people. Quintyne said he could make more money in an office job and would have lots of "creature comforts" and a pension, but that he would not enjoy himself nearly as much as he does now running cycling tours. Walcott, formerly a computer repairman, much preferred spending his day at sea with the *Atlantis* submarine, interacting with people on vacation. Even beach vendor Rosco Roach and jet-ski operator Ricky Hinds, who also once had steady wage-paying jobs in the non-tourism sector, preferred working on the beach despite the facts that they made very little money and their incomes were unreliable.

The positive attitudes of the interviewees toward their jobs are contrary to what some scholars have suggested for Caribbean tourism. Martin Mowforth and Ian Munt (1998), for example, say that "aggressive attitudes often emerge among workers and that a significant number of employees are not proud of what they do, and harbor resentment." They attribute such disgruntlement to the workers' inability to distinguish between service and servitude. Again, it is the issue of black workers having to serve white guests, which some interpret as servility and as a return to the old colonial pattern of relations between blacks and whites. Some workers that I know from the village were initially hesitant to take jobs in tourism. Although they weren't always clear about their reasons, some did mention being unsure about serving white visitors, that it might be demeaning and unpleasant. A few were concerned about having to deal with racial prejudice. In the narratives, though we hear the workers sometimes complain about tourists, there is no evidence of deep-seated resentment. Admittedly this could be due to a sampling problem: unhappy workers might not have been recommended to me as suitable interviewees.

Though satisfied with their jobs for the present, many of the interviewees said they hoped to be doing something different in the future. Some, like bank teller Joyann Springer, who wishes to start her own tour company, plan to stay in tourism; but most were looking outside the industry. I was surprised that individuals with good-paying jobs, like manager Martin Barrow and security chief Errol

Sobers, planned to leave tourism in order to set up their own businesses. It is a common Barbadian sentiment that it is better to work for yourself so you won't have someone always telling you what to do. One disincentive for staying in tourism is the perception that opportunities for advancement are limited. There are, for example, still too few black hotel managers or black head chefs, though that is slowly improving. So, though many people are happy to have a decent salary and work in pleasant surroundings, there is also the sense that they will never reach their full potential in the industry, and that encourages some to look elsewhere for the future.

Acculturation

It has been widely suggested that tourism promotes acculturation toward Western ideas and values (Crick 1989; Pearce 1982; Stronza 2001). The narratives suggest that some exchange of ideas—cultural borrowing—does occur and that it is likely to be greater where hosts and guests are able to talk freely, where there may be a real exchange of opinions on a range of topics. However, we also saw that workers were sometimes influenced by guests simply from observing them. One room attendant described how she mimicked some of the makeup and dress styles she observed in the rooms she cleaned and took some magazines and foreign newspapers the guests left behind home to read. In another example, several of the hotel workers said that seeing the food tourists order for their meals has influenced their own diets. Some now prepare dishes at home that they were exposed to at the hotel.

The narratives show that changes in language—workers becoming accustomed to speaking standard English and to speaking more slowly when interacting with visitors—may be the most pervasive impact of working in tourism. As bartender Sylvan Alleyne put it, "When you're dealing with tourists you've gotta speak English in the way they can understand." Michael Walcott said his guests on the submarine would close their minds to him if he spoke in his Bajan dialect. Having become accustomed to speaking standard English on the job, many workers now speak it routinely outside of work. The friends of one tourism worker I know say she no longer sounds like a Bajan. Michael Walcott and redcap Wendy Husbands, among others, now require their children to speak standard English even at home and scold them for speaking in dialect. This may reflect a desire to emulate the guests and/or recognition that there are advantages and status in speaking standard English.

The narratives suggest that the interactions of the workers with foreign guests can be educational. Many of the workers learned something about the cultural backgrounds of the guests they serve. As Zerphyl Greaves put it, "People share things with you. You learn what it's really like over there." "They learn there's a world out there," said Hospitality Institute director Bernice Critchlow-Earle. "They develop a certain thirst for geography." Several of my village neighbors who work in hotels said that knowing foreign guests made them more interested in world news, especially when the news was from the home country of a guest they had met. That the workers learned about cultural differences was also evident in the stereotypes they developed of the different nationalities represented by the guests. Everyone had notions about cultural difference, such as that the British were more reserved, Americans friendly and talkative, Germans disciplined and rigid, and Italians fun-loving. Sometimes I wondered about the accuracy of such stereotypes, such as Wendy Husbands's belief that American blacks more than British blacks are into "flashy clothes and things," or Joyann Springer's belief that Canadians are cheap, or Ricky Hinds's assertion that Canadian women are "hornier." Even those workers who don't have a lot of contact with guests, such as maids, learn to distinguish among nationalities by their accent, dress, and manner. Rosie Hartmann noted that such stereotyping is a "shortcut to dealing with people [tourists]. When you don't understand people thoroughly, it helps if you can put them in a particular box."

They also learn that the popular image of tourists as all being wealthy is false. They learn there is much variation in the wealth of their guests and that many had to save for a long time to be able to afford their Caribbean holiday. That awareness reduced the mystique and awe some had held for tourists. In the minds of some workers, it put them on the same plane as the guests they served. It also gave some the confidence to travel abroad themselves. And it led some workers to a new awareness that beneath the veneer of wealth and custom, people are all basically alike. "It has led me to think that we are all under the same struggle," said Dwayne Parry. "Their customs may be different, but deep down we're all the same."

Greater confidence and developing curiosity about the larger world through their exposure to tourists gave many of the interviewees an interest in traveling themselves. "Meeting guests and hearing them talk, learning about where they come from," noted one hotel worker, "has made me want to see the world for myself." "When you interact with them, you begin to become a bit like them." Wendy Husbands, Ricky Hinds, and Rosco Roach traveled overseas for the first time after being invited and encouraged by visitors they got to know. As Bernice Critchlow-Earle put it, they now travel "not just to see auntie or uncle in New York on a ticket they sent them but many are striking out on their own, seeing new places."

In a few instances, interactions between guests and the workers developed into friendships that have been maintained over the years through letters and return visits. A pool attendant that I know at a local resort has developed a friendship with a young English visitor who shares his love for soccer. Both are fans of Manchester United, and for the past four years they have exchanged letters, sports news, and magazines through the mail. Sometimes a tourist has even helped finance a home improvement or business venture. One village man I know set himself up in the jet-ski business with the financial help of a tourist woman friend. Occasionally, a Barbadian will travel with a tourist back home for work. A young woman who had looked after an American couple's children during their two-week vacation returned with them to the States to work as a live-in baby-sitter. Beach boys such as Ricky Hinds may travel to Canada, the United States, or Europe to visit or even move in with their lovers.

Workers also learned firsthand of the prejudices and racist attitudes some foreigners hold about black people. They encountered it in the patronizing comments some guests make, such as how surprised they are that Barbados is so developed or that Barbadians such as guide Malika Marshall can speak foreign languages. Recall the American visitor who told Joyann Springer that she was shocked that Barbados had so many black people because she knew the country had tourist attractions and she did not believe that blacks would be capable of running them. A waitress recalled the white Englishman who recoiled when she put her black hand on his shoulder. There was the elderly Australian who told Springer that he didn't know why he had come to Barbados because he "doesn't really like black people." Although Joyann admitted to being hurt by the man's remarks, most workers said they don't take such remarks personally and try not to let it bother them. In fact, even Joyann told her co-worker not to get annoyed over an Englishman's critical remarks about blacks because it would only make the man feel good for having upset her. Despite these vivid examples, the narratives suggest that racist behavior is not an everyday occurrence, that most guests do not pay attention to color or if so do their best to hide it. And the workers do their best to ignore racist remarks. Could there be more racist behavior than the narratives reveal? Certainly. Some interviewees may have revealed less because they thought racism an unpleasant topic to discuss with a white interviewer, even a sympathetic one who lived in Barbados.

Overall, the narratives paint a picture of individuals who have been influenced or changed by frequent interactions with guests who have exposed them to the ideas and customs of the metropolitan countries from which they come. There is no doubt in my mind that my Bajan village neighbors who work in tourism are generally more worldly and more "modern" than are fellow villagers of the same class and educational backgrounds who have little contact with tourism. It is important to keep in mind, however, that tourism is only one of several modernizing influences at work in the developing world. In Barbados, Western ideas are also diffused through the Internet, television, movies, and travel. In even the most remote villages Bajans can now tune in to over a hundred channels of U.S., European, and South American programming via cable and satellite-television hookups. Many Barbadians have relatives living in the metropolitan countries and are in regular contact with them; many have traveled there to visit them, and some have lived abroad themselves. In an environment with so many foreign influences, it can be difficult to distinguish the effects of tourism from other effects.

Furthermore, tourists are not the only people to introduce foreign values. Local elites who travel and vacation abroad also have much exposure to the metropolitan cultures, and they also are the most likely to have prolonged contact with foreigners within Barbados. More than most Barbadians, even those working in tourism, local elites adopt some European and North American traits that, in turn, trickle down to other Barbadians.

There is a good deal of negativism in the literature about the impacts of tourism, some scholars decrying the corrosive effects of tourism on traditional culture. Such concerns over the erosion of tradition are usually justified when dealing with non-Western societies, but less so in the Caribbean. Here the indigenous cultures were wiped out over three centuries ago. In Barbados, the aboriginal Amerindian inhabitants of the island were gone by the time of

British settlement in the 1600s, and from that time until 1966 the island was a colony of Britain. And as discussed earlier, tourism has resurrected and reinforced some traditional activities, such as festivals, dance performances, and crafts from colonial times. In the Caribbean, "development" has long meant becoming Western. At the national level, progress is largely a measure of the country's proximity to the institutions, resources, and even values of British and North American society. Furthermore, black and white Barbadians have always been oriented to the "Mother Country" (and more recently to North America) in their search for social and economic goals. In short, in the minds of most Bajans, the transfer of culture and capital from the metropolitan countries to their island nation is a good thing. To them it is "development." As we have seen, there are costs to this development—dependency, environmental degradation, congestion, drugs, crime, and prostitution, to name a few. But would Barbados be better off without tourism? Most say no. And there is hope that more thoughtful policy-making and planning will minimize, and even remove, many of the negative effects.

Update

In June 2010, I returned to Barbados; it was exactly a decade since I had finished the research for the first edition of this book. A lot can happen in ten years; I had heard about some of the changes from friends, but I really didn't know what to expect. Having moved on to a new research topic, I also wasn't convinced that I wanted to go back to an old research project. While not a well-thought-out plan, the idea for returning finally solidified when two of my field school students in Tasmania, Australia, fervently wanted to do more field research. With funding from a Union College fellowship program, Pearl Jurist-Schoen worked with me and the other student, Chelsea Tussing, assisted my anthropologist wife, Sharon Gmelch, in updating a different book—*The Parish behind God's Back*. In returning to Barbados I was eager to catch up with old friends and to see how the villages we had lived in had changed. As it turned out, they looked much the same, although some housing had improved significantly, with sturdy wall houses replacing many smaller, traditional board houses. More people owned cars and fewer people relied upon the bus service. But the greatest change was not in material culture or in the appearance of things—rather, it was in people's frequent use of the Internet and their connections to the outside world. Through Facebook and e-mail, many Barbadians now have frequent, sometimes daily, contact with their overseas relatives both in large cities (notably London, New York, Miami, and Toronto) and in the rural areas of Canada, the United States, and the UK, where many Barbadians spend their summers on work programs and their winters working in the service sectors. Local Barbadians' social and work-related networks are no longer confined to friends and neighbors in the village or the parish but are now far-flung. No matter how remote a person's location in Barbados, he or she is now directly plugged into the outside world. One consequence of greater connectedness has been a deeper understanding of tourism's importance to the economic well-being of Barbados.

But how had tourism itself changed in the decade that I was absent? The country added some new tourist attractions, including a museum near the airport built around a decommissioned Concorde jet and called "The Barbados Concorde Experience"; there are also Segway rentals and ziplines, and several adventure tourism outfits, variously called, with obvious hyperbole, the "Highlands Adventure Center," "Forest Safari Barbados," and "Adventure Land Tours." A large marine aquarium (Ocean Park) had also opened but proved to be too expensive and its location too remote. It closed within a few years.

When I left Barbados in 2000, a trend toward all-inclusive hotels had begun and people were talking about how much tourists preferred paying for their vacation upfront, knowing before they left home what it was going to cost. So I was surprised to find no change in the number of all-inclusive hotels in Barbados—fifteen. A few notable ones, like Sam Lord's Castle, had closed and a few new ones had opened. Some all-inclusive resorts now encourage their guests to leave the premises for the day in order to reduce their costs. "They are finding that too many guests are indulgent and wasteful, with people ordering multiple courses and only eating a fraction of what they order," noted one tourism official who wished to remain anonymous. "It's getting very expensive to feed them, and they often drink a lot as well." So, some resorts have begun promoting outside excursions and local restaurants. In another cost-saving and socially responsible measure, the Barbados Hotel and Tourism Association has begun a campaign to raise the environmental awareness of hotel owners and to assist them in getting green certification for their properties.

Adopting an idea that first emerged in North America and Europe in response to the global recession, Barbadian tourism officials are promoting "staycations"; that is, urging islanders to stay close to home during the summer season to help the economy get back on track by boosting tourism revenue. "Staycation," a slang term for a vacation spent at home, was among one hundred new words added to the *Merriam-Webster Collegiate Dictionary* last year. Many hoteliers and tour operators—from Atlantis Submarines to Harrison's Cave—are offering attractive discounts for Bajans. There is now so much domestic tourism that, in the words of Hospitality Institute director Bernice Critchlow-Earle, "It can be hard these days to distinguish who is a tourist and who is not because everybody seems to be visiting places today. I've seen more black Bajans sitting in hotel lobbies or eating in restaurants than ever before."

The glass ceiling that had prevented Bajans from being promoted to the top positions as head chefs and hotel managers is showing cracks. With some Bajans now in top positions in hotel kitchens, there is also greater use of local foods in the menu. This not only means less importing of foreign foodstuffs but reduces the leakage of tourism profits overseas. Working in tourism is losing the stigma it once had. Today fewer people regard jobs in the industry as being primarily that of maids and waiters, said Critchlow-Earle; "besides the maids and waiters, more people also see the well-paid technicians, food and beverage managers, marketing professionals, and hotel managers. And that's led to much for a positive image of tourism." As the island's economy and jobs have become more visibly tied to tourism, more young Barbadians now see tourism as the economic sector with the most jobs to offer. When I asked hotel and tourism officials if they perceived any change in "the speed of service," the consensus was that this may be a little quicker today, though nobody could speak with absolute certainty. As Barbadians' impression of tourism improves, the notion of tourism as a form of neocolonialism has even less currency than it did a decade ago.

An interest in developing alternatives to the traditional focus on "sand, sea, and sun" tourism, which I had encountered in my earlier work and described briefly in chapter 7, is even stronger today. While the beach vacation, with its deluxe hotels and modern facilities, will probably always be the mainstay of Barbadian tourism, many visitors today are spending fewer hours on the beach and looking for other things to do. This is not just because today's visitors are more health-conscious and aware of the consequences of getting too much sun; rather they are also interested in more active and varied vacation experiences. These include sport and adventure and learning about Barbados's heritage. Heritage tourism is one of the fastest-growing forms of tourism in the world and is getting a lot of attention in Barbados. The Ministry of Tourism has made a strong push to promote the island's historic places and to open plantation houses for public viewing. Private enterprises and community groups are also investing in popular heritage attractions and events. St. Nicholas Abbey, for instance, now showcases the historic ways of cultivating and processing sugarcane to make fine rum, and the "Foodies" community group in the parish of St. Thomas showcases agricultural and craft products. The central government in 2010 submitted a formal application to the United Nations Educational, Scientific and Cultural Organization (UNESCO) for "Historic Bridgetown and its Garrison" to be inscribed on the "World Heritage List." Recent tourist development in the Garrison area has included guided tours, the opening of the George Washington House, and restoration of other historic buildings.

Ecotourism, which is now a major attraction in some parts of the Caribbean, especially Dominica and Belize, has not gained much traction in Barbados, despite attempts by several tour operators. Barbados doesn't have the wilderness or "bush" of the more remote and less-developed islands, although the island does have some nature-based tourism, such as Andromeda Gardens, the Flower Forest, Welchman Hall Gully, and the Eco-Heritage Farm at Springvale, and there is interest in developing more.

The global recession of 2008–2010 reminded all Barbadians of how fragile and dependent the country's tourism-based economy is on the ability of Americans and Europeans to afford and to desire a Caribbean vacation. Barbados has lots of competition from its neighboring islands and from other destinations. Therefore, to maintain its current share of visitors, it must continue to offer friendliness, safety, political stability, and attractive facilities that are competitively priced. Tourists are highly mobile and can freely change their vacation destinations; in all regions of the world, some popular holiday destinations are declining while others are growing. In today's uncertain global economy, Barbadians are discovering that there is no guarantee that international tourists will always choose their island.

One concern for the entire region is that rising oil and food prices could put the Caribbean out of reach to the low to middle

A guide giving a tour
of St. Nicholas Abbey.
Photo by George Gmelch.

end of the European tourism market. Some observers, like David
Jessop, the director of the London-based Caribbean Council and
publisher of *Caribbean Insight,* believe that continued unrest in the
Middle East and/or another major natural disaster like the earth-
quake in Japan could produce a tourism shock in the Caribbean
equivalent to the one that followed the terrorist attacks on the
World Trade Center in 2001 or the global financial crisis of 2008.
Either one would raise fuel and food prices, thereby pushing the
cost of a Caribbean vacation beyond the ability of some consumers
to pay, particularly in the UK, Ireland, and Spain, which are key
feeder markets for the Eastern Caribbean. Also of concern is the
UK's new Air Passenger Duty (APD). As Colin Jordan explained in
his narrative (chapter 7), the duty discriminates against the Caribbean in favor of travelers to North America. The European Union is
also considering a levy on airlines and a cap-and-trade scheme to
limit carbon emissions. If enacted, the airlines are likely to pass on
these additional costs to their passengers in the form of higher ticket
prices, and that would reduce visitor arrivals. These are serious is-

The recently restored George Washington House.
Courtesy of Barbados Tourism Authority.

sues not just for Barbados but for all of the tourism-dependent nations of the Eastern Caribbean, some of whom count on tourism for
more than 40 percent of their GDP. Some industry insiders, like
Colin Jordan and David Jessop, are urging for a serious consider-
ation of the consequences of increasing energy prices and taxation
and warning that failure to do so could lead to severe economic and
social consequences for the entire region.

But in the long term, the greatest threat to tourism in Barbados,
and to the island's overall economy and the well-being of its people,
is going to be climate change. A rise in sea level and the coastal erosion and flooding it is bringing are a major threat. A large part of
Barbados's population lives along its coasts, which are particularly
vulnerable to flooding during intense storm and swell conditions.
The coastline contains much of the island's infrastructure, particularly that supporting tourism. Most of the island's hotels, for example, are on the beachfront; even central Bridgetown is at risk. The
erosion of the island's world-class beaches due to rising sea levels
and flooding will certainly discourage some tourists from coming or
returning to Barbados. Climate change, which some climatologists
argue should be called "climate weirding," is also predicted to produce periods of extended rain or drought, either of which will
wreak havoc on the tourism industry. Barbados has signed the
Kyoto climate treaty and adopted measures to reduce its own use of

fossil fuels, such as by increasing its use of solar and wind energy. But there is really little that Barbadians can do to mitigate the effects. The entire Caribbean region accounts for less than 1 percent of global greenhouse gas production. It frustrates many educated Barbadians that industrial nations, and certain political parties within those nations, such as Republicans in the United States, seem to care little about the environmental damage they are causing by their indiscriminate pollution of the atmosphere, or worse that they continue to deny in the face of overwhelming evidence that humans are responsible for climate change. Unlike some of the low-lying atolls in the Pacific Ocean, Barbados is certainly not in danger of being submerged by a rising sea level, but the impact of climate change on the economy of Barbadians is likely to be disastrous nonetheless.

EPILOGUE
STUDENT ENCOUNTERS
WITH TOURISTS AND TOURISM

Most of the research for this book was done while I was directing the research of students on anthropology field programs. I learned much about tourism through their experiences. Even though they were living in villages away from the tourist belt, they often visited beaches, nightclubs, and other places frequented by tourists. In those venues they became tourists themselves. A few students studied aspects of tourism that directly contributed to my own knowledge of the subject. Some recommended individuals for me to interview and a few of those interviewees became subjects or narrators in this book. This epilogue looks at my students' experiences, primarily as tourists but also as young American anthropology students living on their own in rural villages in the least-developed and most-remote parish of Barbados, St. Lucy.

Since I began my teaching career in the mid-1970s I have, along with my anthropologist wife, Sharon Gmelch, been taking students abroad to give them hands-on experience doing anthropological fieldwork. From the mid-1970s until 2000, our field schools were based in rural villages—first in Ireland and then over a twenty-year period in Barbados. Here students were placed in different communities where they conducted their own independent field research. In one semester they learned a great deal about culture, both the one they were living in and studying and their own. But the primary aim of the field schools was to teach the students how to do field research—coming up with a research problem or question, designing an appropriate methodology, recording data in field notes, and near the end of the term analyzing that data and writing up a research paper. Good field schools represent experiential learning and deep cultural immersion at their best.

Sharon and I first became acquainted with field schools while we were in graduate school—I in Mexico, where I spent a summer living in a mountain village in the state of Tlaxcala, and the following summer Sharon did her first fieldwork in a fishing village on the southwest coast of Ireland. Our experiences were challenging, with bouts of illness, loneliness, and culture shock. But they were also exhilarating—a real-life adventure—and unquestionably the most memorable and valuable part of our graduate training. So it was natural that once we began our teaching careers we would want to provide our students with a similar opportunity. Before we turn to the students' encounters with tourism, some description of their lives in Barbados is in order.

Arriving

Sara, Eric, and Kristen heave their backpacks and suitcases—all the gear they'll need for the next ten weeks—into the back of the institute's battered Toyota pickup. Sara, a tense grin on her face, gets up front with me; the others climb in the back and try to make themselves comfortable on the luggage.

Leaving Bellairs Research Institute on the west coast of Barbados, we drive north past the island's posh resorts. As we leave the coast the scene changes from tourism to agriculture. Here, amid the green and quiet of rolling sugarcane fields, there are few white faces. Graceful cabbage palms flank a large plantation house, one of the island's former "great houses." On the edge of its cane fields is a tenantry, a cluster of small board houses whose inhabitants are the descendants of the slaves who once worked on the plantation.

Two monkeys emerge from a gully and cross the road. I tell Sara that they came to Barbados aboard slave ships three hundred years ago, but she is absorbed in her own thoughts and doesn't seem to hear me. I've taken enough students to the field to have an idea of what's on her mind. What will her village in this remote corner of Barbados be like?—the one we just passed through looked unusually poor. Will the family she is going to live with like her? Will she like them? Will she be up to the challenge? Many people are walking along the road; clusters of men sit outside a rum shop shouting loudly while slamming dominoes on a wobbly plywood table.

Earlier in the day, Eric told me that many of the ten students on the field program thought they had made a mistake coming to Barbados. If they had chosen to go on the term abroad to Greece or England or even Japan, they mused, they would be together on a campus, among friends. They wouldn't have to live in a village. They wouldn't have to go out and meet people and try to make friends with all these strangers. To do it all alone now seemed more of a challenge than many wanted.

We continue driving toward the northeastern corner of the island to the village of Pie Corner, where Sara will live. Several miles out we can see huge swells rolling in off the Atlantic, beating against the cliffs. This is the unsheltered side of the island. The village has only a few hundred people but six small churches. Marcus Boyce and his family all come out to the truck to welcome Sara. Mrs. Boyce gives her a big hug, as though she were a returning relative, and daughter Yvette takes her into the yard to show her the pigs and chickens and then on a tour of the small house. The bedroom is smaller than Sara imagined, barely larger than the bed. She puzzles over where to put all her stuff while I explain the nature of the program to the Boyces. Sara, I tell them, will be spending most of her time in the village talking to people and participating as much as possible in the life of the community, everything from attending church to cutting sugarcane. My description doesn't fit their conception of what a university education is all about. The everyday lives of people in their community are probably not something they think worthy of a university student's attention.

Back in the truck Eric and Kristen ask me anxiously how their villages compare to Sara's. Kristen begins to bite her nails.

Adjusting to Village Life

The most immediate adjustment the students must make is to the tropical climate. Barbados lies just 13 degrees above the equator; the sun is intense, especially in the middle of the day, and especially for students raised in the Northeast, as many of my students are. The saying "only mad dogs and Englishmen go out in the midday sun" is an apt warning. For the first few weeks the students are debilitated by the heat, from which there is little respite since village homes are not air-conditioned. Inevitably, the skin of some of the women students breaks out, causing them more misery and self-consciousness about their appearance.

Like all peoples in the tropics, Bajans start their day early (most are up by 5 A.M.) to complete their outdoor chores while the air is still cool. I always advise my students to get onto the local schedule—early to bed, early to rise—but after years of staying up late and getting up late, most find this a struggle. It is usually the female students who adapt best and most quickly to local rhythms.

Coming from spacious middle-class American homes, the students are not prepared for the cramped conditions found in most village dwellings, even though they were advised and even shown slides of village housing before coming to Barbados. Bedrooms often have barely enough space to maneuver past the beds, and it is often a squeeze to get around the dining room table when people are seated. The small interiors reflect both modest incomes and the use of the outdoors for some domestic activities. The students discover, however, that there is one advantage to a small floor plan: it's easy to find things. "At home you have to make sure you have everything that you need before you settle down, because you don't want to have to climb the stairs any more than you have to," Craig commented. "Here if I forget something, no big deal because it's never more than a few steps away." Of course, not having more possessions than will fit into a large backpack also makes keeping track of one's things easier.

While the students usually have their own bedrooms, they often offer little privacy since the walls are thin, sometimes just partitions that do not extend to the ceiling. Where curtains instead of doors separate the rooms, the sounds of television, radio, and conversation spread throughout the house. The constant noise can wear on a student's nerves. "It seems like the TV hasn't been turned off since I arrived here five weeks ago," reported Sara. "Even at night when I am alone in my bedroom, I can hear conversations in other parts of the house as though there wasn't a wall between us," complained Dan.

The separation between the indoors and outside so characteristic of housing in northern climates is noticeably absent in the Caribbean. Windows that are usually open during the day to let the breeze in also let in insects and small critters. In village homes students feel like they are living close to "nature," since they often share their bedrooms with green lizards, mice, cockroaches, and sometimes a whistling frog. My home had four resident green lizards that Sharon and I came to know well; each morning we awoke to find some portion of the group staring down at us from the wall above, heads cocked to the side watching our every move. Unwelcome are centipedes, which can seek refuge in houses when the fields of sugarcane are being harvested. Some are large and give a nasty bite, as Sharon discovered when one crawled in our bed and under her nightshirt.

What village homes may lack in material comforts, families make up for in kindness and concern for their student guests. Most homestay families go to great lengths to make the students feel welcome, introducing them to friends, taking them to church and family gatherings and on outings to show them some of the island's tourist attractions. Homestay mothers adjust their cooking to suit their student's tastes. Students joke that they have to be careful about what dishes they say they like because they can end up getting them every night. Just how concerned host families can be about their student's welfare is illustrated by one unfortunate incident. Whenever Sara left her home during the first few weeks, she was harassed by a neighbor's large dog, which would bark loudly and nip at her heels. She tried to sneak by him, but usually to no avail. Then one evening her homestay father said at the dinner table, "Don't worry, Sara, that dog won't bother you no more." She didn't understand, until she later learned that he had poisoned it.

Nearly all of my students grew up in the suburbs or cities and apart from short vacations they had never lived in the countryside before. Barbados is their first experience living with people who are close to the land. Most host families raise a few animals and have a kitchen garden. Each morning, before dawn, students awake to the sounds of animals in the yard and soon learn about their behavior. Some students collect eggs and watch sheep giving birth or pigs being slaughtered. They see the satisfaction families derive from consuming food they have produced themselves. They are also struck by the darkness of the sky at night and the brilliance of the stars with no city lights to diminish their intensity. A student from Long Island, New York, described her village at night as "like living in a planetarium."

The pace of life in Barbados, like all tropical places, is much slower than at home, and that too takes some adjusting. As one host mother explained to Megan, "there are only two speeds in Barbados: slow and dead stop." Compared to Americans, Bajans are in less of a hurry to get things done. At the shop or post office in town, customers wait to be served until the clerk finishes chatting with others. Bajans think little of being late for appointments. Ac-

customed to the punctuality and time-centeredness of North American life, my students are often impatient and frustrated by the lack
of urgency (as are many Bajan returnees who have lived abroad).
But over time, their compulsive haste begins to dissipate. They
sense a different time, one that is unhurried and attuned to the
place. As the term passes, they come to value this unhurried way of
life, and by the time they leave the island most are determined to
maintain a more tranquil, relaxed lifestyle when they return home.
Unfortunately, that's hard to do and before long most have slipped
back into the harried pace of North American college life. But they
have learned that there is an alternative way, and that not everyone
in the world rushes around.

Many students arrive at a new awareness of wealth and materi-
alism. One of the strongest initial perceptions students have of their
villages is that the people are "poor"—their houses are small, their
diets are limited, and they lack some of the amenities and comforts
the students are accustomed to. Even little things may remind students of the difference in wealth, as anthropology major Betsy re-
counted after her first week in the field:

> At home [Vermont], when I go into a convenience store and buy a
> soda, I don't think twice about handing the clerk a $20 bill. But here
> when you hand the man in a rum shop a $20 bill, they often ask if
> you have something smaller. It makes me self-conscious of how
> wealthy I appear, and how little money the rum shop man makes in
> a day.

The initial response of the students to such incidents is to feel embarrassed, even guilty that as Americans they have so much wealth.
However, such feelings are short-lived, for as the students get to
know the families they no longer seem poor, and their houses no
longer seem so small. They discover that most people not only manage quite well on what they have but that they are reasonably content. In fact, most students eventually come to believe that the
villagers are, on the whole, actually more satisfied with their lives
than most Americans. Whether or not this is true, it's an important
perception for students whose ideas about happiness have been
shaped by an ethos that measures success and satisfaction by material gain.

Many students say that after Barbados they became less materi-
alistic. Many said that when they returned home from Barbados
they were surprised at how many possessions they owned; and that
when they came back to campus they didn't bring nearly as many

things with them as they usually did. They had gone through their drawers and closets and given away to Goodwill or Salvation Army the things they didn't really need. Most said they would no longer take for granted the luxuries, such as hot showers, that they are accustomed to on campus and at home. Amy said:

> When I came back I saw how out of control the students here are. It's just crazy. They want so much, they talk about how much money they need to make, as if these things are necessities and you'll never be happy without them. Maybe I was like that too, but now I know that I don't need those things; sure I'd like a great car, but I don't need it.

The social world of the village is also unlike that of the communities the students come from. When they administer an assigned household survey, they discover that individuals know most everyone else in the village. And they often know them in more than one context; that is, not just as neighbors but also as members of their church or as teammates on the village cricket or soccer team. Relationships are multi-stranded, not single-stranded as they often are in suburban America. Most students have never known a place of such intimacy, where people have a shared history and where relationships have so many different meanings. In their journals, some students reflect upon the warmth, friendliness, and frequent sharing of food and other resources that occurs in their out-of-the-way St. Lucy villages and compare it to the impersonality, individualism, and detachment of life at home.

But they also learn about the drawbacks of living in a small community, including the lack of anonymity. People can be nosy and unduly interested in the affairs of their neighbors. To their dismay, students discover that they too can be the object of local gossip. Several female students have learned that there were stories afoot that they were either mistresses to their host fathers or said to be sleeping with their host brothers. Such gossip hurts, for the students, like all anthropologists, have worked hard to gain acceptance. They worry about the damage such rumors can do to their reputations and relationships and to their field research.

Female students must learn how to deal with the frequent and overt sexual advances of Bajan men. "When I walk through the village, the guys who hang out at the rum shop yell comments," wrote Jenny.

> I have never heard men say some of the things they tell me here. My friend Andrew tells me that most of the comments are actually com-

pliments. Yet I still feel weird . . . I am merely an object that they would like to conquer. I hate that feeling, so I am trying to get to know these guys. I figure that if they know me as a person and a friend, they will stop with the demeaning comments. Maybe it's a cultural thing they do to all women.

Indeed, many Bajan men feel it is their right to verbally accost women in public with hissing, appreciative remarks, and offers of sex. This sexual bantering is generally tolerated by Bajan women, who typically ignore men's comments. Most women consider it harmless, if annoying; some think it flattering. Students like Jenny, however, are not sure what to make of it. They do not know whether it is being directed at them because local men think white girls are "loose" or whether Bajan men behave in this fashion toward all women. Not wanting to be rude or culturally insensitive, most students tolerate the remarks the best they can, while searching for a strategy to politely discourage them. Most find that as people get to know them by name, the verbal harassment subsides.

One cultural difference that some female students never get used to is village women complimenting them on having put on weight. The ideal Barbadian female body is heavier than the North American ideal. In fact, villagers consider most of my students to be too skinny and will tell them that they have gained weight (even when they haven't) as a way of saying they are looking good and as a compliment to the homestay mother who is feeding them. Annie wrote a long passage in her journal about how a village shopkeeper's comment that she was getting nice and plump had made her depressed.

Social Class

Most American students, particularly compared to their European counterparts, have little understanding of social class. Even after several weeks in Barbados most students are fairly oblivious to class and status differences in their villages. The American suburbs that they grew up in are fairly homogeneous in social composition and housing—most homes fall in the same general price range. In contrast, the Barbadian villages the students now live in exhibit a broad spectrum, ranging from the large two-story masonry homes of returned migrants to tiny "chattel houses" (Barbadian slang for a small wood-frame house) of farmers who eke out a living on a few acres of land. The students are slow to translate such differences in the material conditions of village households into status or class differences. Barbadians' well-developed class consciousness, fostered by three centuries of British rule, is foreign to American students steeped in a culture that stresses, at least on an ideological level, egalitarianism. Hence, the students, who have never given much thought to social class, tend to view the population of the villages as essentially all the same.

It is largely from the comments their host families make about other people that students start to become aware of status distinctions. But equally, they learn about class and status from making mistakes, by violating norms concerning relationships between different categories of people. Kristen learned that there are different standards of behavior for the more affluent families after she walked home through the village carrying a bundle on her head: "Mrs. C. told me never to do that again, that only poor people carry things on their heads, and that my doing it reflected badly on her family."

As in most field situations, the first villagers to offer the students friendship are often marginal members of the community, and this creates special problems. Most of the students are hosted by respectable and often high-status village families. The host parents become upset when they discover their student has been hanging out with a disreputable young man or woman. Most serious were, in the early years of the field program, female students who went out with the hustlers they met on the beach, such as Ricky Hinds and Rosco Roach (chapter 5). The women entered into these friendships, and sometimes romantic relationships, oblivious to what the local reaction might be, and equally oblivious to how little privacy there is in a village where everyone knows everyone else's business. One student said she wrongly assumed that people would look favorably upon her going with a local man because it would show she wasn't prejudiced and that she found blacks just as desirable as whites. Another student was befriended by some Rastafarians—orthodox Rastas who wore no clothes, subsisted off the land, and lived in caves in an isolated stretch of the nearby St. Lucy coastline. When villagers discovered she had been seeing them, her homestay mother nearly evicted her and others gave her the cold shoulder. The student wrote: "I have discovered the power of a societal norm: nice girls don't talk to Rastas. When girls who were formerly nice talk to Rastas, they ceased to be known as nice. Exceptions: none."

Being of a Different Color

In more than thirty years of directing field school in Barbados, only two of my students have been nonwhite. In the villages, each student is the only white person in his or her community, and the students are part of a racial minority for the first time in their lives. During their first few weeks in the field, they are acutely aware of being white while everyone around them is dark. Some villagers call them "white girl" or "white boy" until they get to know them individually. The students are surprised that Barbadians speak so openly about racial difference, something that is seldom done at home in the United States. Village children sometimes ask to touch a student's skin, marveling at the blue veins that show through it. They sometimes ask students with freckles if they have a skin disease. Others want to feel their straight hair. Characteristically, one student during the second week wrote: "I have never been in a situation before where I was a minority purely due to the color of my skin, and treated differently because of it. When I approach people I am very conscious of having white skin. Before I never thought of myself as having color." A few become overly sensitive to racial difference, especially when they leave their villages and travel on crowded buses where they are the only whites. Often they are stared at. As the bus heads away from the coast and into the countryside, the passengers may worry that the student has missed his or her stop or has taken the wrong bus. Students notice that as the bus fills up, the seat next to them is often taken last.

Concerns about race, even the very awareness of it, diminish as they make friends and become integrated into their communities. By the end of the term, most claim they are rarely aware of being white. Several students described incidents in which they had become so unaware of skin color that they were shocked when someone made a remark or did something to remind them that they were different. Kristen was startled when, after shaking her hand, an old woman remarked that she had never touched the hand of a white person before. Other students reported being surprised whenever they walked by a mirror and got a glimpse of their white skin. One student wrote that although she knew she wasn't black, she no longer felt white.

Students as Tourists

The field school students are almost universally assumed by locals to be tourists. This is especially so whenever they leave their villages and become just another white face in a predominately black society. Even when the students are in their home villages, where most local people know they are part of the field school and that their reason for coming to Barbados is educational rather than recreational, they are still thought of as tourists, even by village friends who appreciate the students' serious interest in their culture. When the students first arrive in Barbados, they don't know much about tourists, and being new to the island they don't pay much attention to how they are identified. But as they learn more about both tourism and Barbados, they begin to resent being labeled as tourists. In fact, many find it infuriating, as they feel it demeans or lessens them. They are quick to point out that they have come to Barbados to study, to learn the culture, and not to vacation. Even when they are out doing typical tourist activities, such as sitting out on the beach, hanging out in a nightclub, or visiting a tourist attraction like Harrison's Cave, they still do not like being regarded as tourists. Here is Megan talking about not wanting her village neighbors to see her traveling in a taxi, which she believes will make her look like a tourist:

> My aunt and uncle were in Barbados on vacation and they called to see if I'd like to meet them for dinner. I asked if Siri [a fellow student] could come along as well. I was thinking it would be nice to catch up with my aunt and uncle, but also selfishly looking forward to a nice and free dinner out! They wanted to meet for dinner at a fancy place near Holetown and they wanted to send a taxi for me. They simply couldn't imagine me taking the local bus or getting a ride. I told them it would be embarrassing for me to be picked up in the village by a taxi. So, Siri and I took the bus. We had a great dinner—I still remember the red snapper—and I also remember my aunt wearing beach-bought jewelry, matching necklace and bracelet, and thinking, "She looks like such a tourist." After dinner they were adamant about putting us in a cab to go home. We gave in but it felt pretty weird being dropped off in a cab in Maynards [her village]. I felt like it took away from our status as students, students who knew the local scene and could get around on their own and that it made us look like tourists. Yuck!

I know exactly how the students feel, because like most anthropologists I too have never liked being regarded as a tourist. I once had a spirited debate with taxi driver Trevor Mapp (see chapter 4), who insisted that despite my being an anthropologist who came to Barbados to teach and to do research, I was still a tourist. I argued that I had made ten trips to Barbados and that I had always lived in a village and in a region far from the tourist belt, and that I had spent nearly three years on the island and that other than going to the beach I no longer participated in the typical tourist activities. He said that made no difference, and then asked me what time of year I usually came to Barbados. I said, "Winter." He responded, "You're not even here year-round. You are a tourist!" To Trevor, like most Barbadians, white visitors are lumped in one broad category, regardless of what they do when in Barbados. It should be no surprise that the real tourists to Barbados also regard my students as tourists, a little younger perhaps but basically just like themselves.

When I ask the students why they so strongly dislike being identified as tourists, two points usually come up. One, that what they are doing in Barbados is something quite different from what tourists do; that in doing fieldwork they acquire knowledge and respect for the local culture, which they believe is sorely lacking among tourists. Second, they have developed a low opinion of tourists, whose behavior they often find culturally insensitive and sometimes outright offensive. The following quotations, taken from my interviews with the students, are illustrative:

> I remember one time we went to a nightclub and there were a bunch of American girls there, I think they were a volleyball team, and they were kind of slutty, . . . drunken, obnoxious, flirting with the guys in the band. It was pretty embarrassing, it was like "Oh God, let's get away from them." You didn't want to be associated with them because they just looked so stupid. In a college setting back home that kind of behavior is common, the girls would have just blended right in, but here in Barbados it was pretty obnoxious. (Chelsea)

> When we'd be walking in town where there were lots of tourists, we'd make comments like, "Don't they know that Bajans are conservative dressers, that no Bajan would ever wear her bathing suit or short shorts in town, and especially in a store?" (Anne)

> When we'd see them [American tourists], we'd be like, "I hate them." We'd sort of be kidding but the truth was we really didn't like them. I didn't like the fact that most tourists just take Barbados for granted and treat it as some kind of Disneyland. They think Barbados is here for their own pleasure. I hated seeing Bajans having to cater to tourists just because they need their money. (Pearl)

> One time we were down in the St. Lawrence Gap area and we saw these American girls in hats with fake dreadlocks and wearing the colors of the Jamaican flag. I thought it was really insulting. (Suzy)

The students are particularly hard on their fellow Americans. I can't say whether this is because the behavior of American tourists is more embarrassing to them or whether American tourists are more likely to be culturally insensitive than tourists from the UK or Canada, the primary nationalities that visit Barbados. I suspect it's both. Some students admitted that they were sometimes unfairly harsh in their condemnation of American tourists. As Emily said,

> I did think they [American tourists] were pretty crass, that they were just in Barbados to have a good time and not really interested in getting to know the people. And I didn't like to see them wear bikinis and flip-flops in public where locals never would, and speaking so loudly that you could always overhear their conversations. However, I now realize that we were a bit hypocritical because we [students] could also be loud when we went out, and although we never wore beachwear in public, we would go to Almond Beach [an all-inclusive resort] and pass ourselves off as tourists staying in the hotel in order to get the free drinks. When we were there we weren't all that different from the other tourists.

On the other hand, when the students were away from their home villages and out in public, they usually made some effort to distance themselves from the other visitors to the island. For example, most would dress conservatively. Chelsea said, "I learned pretty quickly the first time I went to the Speightstown library and the guard said my shorts were too short. I never wore them in town again." In conversation they would let it be known that they lived in a village with a local family and that they got around on the local buses. Likewise, women anthropologists working in other parts of the world where female tourists are assumed to be interested in sex with local men may try to distinguish themselves from tourists by dressing very modestly, in dresses rather than shorts.

The students' attempts to identify themselves as something other than run-of-the-mill tourists often met with only limited success, as Pearl explained: "Even when I tell people I live in Checker Hall [a village] and that I am an anthropology student, I still get comments like 'Not bad, I'll bet you get to spend a lot of time at the beach.' It's like they think that every white person in Barbados must be on vacation." Chelsea described how the tourists she met reacted when she explained she was a student: "They kind of laugh at the idea that I could be doing research in Barbados; I think some of them think I am taking advantage of my college by having a good time on the beach. The attitude is sort of that you can't be doing anything very serious in a tropical resort country." Actually, anthropologists who work in the Caribbean, especially if they are there primarily during the North American winter, also can have difficulty being taken seriously by their colleagues at home. This is a problem that does not occur for anthropologists who work in remote, hot, and dusty—or frozen and barren—places far from pleasure centers or vacation destinations like the beaches of the Caribbean.

Some students said the best way to get around being regarded as a tourist was to go out with their village friends, and when they were out to follow Bajan norms of behavior. As Pearl noted of spending time in Bridgetown nightclubs with the friends she and fellow student Chelsea had made in the village of Checker Hall:

> We wouldn't get wasted like we would at home, because that's not what they do here. Bajans like to talk about how much they party but they don't get really drunk the way American college kids do. And it's not because they can't afford it because rum is super cheap, like 6 dollars a bottle. They like to get a buzz, but not crazy drunk and if we were to do it we'd look like dumb Americans.

Annie recalled: "When walking about the village or making my way into town, I learned the value of looking a passing stranger in the eye and shouting out 'Alright!' like they do with each other."

Almost every afternoon Sharon and I would leave our home in the St. Lucy village of Josey Hill to go snorkeling or swimming at a west coast resort, and if we interacted with the staff or other locals there we would discreetly let it be known that we lived in Josey Hill, which they would know had no tourist accommodation, and in fact no white people other than us. We weren't doing this to appear "native," rather to put our interaction on a different footing, hoping they would relate to us not as tourists and we could avoid having to deal with their attempts to sell us something—jewelry, aloe, a jet-ski adventure, hair braiding, and so on—or having to answer questions like had we been to Harrison's Cave yet or any of the other questions that locals typically ask of visitors.

Every term a few of my students are put in the position of being tour guides to visiting friends and relatives. We don't discourage the students from inviting their parents and others to visit them in Barbados, but we do ask them to have their visitors come at the end of the term, when the disruption to the students' research and field experience will be less. By the end of the term, the students have made many acquaintances and some local friends and have learned a great deal about the culture, all of which contributes to their being excellent tour guides. It's a role that most students enjoy, as it gives them an opportunity to show off their expertise in navigating the culture. Emily's description of showing her parents around the island is fairly typical:

> It was fun and I think I felt a lot of pride because I could show them how much I'd learned and all the places that I knew, and all the people. And I also knew a lot of easier or better ways of doing things—things that I had figured out myself and that you wouldn't find in a guidebook. It was also an opportunity to go to a few places like the Mount Gay Distillery and the Barbados Wildlife Reserve that I hadn't been to before because they were kind of touristy and expensive.

Does spending a term abroad at a field school in Barbados change how students travel and behave when they become tourists on their own? I put this question to a dozen alumni of the Barbados program over the telephone. Everyone, without exception, thought he or she had become a more sensitive and culturally aware traveler because of the experience in Barbados. "I ask a lot of questions; I let people know that I am really interested in their lives, that I want to see how people really live," said Terry. Similarly, Robin noted, "I think I talk to the locals a lot more. Not just brief conversations like 'Hi, you've got a nice place here,' but really talk to them, about their lifestyle and what they think about things. But it's funny because when I do it everyone in my family thinks I'm weird." Another student said it's not just when he travels that he is curious about strangers, but whenever he goes out, "I like to meet people and have real conversations, and that comes from our experiences in Barbados. Like just yesterday I took the train upstate and I talked for a long time to the people sitting near me; these were real conversations and I learned some neat stuff. I didn't just sit there and ignore them and listen to my music." In the words of Annie, who spent two terms at the field school, the second time as a teaching assistant:

> When we went back to Barbados several years ago it wasn't even a consideration to stay at a resort. We rented an apartment up the hill in Gibbs [away from the coast]. In fact, most of the travel that we've done since Barbados [twenty years ago] has been where we try to be more a part of the local culture, like we will stay with a family or in an apartment and not in one of the glitzy tourist hotels that have all the amenities and keep you sheltered away from the locals. I have

the confidence to travel this way, but I know a lot of friends who wouldn't feel comfortable being out on their own so much. It's a lot easier for them to stay at a resort.

Most of the alumni said that when they travel now they eat the local food. Chris added, "Now that I know all about leakage, and how little money actually stays on the islands, I try to spend my money in locally owned places . . . I want to leave my money in the local economy." Likewise, most field school alumni also talked about getting out and exploring and not just going to the well-known and advertised tourist destinations. "I like to take time and just drive around the back roads and see places that tourists don't normally go," said Diane. And many talked about doing their "homework" or "research" before they traveled; trying to learn about the peoples and places they were visiting, so that they wouldn't be quite so uninformed when they arrived.

Portions of this chapter were originally published in Gmelch and Gmelch 1997 and Gmelch 2000.

Acknowledgments

During the years this book was intermittently in progress, many people helped out. I am extremely grateful to my colleagues in Barbados: Jerry Handler, Susan Mahon, Janice Whittle, Rick Stone, Christine Keeler, Dale Mapp, Yvonne Cumberbatch, Richard Goddard, and the late Colin Hudson and Bob Speed, for their guidance. I also owe much to the Union College anthropology students who over nearly two decades (1983–1999) participated in field programs that Sharon Gmelch and I directed in Barbados. They deepened my understanding of Barbadian culture, introduced me to people in their villages, some of whom later became my own teachers and informants, and almost always made my time in the field enjoyable. Guiding the students' field research and showing them the ways of anthropology has been the most satisfying aspect of my teaching career. Just to name a few, I thank Annie Bruhn, Julie Barton, Johanna Campbell, Megan Donovan, Cari Hepner, Nolan Farris, Ellen Frankenstein, Sara Finnerty, Dan Gilbert, Siri Newman, Emily Sparks, and Polly Wheeler.

I owe a debt to Union College student aides and summer research fellows Megan Denefrio, Elizabeth Daigle, Hannah Gaw, Amanda Haag, Jessica Henry, and Justine Willey, who assisted me in everything from transcribing interviews to critiquing narratives. I also thank the dozens of hotel and tourism employees who gave their time and indulgence during this endeavor and especially to Active Vision, Angeline Gittens of the Barbados Tourism Authority, and Mary Kerr, Elizabeth King, Frank Otto, Michalena Skiadas, and Emily Sparks for providing photographs.

Bellairs Research Institute provided a base for my research in Barbados and I especially thank its directors Wayne Hunte and the late Joan Marsden. Librarians Bruce Connolly, Dave Gerhan, Donna Burton, and Mary Cahill at Union College and Michael Gill, Alan Moss, and Carlye Best at the University of the West Indies, Cave Hill, were a huge help. In the parish of St. Lucy where I have spent two and a half years living in several villages, I thank Irmine Greaves, Rudolph and Shirley Hollingsworth, Judy and Roosevelt Griffiths, Uzil Holder, and Eric, Marcus, and Velma O'Neale, Siebert and Aileen Allman, and Marcus and Janet Hinds for their hospitality and for making my stays in Barbados so pleasant.

Friends and colleagues not mentioned above who helped by commenting on the manuscript or portions of it are Morgan Gmelch, Sharon Gmelch, Dan Gordon, Sheila Otto, Jay Poropatich, Melissa Thurston, Bob Wheelock, the late Deb Ludke, and two anonymous reviewers. Rebecca Tolen at Indiana University Press is a splendid rarity, an editor with a Ph.D. in anthropology who knows as much about the field as does the writer. Her suggestions, more than any, have made this a better book. Kate Babbitt did a superb job of copyediting the first edition. I have benefited from discussions with colleagues, especially Karen Brison, Cate Cameron, Ian Condry, Tom Curtin, Kenji Tierney, Sharon Gmelch, Steve Leavitt, Teresa Meade, Charles Bishop, the late Estellie Smith, Anne and Warren Roberts, and Tim Wallace. Some excellent writings on tourism by Erve Chambers, Erik Cohen, Malcolm Crick, Polly Pattullo, and Amanda Stronza greatly influenced my thinking about the subject.

Finally, my deepest debt is to the interviewees in this book who were generous in their trust and time—Sylvan Alleyne, Marilyn Cooper, Robert Quintyne, Michael Walcott, and all the others who elected to use pseudonyms. They gave me a wide window on their world, and I hope they will not be disappointed with the result. Their stories have changed forever the way I view tourism. Finally at Indiana University Press I thank my editor Rebecca Tolen and her assistant Sarah Jacobi for their enthusiasm and for ushering this book through the labyrinth of publication.

Acknowledgments for the Second Edition

This new edition of *Behind the Smile* benefited greatly from the assistance of student research fellows Pearl Jurist-Schoen and Chelsea Tussing, who accompanied me to Barbados in the summer of 2010. For insights on how the tourism landscape had changed since my early work, I thank Bernice Critchlow-Earle, Rosie Hartmann, Colin Jordan, Susan Mahon, Rick Stone, Gale Yearwood, and Janice Whittle. For being wonderful hosts I thank Ermine Greaves and Findlay and Marcia Cockrell. The University of San Francisco, to which I moved in 2007, generously provided financial support for the fieldwork and an ideal intellectual environment. I was especially fortunate to have two excellent research assistants in Diane Royal at USF and summer intern Carolyn Hou from Smith College. Their critical reading of the first edition and their many suggestions for revising it have made this new edition a better book.

Bibliography

Archer, E. D. 1980. "Effects of the Tourist Industry in Barbados, West Indies." Ph.D. diss., University of Texas, Austin.

———. 1985. "Emerging Environmental Problems in a Tourist Zone: The Case of Barbados." *Caribbean Geography* 2: 45–55.

Baldacchino, Godfrey. 1997. *Global Tourism and Informal Labour Relations: The Small-Scale Syndrome at Work.* London: Mansell.

Barbados Digest of Tourism Statistics (BDTS). 1991. Bridgetown, Barbados: Government Printer.

Barbados Improvement Association. 1913. *The Tourist Guide to Barbados.* Bridgetown: Barbados Improvement Association.

Barbados Statistical Service. 1985. *Monthly Digest of Statistics.* Bridgetown: Barbados Statistical Service.

Barrow, C. 1976. "Reputation and Ranking in a Barbadian Locality." *Social and Economic Studies* 25, no. 2: 106–129.

Barry, T., B. Wood, and D. Preusch. 1984. *The Other Side of Paradise: Foreign Control in the Caribbean.* New York: Grove Press.

Bayley, F. W. N. 1830. *Four Years Residence in the West Indies.* London: W. Kidd.

Beckles, Hillary. 1990. *The History of Barbados.* Cambridge: Cambridge University Press.

Boissevain, Jeremy, ed. 1996. *Coping with Tourists: European Reactions to Mass Tourism.* Providence, R.I.: Berghahn.

Briguglio, Lino, Richard Butler, David Harrison, and Walter Leal Filho. 1996. *Sustainable Tourism in Islands and Small States.* Wellington, UK: Pinter.

Bryden, J. M. 1973. *Tourism and Development: A Case Study of the Commonwealth Caribbean.* Cambridge: Cambridge University Press.

Cave, Shepherd and Co. 1911. *Barbados (Illustrated): Historical, Descriptive and Commercial.* Bridgetown, Barbados: Cave, Shepherd and Co.

Chambers, Erve, ed. 1997. *Tourism and Culture: An Applied Perspective.* Albany: State University of New York Press.

———. 2002. *Native Tours: The Anthropology of Travel and Tourism*
  Prospect Heights, Ill.: Waveland Press.
Chandler, A. A. 1946. "The Expansion of Barbados." *Journal of the
  Barbados Museum and Historical Society* 13: 106–136.
Cohen, E. 1978. "The Impact of Tourism on the Physical
  Environment." *Annals of Tourism Research* 5: 215–237.
———. 1984. "The Sociology of Tourism: Approaches, Issues and
  Findings." *Annual Review of Sociology* 10: 373–392.
———. 1993. "The Study of Touristic Images of Native People." In
  Tourism Research: Critiques and Challenges, ed. D. G. Pearce and
  R. W. Butler, 36–69. London: Routledge.
Coleridge, H. N. 1970 [1836]. *Six Months in the West Indies.* New York:
  Negro Universities Press.
Crick, Malcolm. 1989. "Representation of the International Tourism
  in the Social Sciences: Sun, Sex, Sights, Savings, and
  Servility." *Annual Review of Anthropology* 18: 307–344.
———. 1994. *Resplendent Sites, Discordant Voices: Sri Lankans and
  International Tourism.* Chur, Switzerland: Harwood Academic
  Publishers.
Cutsinger, Loran. 1990. "Informal Marketing in Barbados, West
  Indies." Ph.D. diss., Washington State University.
Dann, G. 1979. *Everyday Life in Barbados: A Sociological Perspective.*
  Leiden: Royal Institute of Linguistics and Anthropology.
———. 1984. *The Quality of Life in Barbados.* London: Macmillan.
———. 1987. *The Barbadian Male: Sexual Attitudes and Practice.* London:
  MacMillan Caribbean.
Dann, G. M. S., and E. Cohen. 1991. "Sociology and Tourism."
  Annals of Tourism Research 18: 155–169.
Daye, Marcella, et al. 2008. *New Perspectives in Caribbean Tourism.* New
  York: Routledge.
Deere, Carmen Diana, et al. 1990. *In the Shadows of the Sun: Caribbean
  Development Alternatives and U.S. Policy.* Boulder, Colo.:
  Westview Press.
Din, Kadir H. 1988. "Social and Cultural Impacts of Tourism." *Annals
  of Tourism Research* 25, no. 4: 563–566.
Doxey, G. V. 1975. "A Causation Theory of Visitor-Resident Irritants."
  *Sixth Annual Conference Proceedings of Travel and Tourism
  Research Association* 21, no. 1: 22–28.
Erisman, M. 1983. "Tourism and Cultural Dependency in the West
  Indies." *Annals of Tourism Research* 10: 337–361.
Errington, F., and D. Gewertz. 1989. "Tourism and Anthropology in a
  Post-Modern World." *Oceania* 60: 37.

Evans-Pritchard D. 1989. "How 'They' See 'Us': Native American Images of Tourists." *Annals of Tourism Research* 16: 89–105.

Fraser, H., et al. 1990. *A–Z of Barbadian Heritage.* Kingston: Heinemann Publishers.

Freeman, Carla. 1993. "Designing Women: Corporate Discipline and Barbados's Off-Shore Pink-Collar Sector." *Cultural Anthropology* 8, no. 2: 169–186.

Frere, G. 1768. *A Short History of Barbados.* London: J. Dodsley.

Gee, C. Y., J. C. Makens, and D. Choy. 1997. *The Travel Industry.* New York: Wiley.

Gmelch, G. 1985. "Barbados Odyssey: Some Migrants Fulfill Their Dreams by Returning Home." *Natural History* 94, no. 10: 34–38.

———. 1987. "Work, Innovation, and Investment: The Impact of Return Migrants in Barbados." *Human Organization* 46, no. 2: 131–140.

———. 1992a. *Double Passage: The Lives of Caribbean Migrants Abroad and Back Home.* Ann Arbor: University of Michigan Press.

———. 1992b. "Learning Culture: The Education of American Students in Caribbean Villages." *Human Organization* 51, no. 3: 245–252.

———. 2000. "Lessons from the Field." In *Conformity and Conflict: Readings in Cultural Anthropology,* 10th ed., ed. James Spradley and David McCurdy, 45–55. Boston: Allyn and Bacon.

Gmelch, George, and Sharon Gmelch. 1997. *The Parish behind God's Back: The Changing Culture of Rural Barbados.* Ann Arbor: University of Michigan Press. 2nd ed., Prospect Heights, Ill.: Waveland Press, 2012.

Gmelch, George, and J. J. Weiner. 1998. *In the Ballpark: The Working Lives of Baseball People.* Washington, D.C.: Smithsonian Institution Press.

Gmelch, S. 1991. *Nan: The Life of an Irish Travelling Women.* New York: W. W. Norton.

———, ed. 2010. *Tourists and Tourism.* Prospect Heights, Ill.: Waveland Press.

Graburn, N. 1983. "Anthropology of Tourism." *Annals of Tourism Research* 10: 9–34.

Graburn, Nelson H. H., and Jafar Jafari. 1991. "Introduction: Tourism Social Science." *Annals of Tourism Research* 18, no. 1: 1–11.

Harlow, V. T. 1926. *A History of Barbados, 1625–1685.* Oxford: Clarendon Press.

Harrington, N. 1974. "The Legacy of Caribbean History and Tourism." *Annals of Tourism Research* 2: 13–25.

Herold, E., R. A. Garcia, and T. DeMoya. 2001. "Female Tourists and Beach Boys: Romance or Sex Tourism?" *Annals of Tourism Research* 28, no. 4: 978–997.

Hiller, H. L. 1976. "Escapism, Penetration, and Response: Industrial Tourism in the Caribbean." *Caribbean Studies* 16, no. 2: 92–116.

Hoefer, H., and R. Wilder, eds. 1986. *Barbados.* Singapore: APA Productions.

Holder, J. F., ed. 1979. *Caribbean Tourism: Policies and Impacts—Selected Speeches and Papers.* Christ Church, Barbados: Caribbean Tourism Research and Development Centre.

Holder, J. F., and C. Wilson, eds. 1976. *Caribbean Tourism: Profits and Performance through 1980.* Port of Spain, Trinidad and Tobago: Key Caribbean Publications.

Honey, M. 1999. *Ecotourism and Sustainable Development: Who Owns Paradise?* Washington, D.C.: Island Press.

Hope, K. R. 1982. *Economic Development in the Caribbean.* New York: Praeger.

Hunte, G. 1974. *Barbados.* London: B. T. Batsford.

Hutt, M. B. 1980. *A Report to CADEC [Christian Action for Development in the Caribbean] on "Windows to the Sea."* Bridgetown, Barbados: Cedar Press.

———. 1981. *Exploring Historic Barbados.* Bedford, Nova Scotia: Layne.

Karch, Cecilia A., and G. H. S. Dann. 1981. "Close Encounters of the Third World." *Human Relations* 34, no. 4: 249–268.

Lencek, Lina, and Gideon Bosker. 1998. *The Beach: The History of Paradise on Earth.* New York: Viking.

Lerch, Patricia B., and Diane E. Levy. 1990. "A Solid Foundation: Predicting Success in Barbados' Tourist Industry." *Human Organization* 49, no. 4: 355–363.

Ligon, R. A. 1970 [1657]. *A True & Exact History of the Island of Barbados.* Portland, Ore.: Frank Cass.

Lockhart, Douglas, and D. W. Drakakis-Smith. 1996. *Island Tourism: Trends and Prospects.* New York: Pinter.

Lofgren, O. 1999. *On Holiday: A History of Vacationing.* Berkeley: University of California Press.

Lynch, L. 1972. *The Barbados Book.* London: Andre Deutsch.

MacCannell, D. 1976. *The Tourist: A New Theory of the Leisure Class.* New York: Schocken Books.

McLaren, D. 1998. *Rethinking Tourism and Ecotravel: The Paving of Paradise and What You Can Do to Stop It.* West Hartford, Conn.: Kumarian.

Miller, D. 1994. *Modernity, an Ethnographic Approach: Dualism and Mass Consumption in Trinidad.* Oxford: Berg.

Mowforth, Martin, and Ian Munt. 1998. *Tourism and Sustainability: New Tourism in the Third World.* New York: Routledge.

Moxly, Rev. J. H. Sutton. 1886. *An Account of a West Indian Sanatorium and a Guide to Barbados.* London: S. Low, Marston, Searle, & Rivington.

Nash, Dennison. 1981. *Anthropology of Tourism.* Oxford: Pergamon Press.

Nash, Dennison, and Valene Smith. 1991. "Anthropology and Tourism." *Annals of Tourism Research* 18, no. 1: 12–25.

Nurse, L. 1983. *Residential Subdivision of Barbados: 1965–1977.* Cave Hill, Barbados: Institute of Social and Economic Research, University of the West Indies.

Pattullo, Polly. 1996. *Last Resorts: The Cost of Tourism in the Caribbean.* London: Cassell.

Pearce, P. L. 1982. *The Social Psychology of Tourist Behavior.* Oxford: Pergamon.

Perez, L. 1974. "Aspects of Underdevelopment: Tourism in the West Indies." *Science and Society* 37: 473.

Phillips, J. 1999. "Tourist-Oriented Prostitution in Barbados." In *Sun, Sex, and Gold: Tourism and Sex Work in the Caribbean,* ed. Kamala Kempadoo, 183–200. New York: Rowman & Littlefield Publishers.

Pi-Sunyer, O. 1977. "Through Native Eyes: Tourists and Tourism in a Catalan Maritime Community." In *Hosts and Guests,* ed. Valene Smith, 187–199. London: Routledge.

Pruitt, Deborah, and Suzanne LaFont. 1995. "For Love and Money: Romance Tourism in Jamaica." *Annals of Tourism Research* 22, no. 2: 422–440.

Schomburgk, R. H. 1971 [1848]. *The History of Barbados.* London: Frank Cass.

Smith, Valene L., ed. 1989. *Hosts and Guests: The Anthropology of Tourism,* 2nd ed. Philadelphia: University of Pennsylvania Press.

Smith, Valene L., and William R. Eadington, eds. 1992. *Tourism Alternatives: Potentials and Problems in the Development of Tourism.* Philadelphia: University of Pennsylvania Press.

Spradley, James, and David McCurdy, eds. 2000. *Conformity and Conflict: Readings in Cultural Anthropology,* 10th ed. Boston: Allyn and Bacon.

Stronza, Amanda. 2001. "Anthropology of Tourism." *Annual Review of Anthropology* 30: 261–283.

Trouillot, Michel-Rolph. 1992. "The Caribbean Region: An Open Frontier in Anthropological Theory." *Annual Review of Anthropology* 21: 19–42.

UNESCO. 1977. "The Effects of Tourism on Socio-Cultural Values." *Annals of Tourism Research* 4: 74–105.

Urry, John. 1990. *The Tourist Gaze: Travel and Leisure in Contemporary Societies*. Newbury Park, Calif.: Sage Publications.

Wickham, J. 1975. "The Thing about Barbados." *Journal of the Barbados Museum and Historical Society* 35: 223–230.

Wilson, P. 1973. *Crab Antics: The Social Anthropology of English-Speaking Negro Societies of the Caribbean*. New Haven, Conn.: Yale University Press.

Wirthlin, Karin. 2000. "Tourism and Barbados: An Examination of Local Perspectives." M.A. thesis, Colorado State University.

Worrell, D., ed. 1982. *The Economy of Barbados, 1946–1980*. Bridgetown: Central Bank of Barbados.

———. 1987. *Small Island Economies: Structure and Performance in the English-Speaking Caribbean Since 1970*. New York: Praeger.

Index

Pattullo, Polly, 6, 6n4, 10–11, 57
Pearce, P., 25, 37
Pie Corner, 229
Pi-Sunyer, O., 37
police, 88–89
Pope Paul VI, 7
porters (redcaps), 44–48, 54
privacy, loss of, 25
prostitution, 70, 92. *See also* beach
    boys; romance tourism
Pruitt, Deborah, 33

race relations, 143, 148–50
racism, 28–29, 51–53, 72, 80, 95, 108,
    111, 132–33, 171, 218–19. *See
    also* neocolonialism
Rastafarians, 235
romance tourism, 32–35, 119–20,
    129–32. *See also* beach boys

sailing, 123
sea bathing, 3–4
sexual bantering, 233–34
smokers, problems with, 65, 84, 157
Speightstown, 10
stereotypes (of nationalities), 147–48
Stronza, Amanda, 38
students (American, studying and
    doing research in Barbados),
    228–42; adjusting to village life,
    229–34; attitudes toward tourists,
    236–42; field schools, 228–29;
    race, 236–37; sexism, 233–34; so-
    cial class, 234–35; as tourists,
    236–42; University of the West
    Indies, Cave Hill, 190
sugar cultivation: cutting cane, 118–
    19; decline of plantations, 7, 57
sunning, 5

Tall Ships, 143–46
Tamarind Cove Hotel, 190–91
taxi driver, 61–66, 158–59
taxi stands, 61
television, and public service an-
    nouncements for tourism, 30
tipping, 44–46, 64, 84
Tobago, 186

tour bus, 152–61
tour guides, 140–48, 152–61, 168–
    73, 183, 240–41
tourism: as acculturation, 35, 216–
    20; activities, 138, 181; creation
    of cultural events, 19; demon-
    stration effects of, 35, 35–36,
    215; development of, 6–12, 22;
    and drinking, 92, 178, 181; and
    drugs, 23, 89, 91, 206; econom-
    ics of, 9–12, 15; effect of, on
    work ethic, 26; and employ-
    ment, 15; environmental impact
    of, 20–21, 22, 23–24, 137; future
    of, 150, 194–195; and garbage,
    23; history of, 1–6; history of, in
    Barbados, impacts of, 9–12, 19–
    26, 90–92, 97, 111, 206; impor-
    tance to the economy, 19;
    infrastructure for, 9–10; and jobs
    for women, 36–37; and media,
    204; and neocolonialism, 37–38,
    149; number of visitors, 8; and
    pollution, 20–21; research on,
    201–207; seasons, 6, 63, 77–78,
    116, 161, 206; slogans, 194; so-
    cial impacts of, 25–26; and ste-
    reotypes, 48; training for, 31–32
    (*see also* Barbados Hospitality In-
    stitute); and "vertical integra-
    tion," 10
tourism workers: and acculturation,
    216–18 (*see also* interaction, be-
    tween tourists and locals); and
    camaraderie, 101; and com-
    plaints with guests, 78, 101–102,
    108–109, 124, 156–57, 171–72,
    212–14; and "emotional work,"
    59; and expatriates, 75, 100,
    102–103; glass ceiling for, 59;
    and gossip, 214; impacts of, 35–
    37, 91–92, 166–67, 178–79, 184;
    job satisfaction among, 95, 110–
    11, 183, 215–26; and language,
    changes in, 70, 75, 126, 155,
    166, 170, 216; and "new slav-
    ery" (*see* neocolonialism; rac-
    ism); perceptions of guests,

GEORGE GMELCH

is Professor of Anthropology at the University of San Francisco and Union College. He has studied Irish Travellers, return migrants, commercial fishermen, Alaska natives, Caribbean villagers, tourism workers, and American professional baseball players. He is the author of eleven books, including (with Sharon Bohn Gmelch) *Tasting the Good Life: Wine Tourism in the Napa Valley* (Indiana University Press, 2011). He has written two other books on Barbados: *Double Passage,* which is about return migration, and *The Parish behind God's Back: The Changing Culture of Rural Barbados* (with Sharon Bohn Gmelch). He has also written widely for general audiences, including the *New York Times,* the *Washington Post, Psychology Today,* and *Natural History.*